Ela

"Your worth has been established! Your heart contains the beauty that I cherish. You are Mine! I rewarded Myself... with YOU!"

Your Heavenly Father

All My Love,
Maribeth
Eickhoff

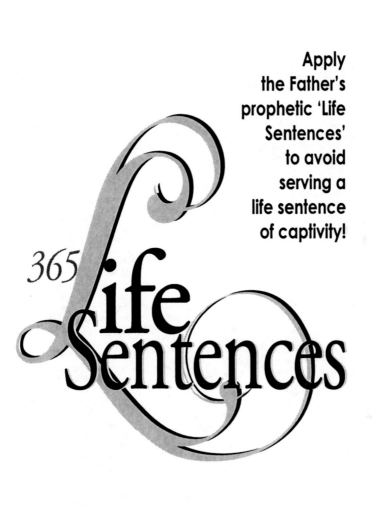

Apply
the Father's
prophetic 'Life
Sentences'
to avoid
serving a
life sentence
of captivity!

365 Life Sentences

365 Life Sentences:
Apply the Father's prophetic 'Life Sentences' to avoid serving a life sentence of captivity!

ISBN 978-0-692-87257-4

Unless otherwise noted, all Scripture quotations are from the New International Version (NIV) of the Bible. Copyright © 1973, 1978, 1984 by International Bible Society.

Scripture quotations marked AMP are taken from the Amplified® Bible, Copyright © 1954, 1958, 1962, 1964, 1965, 1987 by The Lockman Foundation. Used by permission.

Scripture quotations marked AMPC are taken from the Amplified® Bible, Classic Edition, Copyright © 1954, 1958, 1962, 1964, 1965, 1987 by The Lockman Foundation. Used by permission.

Scripture quotations marked NLT are taken from the New Living Translation Holy Bible unless otherwise noted. New Living Translation copyright © 1996, 2004, 2007 by Tyndale House Foundation. Used by permission of Tyndale House Publishers Inc., Carol Stream, Illinois 60188. All rights reserved.

Scripture quotations marked NLV are taken from the New Life Version. Copyright © 1969 by Christian Literature International. All rights reserved.

Scripture quotations marked TLB are taken from The Living Bible. Copyright © 1976 by Tyndale House Publishers, Wheaton, Ill. 60187. Used by permission. All rights reserved.

Scripture quotations marked NASB are taken from the New American Standard Bible, Copyright © 1960, 1962, 1963, 1968, 1971, 1972, 1973, 1975, 1977, 1995 by The Lockman Foundation. Used by permission.

Scripture quotations marked KJV are taken from the King James Version of the Bible. Public Domain.

Scripture quotations marked CEV are taken from the Contemporary English Version of the Bible. Copyright © 1995 by American Bible Society.

Scripture quotations marked MSG are taken from The Message Version of the Bible. Copyright © 1993, 1994, 1995, 1996, 2000, 2001, 2002 by Eugene H. Peterson by NAV Press.

Scripture quotations marked NKJV are taken from The New King James Version of the Bible. NKJV, Copyright © 1979, 1980, 1982, Thomas Nelson, Inc. All rights reserved.

Scripture quotations marked CJB are taken from Complete Jewish Bible. Copyright © 1998 by David H. Stern. All rights reserved.

Scripture quotations marked ERV are taken from the Easy-to-Read Version, Copyright © 2006 by World Bible Translation Center. Used by permission.

Scripture quotations marked ESV are taken from the English Standard Version, The Holy Bible, English Standard Version Copyright © 2001 by Crossway Bibles, a publishing ministry of Good News Publishers.

Scripture quotations marked DRA are taken from the Douay-Rheims 1899 American Edition. Public Domain.

Scripture quotations marked GW are taken from GOD'S WORD Translation, Copyright © 1995 by God's Word to the Nations. Used by permission of Baker Publishing Group.

Scripture quotations marked CEB are taken from the Common English Bible, Copyright © 2011 by Common English Bible.

Scripture quotations marked "Darby" are taken from the Darby Translation Bible. Public Domain.

Scripture quotations marked JUB are taken from the Jubilee Bible 2000. Copyright © 2000, 2001, 2010 by LIFE SENTENCE Publishing Used with Permission.

Scripture quotations marked "Phillips" are taken from the J. B. Phillips, "The New Testament in Modern English", 1962 edition, published by HarperCollins.

Scripture quotations marked NRSV are taken from the New Revised Standard Version Bible, copyright © 1989 the Division of Christian Education of the National Council of the Churches of Christ in the United States of America. Used by permission. All rights reserved.

Emphasis within Scripture quotations are the author's own. Please note that Abba's Heart Publishing style capitalizes certain words in Scripture, including those referring to the Father, Son, and Holy Spirit. Also take note that the word enemy is used in place of the devil or the name Satan, as we choose not to acknowledge him (except to differntiate him from others).

Published by Abba's Heart Publishing.

Printed in the United States of America.

Apply
the Father's
prophetic 'Life
Sentences'
to avoid
serving a
life sentence
of captivity!

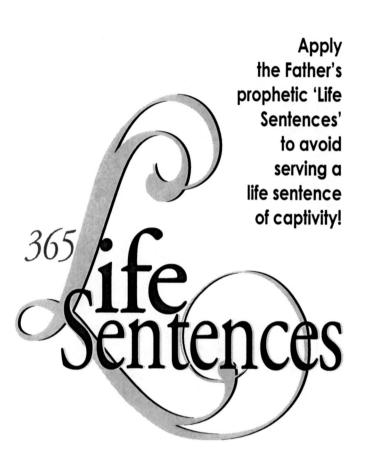

365 **Life
Sentences**

Maribeth Eickhoff

Foreword by
Steve Sampson

Foreword

My friend, Maribeth Eickhoff, has written a masterpiece! Filled with colorful truths, which are daily delicacies, each "sentence" is created to offer you encouragement, strength, and a daily spiritual boost.

Because she has been through many hard places in her life, she has found wisdom and strength from God that will greatly benefit each of us. I am personally amazed how she has capsulized great insights in such succinct expressions.

As I read through this, I was captivated by the creativity and substance of each daily reading. These are words that will stick with you and will challenge you to avoid pitfalls — and hopefully confront, with honesty and a fresh perspective, a battle or situation you may be facing.

As you take time to meditate on each sentence, you will receive the freshness from the mind of the Lord that will navigate you through your day. Each day is filled with a uniqueness and genuineness that is guaranteed to lift your heart.

It is a delight to open this book to a new thought every morning. With the brilliance and wisdom of the Holy Spirit, so much *Life* is contained in each power-packed sentence and exhortation.

This book is truly a "life sentence" for every day of the year.

– Steve Sampson,
Author and Conference Speaker

Dedication

First and foremost, I dedicate this book to The Almighty God — Father, Son, and Holy Spirit. I give You all of the honor and glory for this book! Thank You, Heavenly Father, for revealing your heart to me in these pages!

Secondly, I dedicate this book to my precious family: To my husband, Tom, of 34 years, you are my best friend and my one and only! You walk in such integrity and character and you are a champion in every part of your life. I love you more than you will ever know! To my amazing daughters: Malisa, Jenny and Mackenzie, inside and out, you all are the most beautiful of anyone I have ever met on earth! Your love and encouragement during very dark decades in my life literally saved my life! Thank you for teaching me so much about God and true love! You made me believe that I could! You three make my life beautiful! I love you.

A very special and heartfelt thank you to my dear friends, Autumn Cherry and Marjorie Russell Kough! This book would not be finished if it were not for your very hard work. Thank you does not seem adequate! I love you.

Introduction

*But when He, the Spirit of Truth (the Truth-giving Spirit) comes, He will guide you into all the Truth (the whole, full Truth). For He will not speak His own message [on His own authority]; but **He will tell whatever He hears [from the Father; He will give the message that has been given to Him], and He will announce and declare to you** the things that are to come [that will happen in the future]. He will honor and glorify Me, because **He will take of (receive, draw upon) what is Mine and will reveal (declare, disclose, transmit) it to you.** Everything that the Father has is Mine. That is what I meant when I said that He [the Spirit] will take the things that are Mine and will reveal (declare, disclose, transmit) it to you.*

– John 16:13-15 AMP

When you **apply** the **Life Sentences** in this book, written by the Father, then you will not have to **serve** a life sentence in deception and captivity from the enemy! I believe God — the Father, Son, and Holy Spirit — is always revealing Himself to us (John 16:15)!

I began hearing the Lord's voice in 1985 when I was baptized in the Holy Spirit (Acts 2). He began to teach my ear to hear and my eyes to see (Matthew 13:16). At around this same time, at age 24, I began

11

getting very sick. I started experiencing electrical shocks in my teeth and on the left side of my face, including my eye, nose and jaw. For decades, I was in so much pain that I would count from 1 to 10, over and over, to keep from taking my life because of the unbelievable pain. I would challenge myself to just make it to 10 seconds without killing myself. We now know that what I had was Trigeminal Neuralgia. (This disease has recently been named Suicide Disease because of the vast number of people who commit suicide in attempt to be free of this disease's pain, which has been called the worst pain known to man.) Trigeminal Neuralgia affects the part of the brain where an artery connects with the trigeminal nerve; the artery whips that large nerve with every pulse. I spent 28 years in this horrible pain, also suffering from migraines and migraine clusters 24/7 for 27 of those years — along with pain from a back injury from a horse accident. After a botched brain surgery at Cedars-Sinai Medical Center in Los Angeles, my face was scarred with a third-degree burn from doctor-prescribed medication, my lips were severely disfigured, and I lost my left eye. I was left in a much worse and more painful condition than before surgery. I was told by doctors at both Barnes Hospital in St. Louis and at Mayo Clinic that this pain level is where many people literally lose their minds. These were just a few of the painful and hard diseases that I was diagnosed with. Although I am still overcoming some health issues, the Lord has used natural products to heal me in several areas. Then on September 21, 2012, the Lord completely healed me of Trigeminal Neuralgia at a Joyce Meyer conference in St. Louis!

During these years prior to my healings, as I was confined to my bed most of the time, I sought to hear the Lord's voice as fervently as if I were seeking the light switch in a dark and strange room! During these very hard times of torture, I would hear the Lord's sweet voice giving me such beautiful words of comfort and love. Scriptures in the Bible, along with these words, became as beams of sunshine shining through a very difficult and scary storm. This is when I began writing His words and filling notebooks with them. Hearing His voice is what kept me alive during seasons and decades of such intense pain. I drew much strength, faith, comfort, and encouragement from these words of love, correction, wisdom, and revelation from the heart of the Father. He showed me revelations of His Kingdom, as well as great insight into the strategies of the enemy, and how the kingdom of darkness operates and deceives.

This book was written in First Person, from the Father, because that is how I heard it spoken to me. I pray, as you read this book, that *every* day will be relevant to your day and that you will feel His Love in every sentence you read and meditate upon — whether it is His celebration of you or His gentle correction. I long for you, my dear friend, to be comforted as I have been comforted by the Father's Love and Wisdom. I know many suffer much in their lives. My prayer is that this book provides answers in your life, especially during dark and lonely seasons. It is my desire that you feel the heartbeat of the Father, Son, and Holy Spirit through His warnings, His words of Wisdom, and His wonderful Love for you. When reading this book, be diligent to set aside this time to hear your Heavenly Father. Read every sentence very carefully and ask Him to show you what you have never seen before! Allow Him the time to speak to you personally. Do not allow distractions to steal what the Father wants to reveal to *you*! Only He knows what you will face every day. He wants you to know that He is not indifferent to your struggles, trials, and triumphs! My prayer is this: If you are in need of His Wisdom, may He lavishly grant you wisdom and understanding. If you are not certain of His Love, may you be filled and overflowing with the assurance of His Love! If you are in pain, may you be completely comforted as only your Father can comfort! If you have been ensnared by lies of the enemy, may you see the Truth that will set you free! And if you are in need of revelation, may you be completely satisfied!

The Father longs for you to understand that you are treasured! He wants you to understand that He is bound by His Word and by the Laws of His Kingdom. He honors His Word above His name (Psalm 138:2-3). He wants you to know that Love always comes with choices, and He will never override your choices (Deuteronomy 30:19).

I bless you, my dear friend, to hear from the Father's heart as you continue your journey as a child of the Most High God!

— Maribeth Eickhoff

Testimonials

It's an honor and my pleasure to recommend to you this book by Maribeth Eickhoff. I have always been amazed at her sensitivity to the Holy Spirit, and have found her prophetic gifting to be very unique, with her witty use of words and riddles.

As you read the Kingdom power nuggets in this book each day, I believe you will enter into a new dimension of hearing for yourself the Lord speak in so many ways and facets.

Maribeth's words and keen insight in each of these **365 Life Sentences** will inspire you, as well as challenge you, to continue to press into *all* of what Holy Spirit is saying.

I encourage you to take one a day and fully digest it — then experience the strength and vitality contained in these prophetic nuggets.

This book carries with it an anointing that will impart to you a greater understanding and level of hearing from the Lord for yourself, thereby unlocking your future and destiny.

As you progress forward each day, you will find your own life being impacted and advancing into God's original design for you.

Thank you, Maribeth, for sharing your intimate times and power nuggets with all of us.

— Gaye Rogers, Healing House,
Kentucky Awakening,
Center for Kingdom Development,
Owensboro, Kentucky

What a joy and honor it is to know Maribeth! We are part of a prophetic ministry team. She has such a sense of humor and she knows the Lord intimately. She flows strongly in revelation gifts, especially in the prophetic. She hears clearly from the Lord and is very balanced in her gifting. She is a good friend and a great blessing to the Body of Christ. You are going to be blessed!

— Rev. Gail Morgan,
Prayer Center,
Mt. Carmel, Illinois

I have known Maribeth Eickhoff for several years as her pastor and friend. She is one of the most delightful prophetic voices speaking today. Maribeth hears from God in such unique, accurate and profound ways. She has come through many hard times, but her close relationship with the Lord has always brought her through with glorious victory. I know this book will bring healing, insight, and joy to many.

— Pastor Betsy Pfohl.
Rhema graduate and
Pastor of Destiny Of Faith
Community Church

There is an anointing on this author, Maribeth Eickhoff, that will bring you into the presence of the Lord. These *365 Life Sentences* are sprinkled with salt and light. When you apply the wisdom in these sentences, it is truly Proverbs 25:11. ... "*A word fitly spoken and in due season is like apples of gold in settings of silver.*"

— KIM KEEPES,
DIRECTOR, OUT OF ZION PRAYER CENTER

Maribeth is one of those clean prophetic voices coming on the scene now. This book comes from her relationship with Christ Jesus. He has taught her His voice. That is how she hears so clearly His words for herself and others that she has been called to speak into.

— JANE SIMMONS,
HEALING ROOMS OF WABASH COUNTY

Prologue

My child, I AM Love! My Love for you is a language that never needs an interpreter. My Love and mercy are so vast that I need a new day, every day throughout eternity, just to express and display a new dimension of Me. My Love for you cannot ever be contaminated or contained. My Love never changes! You are perfectly loved and perfectly Mine — even when you, as dust, are not perfect! Oh, seek Me! Call on Me! I AM ever approachable and will never reproach you. Can you feel Me wooing you to draw closer to My heart? Do you know that you have given My heart the reason to sing? You have been tattooed on My flesh by the indelible Ink of My Son's Blood! You are forever and eternally loved! You did nothing to cause Me to love you — except you were born. You are loved because you exist! Your Heavenly Father

Behold, I have indelibly imprinted (tattooed a picture of) you on the palm of each of My hands; [O Zion] your walls are continually before Me.

— Isaiah 49:16 AMPC

It is because of the Lord's mercy and loving-kindness that we are not consumed, because His [tender] compassions fail not. They are new every morning; great and abundant is Your stability and faithfulness.

— Lamentations 3:22-23 AMP

Isaiah 43;18-19; Proverbs 11:20;
Psalm 136:2; Romans 8:39; 1 John 4:8

If you do not know
Who I AM, you will
never know who you are!

I AM! I AM Alpha and I AM Omega. Everything that exists came from Me. I AM as the earth and I AM Living Water! I AM as lightning and I AM as thunder. *I AM as a baby's smile and I AM as a lion's roar. I AM too large to contain and too impressive to ignore.* I AM in you! I AM what gives you significance. Without Me, you would still be dust. Know this: I refuse to live in the ordinary; this makes you extraordinary! When you understand My vastness, you will understand yourself as the miracle from the blast of My Breath. My Breath is Love, and My Love is My Breath! Is your breath for love? *Do you breathe to love as you love to breathe?* You must know your significance because I AM your Father. Your bloodline is that of the Royal Alpha bloodline. Your destiny is compacted with eminent purpose. Make no mistake. I make no mistakes! Wisdom says: When you see that I AM limitless, you will stop limiting yourself. I know you by name. You are My reason to smile every day! The closer you become to Me, the more you will see Me in you!

> *See what great love the Father has lavished on us,*
> *that we should be called children of God!*
> — 1 JOHN 3:1

SEE ALSO: PSALM 82:6; 1 JOHN 4:7; PSALM 139:14-16; ROMANS 8:39

Have the courage to let go of what sustained you during the 'last' season!

This is key to movement and success in this new season that I AM leading you into! My Kingdom is in constant movement forward. Are you willing to let go of what was vital during the last season, but has now become a hindrance to you? The afterbirth is the perfect example of this Kingdom key! Before your birth, all of it was vitally necessary to your growth and ability to survive. In this new season, the afterbirth must be discarded because the blood is no longer connected; it is dead! Never cling to what has already died! Allow Me to show you what you are clinging to that is old and dead — what is no longer connected to My Son's Blood! Wisdom says: You must let go of things you think you know before I reveal My all-knowing Truth! Ask Me for the courage and the bravery to let go of what has become old and dead and to grab hold of what is alive and necessary for this new season. I always ask you to let go of what was good, so you will reach for what is better!

SEE ALSO: PHILIPPIANS 3:12-19; ECCLESIASTES 3:1; HEBREWS 12:1

Do not allow familiarity to contaminate My Word's purity.

This Gift of My Word has been given freely to **you.** Whose tongue is pure enough to even utter such a prize and treasure? Whose eyes are so undefiled as to even gaze upon this Master's Peace? Whose ears are pure enough to be counted among the blessed to hear such a symphony of power? Whose hands are holy enough to even carry this Ark of the Covenant, My Word? Whose heart is counted among the most fortunate to have Me, My Word, growing as a Holy Garden inside of them? You, Child of the Most High God. With My Word in you, you are literally pregnant with the King of kings. Just as Mary agreed to be My chosen vessel, so are you carrying this Holy Life. From her belly she brought forth the Source of All Life, Jesus; so from your belly shall flow rivers of Living Water. Wisdom says: Do not allow familiarity to contaminate My Word's purity. Read My Word with expectation and holy reverence. The Israelites carried My Ark at the risk of death, but you carry My Ark that resists death.

> *"Whoever believes in me, as Scripture has said, rivers of living water will flow from within them."* – JOHN 7:38

SEE ALSO: JOHN 15:7; LUKE 1; ISAIAH 58:11

If you suffer from an identity crisis, it is because you have not *yet* found your name in My Word.

You can find your identity every time you read My Son's name — "in Him" — in My Word. Pray for the revelation that you are "in Jesus" and Jesus is in you. It is so crucial that you know *why* you have the privilege and right to use My Son's holy name by proxy in the Courtroom of Heaven. When you use His name, you decree by legal right that you are one with Him, just as a spouse has right to everything the other spouse owns. Just as two become one flesh in the marriage of one man and one woman, so it is with Jesus and His Bride. You, the Bride, have taken the Groom's name and have rights to everything — all power and authority — that is His. A Bride is never a beggar of her rights! Every Bride knows her position as being loved and at the center of the Bridegroom's heart. Be secure in your position of being seated with King Jesus. Wisdom says: Only you have the legal right to use your own name. Consider this: You have been given the legal right to use the name of Jesus. This is because you died and Jesus now lives in you.

I promised you as a pure bride to one husband — Christ.
— 2 CORINTHIANS 11:2 NLT

"... so that they may be one as we are one." — JOHN 17:11

SEE ALSO: JOHN 15:5; GALATIANS 2:20

You were born with the option to quit, but not the right.

Every decision and choice that you make not only affects you and everyone around you, but it affects Me and My Kingdom. Soldiers do not have the right to decide if they want to follow orders or complete assignments. They lose these rights when they join the military. They now belong to their commander in chief. As your Commander in Chief, I give you assignments that have an eternal purpose. The lives of many people are at stake. They are depending upon you! Wisdom says: I AM determined to bless those who are determined to keep going! You do not have the right to quit on your Kingdom assignment. Seek Me today for the strength to carry out *your* personal assignment with perseverance! Know this today: I will never quit on you, even if you choose to quit on Me.

> *Since we are surrounded by such a great cloud of witnesses, ... let us run with perseverance the race marked out for us.*
> — HEBREWS 12:1

> *We are hard pressed on every side, but not crushed; perplexed, but not in despair; persecuted, but not abandoned; struck down, but not destroyed.*
> — 2 CORINTHIANS 4:8-9

SEE ALSO: ISAIAH 40:31

January 6

Live a life of excellence, and watch promotion hunt you down!

Doing things with excellence gets My attention! A king is called "Your Excellency." As your King, I seek excellence *from* you, because I give nothing less than excellence *to* you. Do not confuse excellence with perfection. There is a vast difference. An excellent spirit comes from Me. A perfectionist spirit comes from a root of inadequacy and is torment. To live in excellence is to make *Me* look good. To be a perfectionist is to make *you* look good. This one area is keeping so many people from promotion. In My Kingdom, to live a life of excellence should be the norm, not the exception. Wisdom says: To be excellent is to do everything for My Glory and Honor. This means to serve Me and My children with your whole heart, without complaining. Know today that I do not require you to be perfect. *But, choose to represent Me well by living a life of excellence!* Those who are **excel**ling in My Kingdom are those who are **excel**lent in My Kingdom.

*O Lord, our Lord, how **excellent** (majestic and glorious) **is Your name** in all the earth!* — Psalm 8:1 AMP

*Then this Daniel became distinguished ... because an **excellent spirit** was in him. And the king planned to set him over the whole kingdom.* — Daniel 6:3

24

See also: Colossians 3:23; 2 Peter 1:3-4

Those who choose to war in My Spirit get the spoils of war; those who stay in the palace just get spoiled!

Are you willing to leave the comfort of the palace for the uncomfortable position of the foxhole? The only way to get the spoils of the enemy is to plunder the enemy! Just because you have been reborn in the position of a king does not mean that you do not have to leave the comfort of My Palace. Learn the lesson from King David. When he refused to go to war with his men, he became ensnared in the sin of lies and murder! When you stay in the palace too long, you become selfish and entitled. Staying in places of comfort will breed complacency. Those who become complacent become self-serving! You cannot serve yourself and Me at the same time! I have assigned you to the foxhole of prayer and praise! Wisdom says: To be a warrior in My Kingdom, you must be willing to engage the enemy with My weapons of prayer and praise! I AM your firm Strength Who teaches you to war. Fall in love with My people, not your palace!

See also: Psalm 144:1; 2 Samuel 11

January 8

You cannot be in two places
— fear and faith —
at the same time.

Fear is not a fact! Fear is a lie! The enemy lies to you about Me because every lie is designed to twist and pervert My character so that you will question My Love for you as your trustworthy Father. If you take this bait, then you will be full of fear! Every fear is simply faith in the enemy to hurt you, instead of faith in Me to protect and love you. Fear is a choice, as is faith. When you are fearful, you miss the opportunity to enact the spiritual force of faith — which is power, love, and a sound mind. Fear makes you powerless; faith makes you powerful in Me. Every fear is an issue of not trusting Me and My Love for you. Every fear is designed to make Me seem weak. Every fear is a lie disguised as truth. Wisdom says: Choose today not to *entertain* fear, but to *enforce* the power of faith! I AM for you. There is nothing to fear! I know you by name and you are Mine. Fear not, for I AM with you. You are My top priority today.

And without faith it is impossible to please God, because anyone who comes to him must believe that he exists and that he rewards those who earnestly seek him.
— HEBREWS 11:6

For God has not given us a spirit of fear, but of power and of love and of a sound mind. — 2 TIMOTHY 1:7 NKJV

Your enemy sees
passive as permissive.

You do not have to sit back and take everything that the enemy throws at you! Being passive is being spiritually lazy. Why would I have given you My armor to use against the enemy if I expected you to be passive? There is nothing passive about war. My Kingdom suffers violence, but the violent *take* it by force. If you are passive with the enemy, he will steal from you. In being passive, you are giving him permission to destroy your life. *You cannot be passive and passionate about Me at the same time!* I see you as one with great valor! Wisdom says: Do not make it easy for the enemy to steal from you. Use the power and authority that I have given you to enforce your rights. You are made in My image, and nothing about Me is passive! You are already seated with Christ in heavenly places. Be passionate about your position in Christ.

The kingdom of heaven has endured violent assault,
and violent men seize it by force [as a precious prize
— a share in the heavenly kingdom is sought with
most ardent zeal and intense exertion].

— MATTHEW 11:12 AMP

SEE ALSO: JOHN 10:10; HEBREWS 11:6; 2 CORINTHIANS 10:4-7

I do not condemn you.
I commend you.

When I think of you, I think of what is true, lovely, pure, admirable, and excellent. This is what I see in you when you are reborn in the likeness of My Son, Jesus. ***These praiseworthy thoughts toward you outnumber the grains of sand.*** Could anyone even estimate the number of grains of sand on all the beaches, in the oceans, and in the deserts? Neither can My thoughts toward you be numbered! Wisdom says: When you realize how I see you through the eyes of grace, love, and mercy you will understand that I do not condemn you; I commend you. I think the best of you, even when you do not! Draw near Me today, knowing that My thoughts of good toward you outnumber the sand! I AM never ***appalled*** at you; I AM ever ***applauding*** you.

Finally, brothers and sisters, whatever is true, whatever is noble, whatever is right, whatever is pure, whatever is lovely, whatever is admirable — if anything is excellent or praiseworthy — think about such things.
— PHILIPPIANS 4:8

How precious also are Your thoughts to me, O God! How vast is the sum of them! If I could count them, they would outnumber the sand.
— PSALM 139:17-18 AMP

SEE ALSO: PSALM 139: 1-5; GENESIS 32:12

My woman is the perfect collaboration of Me.

My woman is as the sweet and holy blend of spices that burn before My throne. I have crowned and anointed her with the perfect portion of Me, the Father — and the Son, and Holy Spirit. In her I have given these attributes of My heart as Father: She is a life giver. She is all about love, compassion, and genuineness of heart. She cannot accept deception in love. She is the protector of the weak and helpless, as in the case of children. She will fight anything and anyone to protect life. Can you see how she is also just like My Son, Jesus? With great love, she is willing to carry life in her body. She does not back away from serving and sacrifice. She runs toward it, just as Jesus did. No matter the cost, she gives her life to bring forth life. ***She will take her last breath thinking of her children, just as My Son took His last breath thinking of My children.*** Can you also see My Holy Spirit in her? She is wonderful and full of wonder. She is named helpmeet, which is similar to the Holy Spirit's name, Helper. She nurtures, comforts, and teaches with the gentle Love of My Holy Spirit. Wisdom says: She is named "woman"; *woe* to *man* who mistreats, misuses, or dismisses her, because I made her gender. Woe to man who cannot see Me in her. Honor all the women in your life today. They are one of My reflections to the world.

While the king was at his table, my perfume spread its fragrance. — Song of Solomon 1:12

29

1 Corinthians 11:9; 1 Peter 4:16-19; Genesis 2:23; Song of Solomon 1:13-16

The most deadly words are not curses said by others; they are curses that you speak about yourself.

What you say or think about yourself will become a self-fulfilling prophecy. What you say about yourself will either bless or curse you. There is no such thing as a harmless thought or a harmless word. What you say and think about yourself will become the truth you will have to live by — for good or for evil. You are given the privilege to think and speak for yourself to *rule* your life, not *ruin* your life. You pay for what you say. So spend your spoken words and thoughts wisely. Wisdom says: Choose to think and speak words of *life* today. Meditate on what I have already decreed about you in My Word! Since I cannot lie, My Love for you is absolute Truth. Trust in My Truth that you are deeply and dearly loved!

The tongue has the power of life and death, and those who love it will eat its fruit.
— Proverbs 18:21

For as he thinks in his heart, so is he.
— Proverbs 23:7

Peter swore, "A curse on me if I'm lying — I don't know the man!" And immediately the rooster crowed.
— Matthew 26:74 NLT

You are My gift to this world!

You will never know how many lives you have changed and how many lives you have saved — just by being alive! I blessed the earth with your presence. If you did not exist, it would alter the course of more lives than you can ever fathom! You are the answer to many prayers. You are the answer to many cries. Because of you, the world is a better place. Because of you, My Son is **duplicated**. You are My hands reaching out to the sick and hurting! Your mouth is My mouth to speak Life in a dying world. Never underestimate your worth! Your birth is proof of your worth. I AM captivated by you! ***When you are captivated by My Love, you will not be easily held captive by the enemy.*** Wisdom says: You can change the world by loving just one person today! Know this: You changed My world just by being born.

Every good and perfect gift is from above.
— JAMES 1:17

*This [peace, righteousness, security, triumph over opposition] is the heritage of the servants of the Lord [**those in whom the ideal Servant of the Lord is reproduced**].*
— ISAIAH 54:17 AMP

Follow the example of Christ.
— 1 CORINTHIANS 11:1

Be unpredictable to the enemy!

When someone is predictable to the enemy, they are *foretelling* with precision the calculations and knowledge of precise details about what they will do next. This one strategy alone can win or lose wars. To win a battle, the enemy *depends* on your predictability. Then he can stay one step ahead in the attacks. Being unpredictable frustrates him. It sends confusion into the enemy's camp. Use My Wisdom in warfare. Be very predictable to Me alone. This is being faithful. I will always use someone to advance My Kingdom when I can predict their obedience. I reward those who are predictable to *Me*! Wisdom says: Remember today that the easier you make it for the enemy to *predict*, the easier you make it for him to *afflict*.

> *Put on God's whole armor ... that you may be able successfully to stand up against [all] the strategies and the deceits of the devil.* — Ephesians 6:11 AMP

> *Wisdom is better than weapons of war.* — Ecclesiastes 9:18 AMP

> *For though we walk (live) in the flesh, we are not ... using mere human weapons.* — 2 Corinthians 10:3 AMP

Winning in life is always by choice, not chance!

Do not wait until you are in a crisis before you make a decision to walk out of *every* trial victoriously! Be proactive! Make the decision now that you will press on, regardless! Settle your mind now that nothing will take you out of your race! Set your mind today on My Promises of victory. And remember, the trials from the enemy that you overcome in victory in Me are not just for you. They are designed to always help someone else too. Your testimony will give glory to Me and help others. Wisdom says: To quit never happens by accident. It is always by choice. Those who quit are those who forget that I AM with you and holding you closely! I AM deeply acquainted with those who refuse to quit! Never forget: The enemy quakes in absolute fear when you absolutely refuse to quit.

> *Do you not know that in a race all the runners run, but only one gets the prize? Run in such a way as to get the prize.*
> — 1 Corinthians 9:24

> *But thanks be to God! He gives us the victory through our Lord Jesus Christ.*
> — 1 Corinthians 15:57

See also: Deuteronomy 30:19

To make your Christian walk about **you** is the same as starting a false religion.

The Kingdom is all about the King — My Son, Jesus. It is not just about you! You are an important part of My Kingdom. I have a divine purpose for creating you. But you are not to get any of the glory that is due My Son. He is King of kings and the Lord of lords. To make your Christian walk about you is to set yourself up as an idol. You cannot have idols without pride. In My Body, there is no room for pride. I oppose the proud, but give grace to those who walk with Me in humility. If Christianity becomes more about you than about Christ, it can no longer be called Christianity. Wisdom says: Do not disregard or dismiss My gifting that I placed in you! I made you wonderfully with amazing gifts. But always acknowledge My Gift, Jesus, who is continually working through you to reach this hurting world.

*But if God himself has taken up residence in your life, you can hardly be **thinking more of yourself** than of him.*
— ROMANS 8:9 MSG

*But **seek first his kingdom** and his righteousness.*
— MATTHEW 6:33

*"He must become greater and greater, and **I must become less and less."***
– JOHN 3:30 TLB

If the enemy cannot cause **destruction**, he will gladly settle for **distraction**!

A magician deceives by distraction! Likewise, that is how your enemy tricks you — by distorting your perception of reality. What could you really see if you refused to be distracted? When you are being *tempted* by distraction, be still and know that *I AM* your Father. Seek My perception and My reality. If you are without peace, then you are being *attacked* by distraction. Wisdom says: Today, take the time to quiet yourself and seek My Presence. Protect our time together, and do not allow the enemy to steal it with distractions. When you grant Me attention, I grant you My affection.

> *[And I am distracted] at the noise of the enemy.*
> — Psalm 55:3 AMP

> *Looking away [from all that will distract] to Jesus, Who is the Leader and the Source of our faith [giving the first incentive for our belief] and is also its Finisher [bringing it to maturity and perfection].*
> — Hebrews 12:2 AMP

See also: 1 Corinthian 7:35; Ecclesiastes 8:16

January 18

Being grateful is perfect spiritual warfare!

I dwell in the midst of gratefulness. Being grateful is not an attitude only. It is appreciating Me and My Covenant Promises *in your heart*. Being grateful, even through hard times, does not mean that you are grateful for the circumstances; it means that you are grateful for My promises to help you and never leave you. Meditate upon all the times in the past that I have saved and delivered you. This builds faith to fight in your current situation. A grateful heart is a faith-filled heart, and will certainly see My blessings! The enemy is defenseless when you are grateful to Me. Wisdom says: Remember today that being grateful cuts off the enemy's access to your heart. It is hard to steal from a grateful heart. That is why being grateful is perfect spiritual warfare.

Praise the Lord, my soul; all my inmost being, praise his holy name. Praise the Lord, my soul, and forget not all his benefits. — PSALM 103:1-2

Praise the Lord, all his heavenly hosts. — PSALM 103:21

Remember what Christ taught, ... singing to the Lord with thankful hearts. — COLOSSIANS 3:16 TLB

SEE ALSO: ROMANS 8:37; JONAH 2:9

The enemy is not afraid of your information about Me; he is terrified of your revelation from Me!

Have you ever wondered why the enemy asked to sift Simon Peter as wheat? When Jesus asked, "Who do people say the Son of Man is?" The disciples answered Him by saying, "Some say John the Baptist; others say Elijah..." This was *information*! This is just second-hand information or opinions, which *never* requires a relationship with Me! Only Simon Peter answered with *revelation* from Me because *information* did not satisfy his appetite for Me! Information will never satisfy! Only revelation will sustain your hungry heart when you want an authentic relationship with Me, your Father! When you are graced with revelation from My heart and My Kingdom, you are such a threat to the defeated kingdom of darkness! Wisdom says: *Authority is never granted through information, but through revelation! My Body can be built only on revelation. The keys to My Kingdom are given to those who desire intimacy with Me!* Notice how revelation of Who I AM changed Peter's identity and destiny. I changed Peter's name from Simon Son of Jonah to Peter, My son. Revelation always reveals sonship. Today, ask Me to reveal Myself to you.

Hypocritical prayer and worship is as the kiss of Judas!

Hypocrisy is the practice of claiming to have moral standards or beliefs to which one's own behavior does not conform. Hypocrisy is pretense. Deception. Betrayal. Don't be a hypocrite like Judas and betray My Son with a kiss (hypocritical prayer and worship). Judas greeted My Son not only with a kiss, but with pretended warmth and devotion. He greeted Him with "Hail!" — meaning "greetings of good health and long life." This is hypocritical prayer and worship, because he was just pretending to love My Son. Prayer means to talk to Me, face to face. When you pray and worship Me, you actually kiss My cheek! Wisdom says: Your eloquent speech does not impress Me. I desire you to have pure motives and a genuine spirit. Beware that the enemy will position a Judas around the authentic move of Jesus. Kiss My cheek with authentic prayers of faith that not only move mountains, but also move My heart and hands to help you in the situation that you are facing this day. Seek and love Me with a pure heart.

*And he came up to Jesus at once and said, **Hail (greetings, good health to You, long life to You), Master! And he embraced Him and kissed Him with [pretended] warmth and devotion.*** — MATTHEW 26:49 AMP

Jesus asked him, "Judas, are you betraying the Son of Man with a kiss?" — LUKE 22:48

SEE ALSO: *MATTHEW 6:5-6*

If life has lost its flavor, could your tongue be the reason?

Taste and see that I AM good! I have placed taste buds on your tongue not only for your enjoyment of food, but also to remind you of your ability to choose how you want to season your life and the lives of those around you. There are four main categories of taste buds: salty, sour, bitter and sweet. Choose to season lives with the sweetness of My Word — with blessing — instead of harming others with bitter, and sour words. Choose My Words of Salt and Light to release My anointing that breaks yokes of bondage in your life and the lives of those around you. When you speak My Word into any situation, My Word releases the richest flavors, seasonings, fragrances, and oils of My anointing that change the entire atmosphere for My power! Wisdom says: Make the decision to be seasoned in My Word and in the things of My Kingdom. Speak My Words very strategically to change the circumstances in your life.

Let your conversation be always full of grace, seasoned with salt, so that you may know how to answer everyone.
– COLOSSIANS 4:6

Taste and see that the Lord is good.
– PSALM 34:8

*From your **sweet words** I have gathered the **richest perfumes and spices**.*
– SONG OF SOLOMON 5:1 AMP

SEE ALSO: JAMES 3:3-13; MATTHEW 5:13; PROVERBS 18:21

You cannot survive on **yesterday's faith** any better than you can survive on **yesterday's food.**

Now faith is... You will never be able to survive on yesterday's faith any better than you can survive on yesterday's food. The only time your soul will be at peace is when you are thinking and living in the ***now*** — the present tense — with Me! Meditating on and living in the past leads to regret. Living in regret is living in constant torment. To regret is to regress in your faith, hope, and peace. Regret touches every part of your life! Meditating on and living in the future brings anxiety and fear. Anxiety is exhausting and paralyzing. It is designed to steal and consume your energy that could be used for the present. Wisdom says: You cannot change the past, but I can heal and redeem it so it brings Me glory! If you desire Peace today, you can find Me when you live in the present — the now. ***Now faith is...***

> ***Now faith is*** *confidence in what we hope for and assurance about what we do not see.*
> — HEBREWS 11:1

> *... through whom we have gained access by **faith** into this grace in which we **now** stand.*
> — ROMANS 5:2

> *And **now** these three remain: **faith**, hope and love.*
> — 1 CORINTHIANS 13:13

SEE ALSO: MATTHEW 6:34; MATTHEW 6:11; HEBREWS 13:8

Do you have a heart murmur?

Murmuring is a heart problem, not a mouth problem. In the physical realm, a heart murmur is a disease; it is a recurring, abnormal sound heard in the heart through a stethoscope. It is usually a sign of disease or damage. *Likewise, when you murmur and complain, it is a low, indistinct, continuous and abnormal sound — from your heart to Mine.* To "myrrh-myrrh" is a double portion of bitterness. When you murmur and complain, it contaminates you with bitterness! Wisdom says: When you are My child, it is not normal to murmur and complain. I receive your praise and gratefulness, but not your grumblings. Today, listen to the sound that you hear flowing from your heart through your mouth. It is a clear indication of what you have been meditating upon: My Word or the enemy's words. When you are thanking Me for My faithfulness, it is very easy to be grateful! Gratefulness is reminding yourself that I AM full of greatness!

> *"The Lord has heard your grumblings which you murmur against Him... Your murmurings are not against us* [Moses and Aaron], *but against the Lord."* — Exodus 16:8

Do all things without murmurings and disputings.
— Philippians 2:14 KJV

See also: Matthew 12:34

To **resist** change is to resist Me.
To **embrace** change is to embrace Me.

If you do not *embrace* change, you will *resist* it! If you resist Me in an uncomfortable season, you are resisting My grace to help you walk through it! Familiarity thrives where there is little or no change. When you look for Me in the new season (see Son), you will be amazed at the amount of new growth you will experience. But if you get too comfortable, you will stop growing. Wisdom says: Change will come, whether or not you choose to receive it or embrace it! Consider this: If you are too comfortable in your current season of life, you are most likely not growing or moving forward. With every uncomfortable season, I provide My grace to carry you through it. Whenever you resist change, you resist Me. Today, choose to embrace change, and embrace Me!

> *To everything there is a **season**, A time for every purpose under heaven: ... A time to plant, And a time to pluck what is planted; ... A time to break down, And a time to build up; ... A time to mourn, And a time to dance; A time to cast away stones, And a time to gather stones; A time to embrace, And a time to refrain from embracing.*
>
> — Ecclesiastes 3:1-5 NKJV

See also: Daniel 2:21; Jeremiah 8:7

Insecurity is a war within, not out!

If you are insecure, it is because you do not see yourself like *I* see you — and you are not convinced within yourself that I truly find you worthy of My Love. Insecurity leads you to war with other people. Thus, insecurity is a favorite in the enemy's arsenal, because it leaves you powerless. The enemy will try to deceive you into thinking that your problem is with people. It is not. The fact is: You are not comfortable in your own flesh. Your fight is with your flesh. Insecurity is a war within, not out! A war within will make you sick! And the only cure is to find your identity in Me alone — not in things and people. Wisdom says: I AM the only cure for this heart condition of insecurity. Today, you will only find true Security and Safety when you learn to trust in the fact that I love you unconditionally! I gave My Best, Jesus, so that you could rest in the Truth that you are completely loved!

> *"'Love the Lord your God with all your heart and with all your soul and with all your mind and with all your strength.' The second is this: 'Love your neighbor as yourself.' There is no commandment greater than these."*
> — MARK 12:30-31

> *You will be **secure**, because there is hope; you will look about you and take your rest in safety.* — JOB 11:18

Your body affects My Body.

Your body truly affects the Body of Christ. Remember, you are just a guest in your body! How would you expect a guest to treat your house? I expect the same respect. You are no longer on the title deed to your house (body). I AM. You have become such an important part of My Kingdom and are the temple of My Holy Spirit. If I did not need you in My Kingdom, I would not have created you. A sick and poorly-kept body not only affects Me, but the world. Wisdom says: Be obedient and make wise choices in how you steward My temple. Today, make Me feel welcome in My house! Make My Holy Ghost your Holy Guest.

Didn't you realize that your body is a sacred place, the place of the Holy Spirit? Don't you see that you can't live however you please, squandering what God paid such a high price for? The physical part of you is not some piece of property belonging to the spiritual part of you. God owns the whole works. So let people see God in and through your body.

— 1 CORINTHIANS 6:19-20 MSG

Therefore, I urge you, brothers, in view of God's mercy, to offer your bodies as living sacrifices, holy and pleasing to God — this is your spiritual act of worship.

— ROMANS 12:1

You are not an only child!
You are in My holy family.

I instructed you to pray "Our Father," not "My Father"; give "us" this day, not give "me"; forgive "us" our debts, not "my" debts; lead "us" not into temptation, not lead "me"; deliver "us" from evil, not deliver "me." That's because you are not an only child! You have many brothers and sisters. My Son, Jesus, taught you this holy prayer to engage the Law of Agreement and the force of unity. When you pray My Covenant prayer, know this: When I hear you say this prayer, My heart sings for joy. This is not just an ordinary religious prayer. This is a ***declaration*** of My Covenant with you. This prayer paralyzes hell and enforces My Kingdom of power on earth. Wisdom says: I give you the authority to use My holy name to access the Kingdom of Heaven and make My Kingdom manifest on earth. Unite in agreement with your brothers and sisters. Today, declare that My will be done in your life, just as it is in heaven.

In this manner, therefore, pray:
Our Father in heaven, Hallowed be Your name.
Your kingdom come. Your will be done
On earth as it is in heaven.
Give us this day our daily bread.
And forgive us our debts, As we forgive our debtors.
And do not lead us into temptation,
But deliver us from the evil one.
For Yours is the kingdom and the power
and the glory forever. Amen.

– MATTHEW 6:9-13

Don't fight in your strength. Rest in Mine.

If I AM for you, who can be against you? People will try to rise up against you. The enemy *must* use people to attack you. This has been a very effective way to steal, kill, and destroy from you! ***Do not take it personally when someone hurts you.*** When you do, the hurt can grow into bitterness and unforgiveness. This is a setup from the enemy. Give Me the hurt. It belongs to Me. It is My battle. When I AM for you, what do you *ever* have to fear? Wisdom says: Rest today, knowing I AM your Defender. When you are *resting* in Me, you are *resisting* the enemy. I will never leave you defenseless! You have access to ***all*** of My power as well as My heavenly host to help you in every situation. Rest in the Truth that, long ago, I began fighting the battle that you are facing today! Rest in My Strength.

> *He who dwells in the shelter of the Most High ... will ... **rest** in the shadow of the Almighty [whose power no enemy can withstand].*
> — Psalm 91:1 AMP

> *"All those gathered here will know that it is not by sword or spear that the LORD saves; for the **battle is the LORD's**, and he will give all of you into our hands."*
> — 1 Samuel 17:47

> ***If God is for us, who can be against us?***
> — Romans 8:31-33

Can you see the 'sham' in shame?

You were never meant to be clothed in shame. My Son, Jesus, bore shame for you. When He died on the cross, he made a bold display and public example, triumphing over the enemy. He was stripped and crucified to carry your shame with nakedness so that you would never be clothed with shame. You are now adorned in a royal robe of righteousness, and the enemy is now clothed with disgrace and cloaked in shame. Shame on the enemy — not you! ***No one on earth has the power to shame you.*** That would be a sham — falsely presenting something as truth. Wisdom says: Do not allow anyone to ***clothe*** you with shame! Remember today: Shame is a garment you were never intended to wear! Know that because you are Mine, you will never be put to shame. In Christ, you are blameless and shameless.

> *May my accusers be **clothed** with disgrace and wrapped in **shame** as in a cloak.*
> — Psalm 109:29

> *I will **clothe** his enemies with **shame**.*
> — Psalm 132:18

> *May all who gloat over my distress be put to **shame** and confusion; may all who exalt themselves over me be **clothed** with **shame** and disgrace.*
> — Psalm 35:26

You were designed to carry My Glory, not your cares!

Are you bent over trying to carry your cares? Oh, how I long to release you of those burdens that some insist on carrying! Everything that can afflict you, physically and mentally, was nailed to the cross of My Son, Jesus. How He strained under the weight of your cares and sin. He carried everything that could ever torment your beautiful heart! To cast your cares means to **throw** them, as hard as you are able, on My shoulders, where they belong. To carry your own cares and concerns is a decision that is birthed from pride. Why carry what was already strategically and lovingly placed on My Son? My desire is for you to live completely free of the weight of problems. When you live free of the burdens and cares of life, this is bowing down to Me, your Daddy, in perfect praise. When you allow the enemy to load you down with burdens that Jesus already carried, it is as if you are bowing down to the enemy under the strain of worry. Wisdom says: I designed you to carry My Glory, never your cares! You will not carry My Glory if you are carrying your burdens! *So, release your cares to Me. Don't rehearse your cares to others!* You can share your cares with a few close friends, but remember that rehearsing your cares with people is to enlarge them. Because of My great love for you, allow Me to carry what no one can. When Jesus uttered the words, "It is finished," He utterly destroyed the works of the enemy forever! Give Me everything that concerns you today.

SEE ALSO: 1 PETER 5:7; PSALM 55:22; NAHUM 1:7; PSALM 68:19

No one **owes** you an apology.

To say that someone *owes* you means that you believe someone is in *debt* to you! This implies some ownership of that person; you are holding them hostage emotionally. Do you feel you need an apology before you are able to forgive someone? If you *expect* an apology from someone who has hurt you, then you are walking in unforgiveness! If that is the case, then you would not truly forgive that person, even if you did get the apology! You should not need an apology to be able to forgive. The apology is actually a gift from the person who did the hurting, and it is more for that person than to cover your hurt. The enemy uses this transaction to keep you in bondage to unforgiveness. Although offering an apology would be the right thing to do, it should never be the catalyst for forgiveness. Wisdom says: You forgive for this purpose: so that I, your heavenly Father, can forgive you. Keep in mind today: No apology needed!

"If you forgive people their sins, your Father in heaven will forgive your sins also." — MATTHEW 6:14 NLT

Do not owe anyone anything, but love each other. Whoever loves his neighbor has done what the Law says to do. — ROMANS 13:8 NLT

Are you standing still in **fear**? Or, are you choosing to be still (in **faith**) and know that I AM.

Fear will always stop any forward momentum; faith always moves you forward. Having faith simply means making the decision to believe My Word over the world! It means believing that you receive from Me what you ask when you pray. If you have stayed in the midst of the same trial for a while without making progress, ask yourself where you have let fear creep in. Then have faith by agreeing with My Word. Wisdom says: Remember, faith moves you forward; fear cancels progress! Today, be still, in the confidence that I AM your Father! I have sent My Holy Spirit, the Standby, to help you through every situation. Having faith in My Standby will keep you from standing still in fear.

Be still, and know that I am God.

— Psalm 46:10

*The Lord God is my Strength, my personal bravery, and my invincible army; He makes my feet like hinds' feet and will make me to walk [**not to stand still in terror,** but to walk] and make [spiritual] progress upon my high places [of trouble, suffering, or responsibility]!*

— Habakkuk 3:19 AMP

If we ask anything (make any request) according to His will (in agreement with His own plan), He listens to and hears us.

— 1 John 5:14 AMP

Working for My Love
never **works**.

My Love for you is not based upon performance or doing good works. Yes, your life should yield good works. But these good works should merely be an extension of your faith in Me — not an attempt to earn My Love. Know that My Love for you is unconditional and always consistent because it is based upon the ***finished work*** of My Son, Jesus. When you are born again into the likeness of Jesus, I see Him in you. If I would reject you, I would be rejecting My beloved Son. You are My child. I dearly love you with a love that you do not have to earn or work for. I desire your love in return. Your works merely prove your faith in Me. Your faith without your works is dead. Wisdom says: When you offer Me "works" to earn My Love, I consider them dead works. Today, let your faith show itself by your good works!

No one will be declared righteous in God's sight by the works of the law. — ROMANS 3:20

Faith that doesn't show itself by good works is no faith at all — it is dead and useless. — JAMES 2:17 TLB

For as the body without the spirit is dead, so faith without works is dead also. — JAMES 2:26 NKJV

SEE ALSO: ROMANS 3:27

There is much achieved when heaven and earth agree!

I AM in need of your agreement, not your approval. Do not just try to get Me to agree with what you are praying. Pray My will and not just say prayers of your will. Never confuse prayers of My will with your willful prayers. Remember always that you are setting up My Kingdom on earth, not your own. *There is much power available when you pray My will in heaven on earth, instead of your will on earth to heaven!* I always have the final Word! Do I have the final Word in your life? If not, then you just want My agreement to your will. Wisdom says: Do not say to Me that I must move within the boundaries of religious teachings and man-made doctrines. I have such a lavish reward for those who are willing to lay down their preconceived ideas and past revivals, and who will trust *Me* with obedience as their Father. *You will either do this My way, or you will be in My way!* Listen with great intensity to My instructions, then obey. Ask, and I will grant to you the wisdom and revelation of what I AM doing, so you will not resist Me. I invite you with the greatest of love to agree with what I AM doing and saying.

I appeal to you ... that all of you agree with one another so that there may be no divisions among you and that you may be perfectly united in mind and thought.
- 1 CORINTHIANS 1:10

MATTHEW 6:1-13; MATTHEW 18:19; HOSEA 8:4; 1 JOHN 5:8

Never confuse **resting**
with lack of movement!

Resting in My Promises never means you are to be stationary. My Kingdom is always moving forward! Rest in the fact that I *enjoy* answering your prayers. Resting in My Promises means believing that what you have asked for is already the present possession in your heart. No striving. No working in the flesh. No struggling. No twisting My arm to get My attention. Simply receive My answer by faith. I ask you to pray because I listen and answer your prayers! Wisdom says: Today, choose to rest *in Me* — and indeed, you will truly be moving forward. Rest knowing that you are dearly loved! Rest not in your religion; rest in your reliance on Me! *Rest, not stress!*

Therefore I tell you, whatever you ask for in prayer, believe that you have received it, and it will be yours.
— Mark 11:24

*And if (since) we [positively] know that He listens to us in whatever we ask, we also know [with settled and absolute knowledge] that we have [granted us as our **present possessions**] the requests made of Him.*
— 1 John 5:15 AMP

There remains, then, a Sabbath-rest for the people of God.
— Hebrews 4:9

I only create masterpieces!

What if *your* past — with all its success and mistakes — truly could be a work of art that I would hang in My special place of honor, My gallery of masterpieces? When you surrender your past for **My Glory**, I call it beautiful and a work of art. An artist takes what is basic, ordinary, and even messy, then creates something that is valuable. So allow Me to re-frame the picture of your past into a work of art for My Glory. I AM sharpening My pencils and drawing you into a masterpiece (Master's Peace). I AM not only *drawing* your life into a collector's piece, but I AM *drawing* you closer to My heart. Wisdom says: As the skilled Artist, I AM brilliant at using the dark seasons in your life to "shade" and to add contrast and beauty to My work of art! Trust My gentle hand. Whether I use the slightest touch — or the bold and hard strokes of My pencil — I AM always creating you into a beautiful masterpiece! Today, know that I AM the One Who gives you value! Know that I AM a Miracle Maker. This makes you a miracle and a valuable work of art for My Glory!

For we are God's masterpiece. He has created us anew in Christ Jesus, so we can do the good things he planned for us long ago.
— EPHESIANS 2:10 NLT

SEE ALSO: SONG OF SOLOMON 7:1; JOB 14:15; LAMENTATIONS 4:2

Your body is voice activated.

Your voice carries power in your life! Your body and soul really do believe what you are saying! Even the most cunning and influential lies told by someone else cannot touch the power that your words carry over you. Your entire being is activated by voice recognition. Your cells recognize and obey your voice, not anyone else's — unless you decide what someone else says is truth and choose to believe it. So, what are you telling yourself? Tell yourself the Truth of My Word. My Word is Power. I AM Truth. Wisdom says: Your body recognizes My Word because your body recognizes Me as Creator in you. Give your body instructions today. Use your voice and My Word. Then watch your body respond.

> *It is written: "I believed; therefore I have spoken."*
> *Since we have that same spirit of faith, we also **believe***
> ***and therefore speak.*** — 2 CORINTHIANS 4:13

> *Jesus answered, "I am the way and **the truth** and the*
> *life. No one comes to the Father except through me."*
> — JOHN 14:6

Are you wanting **access to** My throne, or **excess from** My throne?

What are your motives for wanting to approach My throne? Are you longing for time with Me? I AM always longing for your affection, your attention, and your love. I AM like a heart-sore Father who longs for the embrace of His child! No one can comfort Me like you can. Even though I have many children, I have only one of you! There is no other child who can replace what only you can give Me. *You are unquestionably irreplaceable!* While many are approaching My throne with right motives, some have unknowingly slipped into just wanting access to My throne for excess of things. I love to bless My children, and this is part of My Covenant with you. But take heed to this warning: Do not let your heart become polluted by desiring things over Me! Wisdom says: You may have *access* to My throne to express your heart and love for Me. When this is in order, you can expect *excess* from My throne, including grace and mercy in your time of need!

Let us then approach God's throne of grace with confidence, so that we may receive mercy and find grace to help us in our time of need. — HEBREWS 4:16

SEE ALSO: REVELATION 3:21; HEBREWS 1:8; MATTHEW 6:33

A scar is not proof of an injury, but proof of My healing!

A scar is a mark left by a healed cut or wound. It is proof that I heal! When you see your scars, do not meditate upon the injury, but upon My healing power. Focus upon how My Son willingly chose to be scarred so you would not have to be. Scars are reminders that "by His wounds, you were healed." Wisdom says: Learn the lesson of a scar. When skin is cut or injured, it heals even stronger and with thicker skin than before it was ever damaged. When you are cut or hurt, decide to grow stronger and with thicker skin than before. Be determined that you will grow stronger with every attack from the enemy, because of the resurrection power of My Son in you and My great Love for you. Know today that if you have been scarred, I call you as beautiful as My Son, Jesus!

> *He heals the brokenhearted and binds up their wounds.*
>
> — Psalm 147:3

> *Himself bore our sins in His body on the cross, so that we might die to sin and live to righteousness; for by His wounds you were healed.*
> — 1 Peter 2:24 NASB

See also: Luke 10:34

February 9

Unforgiveness is the same as slow suicide!

Unforgiveness evokes the law of sin and death upon yourself — for eternity. ***It is a sin that keeps on killing, from generation to generation.*** Choosing forgiveness, however, evokes My Law of Life and Peace. My Law of Sowing and Reaping is also involved with forgiveness. You cannot be forgiven unless you "sow" forgiveness first. Wisdom says: When you sow forgiveness, you allow Me to make you whole. You cannot remain in wholeness and unforgiveness at the same time. Unforgiveness is a source of self-hatred and self-punishment. Choosing unforgiveness is like choosing a slow and painful death. Every time you choose to forgive, you are choosing to destroy the plans of the enemy instead of destroying your life. When you forgive, you are taking the chains off of yourself and putting them back on the enemy! Today, choose to forgive, and choose to live!

Choose life, that you and your descendants may live.
— Deuteronomy 30:19 AMPC

If you forgive other people when they sin against you, your heavenly Father will also forgive you. But if you do not forgive others their sins, your Father will not forgive your sins.
— Matthew 6:14-15

*He punishes the children and their children for the sin of the parents **to the third and fourth generation.***
— Exodus 34:7

58

See also: Romans 8:2; Deuteronomy 7:9

Avoid dead religion
that will **void** My Word.

Some people want religion instead of relationship because it does not require time and commitment. How can a loving relationship flourish with only scheduled routines that have lost their passion? Dead religion does not require faith because it consists primarily of structure, instead of a personal relationship *with* Me. Religion, by itself, simply rehearses past routines and habits. Religious people, like the Pharisees, want "formulas." Nothing about a relationship with Me requires predetermined steps or formulas. Just because something worked in the past does not mean it will work now — nor will the same instructions work for every struggle. I gave the Israelites different instructions for every battle. Likewise, communicate with Me and get new instructions for each new day. I covet your time and affection! Wisdom says: Who would want *dead* religion when I AM the *Living* God?

> *Thus you are nullifying and making void and of no effect [the authority of] the Word of God through your tradition.*
> — MARK 7:13 AMP

> *"Woe to you, teachers of the law and Pharisees, you hypocrites! You are like whitewashed tombs, which look beautiful on the outside but on the inside are full of the bones of the dead and everything unclean."*
> — MATTHEW 23:27

When you doubt My approval, you will seek man's approval.

I approve of you! If you are seeking man's approval, then you are not seeking My approval. People-pleasers rarely please Me. Thus, when you choose to please people, you are choosing to be in opposition to Me! When you seek man's approval, you give man the power to hurt you — and the enemy will make sure that man destroys you. Wisdom says: *If you know that you have My approval, man's approval means absolutely nothing!* This is true freedom to be yourself — and to be free of the fear of man! Today, I give you permission to be yourself. When I *approve* of you, you have nothing to *prove* to man.

> *Am I now trying to win the approval of human beings, or of God? Or am I trying to please people? If I were still trying to please people, I would not be a servant of Christ.*
> — GALATIANS 1:10

> *Do not work for food that spoils, but for food that endures to eternal life, which the Son of Man will give you. For on him God the Father has placed his seal of approval.*
> — JOHN 6:27

> *So if the Son sets you free, you are truly free.*
> — JOHN 8:36 NLT

SEE ALSO: 1 CORINTHIANS 11:19

If you are being rejected, it is because I AM not being respected.

When someone rejects you, they are rejecting My creation whom I love. They are rejecting Me *in* you! The enemy wants you to take this personally. If he can get you into the trap of taking this personally, then he can steal, kill, and destroy you. Render the enemy harmless and of no effect. See rejection for what it is — to take you down and out! Never forget: When you take rejection personally, you are keeping this attack in your flesh realm where the enemy can win. But when you release all rejection to Me, this battle is kept in My Spirit realm, where I have already won. People reject you when they do not understand something or when they are intimidated by My Presence in you. *It is nothing personal.* Wisdom says: You are My inheritance. I will never reject you. Today, if someone rejects you, consider it a rejection of Me!

Everyone will hate you because of me.

— Luke 21:17

*For the Lord will not reject his people; he will never forsake his **inheritance**.*

— Psalm 94:14

Jesus said to them, "Have you never read in the Scriptures: 'The stone the builders rejected has become the cornerstone.'"

— Matthew 21:42

Rain bow!

If you seem to be experiencing a dark storm with noisy thunder, let My rainbow always be a reminder of My Covenant Promise. The rainbow is a reminder that I commanded the *rain* to *bow* down to Me! That is why My Son, Jesus, had the authority to walk on the water and hush the storm and make it obey and bow down! Know this: After a storm, I send you a rainbow, and I cause the rain to bow its knees in obedience. My Covenant Promise will always carry you through. I promise to never leave you, nor forsake you — no, never. My rainbow proves that I keep My Covenants. Every time that you see a rainbow, you witness again Jesus hushing the storm. Then, once again, without exception, *the rain has to bow*. When the enemy brings the perfect storm, I will always bring you the perfect solution. Wisdom says: Today, use your authority to make the storm bow its knee to you! Know that you reign in life, and everything must bow before you in the name of Jesus!

> *And the one who sat there had the appearance of jasper and ruby. A rainbow that shone like an emerald encircled the throne.*
> — Revelation 4:3

> *I have set my rainbow in the clouds, and it will be the sign of the covenant between me and the earth.*
> — Genesis 9:13

See also: Luke 8:24

I memorized **you** by heart!

When you memorize something or know something *very* well, you say that you know it "by heart." Well, I know *you* by heart. No one has the willingness or the capacity to know and love you like *I* do. You can trust your Father's heart. My heart is ever looking for the prodigal son and earnestly rewarding the faithful at home, as well. Before you even call Me, I AM running to you. I AM the One Who holds you at night and rejoices over you while I sing you to sleep. I know what you like even better than you do. I know all about you. Wisdom says: ***Know that I not only molded you by hand, but I memorized you by heart!***

> *You have searched me, Lord, and you know me. You know when I sit and when I rise; you perceive my thoughts from afar. You discern my going out and my lying down; you are familiar with all my ways. Before a word is on my tongue you, Lord, know it completely.*
> — PSALM 139:1-4

> *The Lord your God ... will take great delight in you; in his love he will ... rejoice over you with singing.*
> — ZEPHANIAH 3:17

> *Yet you desired faithfulness even in the womb; you taught me wisdom in that secret place.*
> — PSALM 51:6

SEE ALSO: PSALM 139: 16-18; PSALM 41:11

If it is easy to compromise in one thing, you can compromise in anything!

To compromise means that you are willing to settle instead of standing up for your values, morals, or the truth. Know this: If you are willing to settle in one area of your life, then you are making it easier to settle in **any** other area of your life, including relationships, habits, or spiritual truths that do not glorify Me. Compromising becomes easier each time you decide to settle. Before you know it, you may compromise in your walk with Me and do things you never thought you would. Wisdom says: Be careful not to compromise your integrity. Compromising, even in what may seem to be small, can lead to settling in life and death issues. Today, trust that I AM your Good Father, and My Love for you will never fade away or be compromised!

"Don't become partners with those who reject God. How can you make a partnership out of right and wrong? That's not partnership; that's war. Is light best friends with dark? Does Christ go strolling with the Devil? Do trust and mistrust hold hands? ... So leave the corruption and **compromise**; *leave it for good," says God. "Don't link up with those who will pollute you. I want you all for myself. I'll be a Father to you; you'll be sons and daughters to me."*

– 2 Corinthians 6:14-18

Supplement your faith with a generous provision of moral excellence.

– 2 Peter 1:5 NLT

My Son, Jesus, wants a Bride that **loves** His name, not just **uses** His name!

"Far above all rule and authority and power and dominion and every name that is named [above every title that can be conferred], not only in this age and in this world, but also in the age and the world to come."

— EPHESIANS 1:21 AMP

My Son, Jesus, deserves a Bride that takes His name in holy matrimony with love and adoration. I have bequeathed to you the highest and the most holy and powerful name that any mouth can speak! No greater honor has been bestowed upon to you, the Bride of Christ! This is proof that you are My child and His Bride. The name of Jesus gives you access to My throne! ***Heaven, earth, hell, and all of creation stand at complete attention every time the name of Jesus is spoken or heard!*** My Son not only wants a Bride that does mighty exploits in His name, but a Bride that honors, loves, and understands the mighty power in My Son's name! Wisdom says: When you, the Bride, ask for anything in the name of Jesus, you are standing in and taking His position of power and authority, because Jesus is the Word. When you say His name, you are enforcing My Word (from Genesis 1:1 to Revelation 22:21). ***Never treat the name of Jesus as just a word. He is the Word!***

SEE ALSO: *1 JOHN 3:23; MATTHEW 7:21-23; JOHN 1:1-13*

There is no such thing as a rational fear when you are in Christ Jesus!

Every form of fear is unnatural to the born-again believer. I have not given you a spirit of fear. I have given you *My* Spirit of power, love, and a sound mind. This crushes all fear. *Fear is a decision, not a reaction.* Fear is optional. *You choose* how to react. If you choose fear, you have not grown into a mature and sufficient understanding of My Love. Wisdom says: Do not fear, for I AM with you. Do not be dismayed, for I AM your God. I will strengthen you and uphold you with My righteous right hand. Make the decision today to not react with fear. Instead, choose love, faith, and peace. Be secure in the truth that I love you with an everlasting love! I AM closer to you than your next breath. You are safe and sound in My arms of love!

There is no fear in love. But perfect love drives out fear.
— 1 JOHN 4:18

A good man ... will never be shaken.
He will not be afraid of evil tidings;
His heart is steadfast, trusting in the Lord.
His heart is established; He will not be afraid.
— PSALM 112:5-8 NKJV

For God has not given us a spirit of fear.
— 2 TIMOTHY 1:7

SEE ALSO: ISAIAH 41:10

A **worrier** will never be a **warrior!**

You were born a worrier, but reborn into a warrior. True warriors are never worriers. Worrying makes you weak. Warriors know they have the victory *before* they go into battle. They do not meditate on fear. Warriors are not filled with dread. Worry disqualifies you as a warrior. You cannot engage in battle over anything that you fear. Faith and peace are in the heart of a warrior. Wisdom says: I AM a Warrior. I AM the Lord of Hosts, the Commander of the armies of Israel. Know that you frustrate the enemy when you refuse to fall for the trap of worry. When you refuse to worry, you engage in the battle as My Warrior, Jesus! I AM Faithful and Trustworthy. Do not worry!

The Lord is a warrior.
— EXODUS 15:3

*David said to the Philistine, "You come against me with sword and spear and javelin, but I come against you in the name of the Lord Almighty, the **God of the armies of Israel**, whom you have defied."*
— 1 SAMUEL 17:45

Do not be anxious about anything, but in every situation, by prayer and petition, with thanksgiving, present your requests to God.
— PHILIPPIANS 4:7

Though an army besiege me, my heart will not fear; though war break out against me, even then I will be confident.
— PSALM 27:3

67

February 19

You govern the measurement of how much you receive from Me.

I AM a measure-for-measure God. I do not set the standard for measurements in your life. *You do!* Your measurement can either tie My hands or it can free My hands to bless you. I cannot make exceptions for you. I must follow the Laws of My Kingdom. This standard of measure actually makes it fair for everyone to receive the same opportunity to receive from Me. You cannot accuse Me of any preferential treatment. Wisdom says: When you release 1/8 teaspoon of faith, do not blame Me when you receive the same measurement in return. When you cooperate with My Laws, I can operate in your life. I will not override your free will in choices. When you choose to abide by My Laws in My Kingdom, you are abiding in Me. Choose to come to My Secret Place today and just rest in the Truth that I AM for you and I AM fair.

God hath dealt to every man the measure of faith.

– ROMANS 12:3

With the measure you use, it will be measured to you — and even more.

– MARK 4:24

SEE ALSO: DEUTERONOMY 25:16; ROMANS 8:39; 1 TIMOTHY 1:14; ROMANS 2:11

I AM not cross with you.

Have you ever wondered why the word "cross" means angry? *All* of My anger was poured out on the cross! My Son literally carried the cross on His shoulders for you. This cross was My anger against your sin. You cannot have faith in Me if you think I AM angry at you. It is also hard to know how much I love you when you think I AM against you. I AM *for* you! Who can be against you? Because of My Son's sacrifice, you do not ever need to be tormented by the thought that I AM angry with you! I put all of My anger on the cross. Wisdom says: To understand Me, you must comprehend My intense love for you. To love like I do means that you would die like My Son died for those that you love! I held nothing back from you and gave My Best to gain those who despised and rejected Me. I went through all of this without a guarantee that anyone would accept My incredible Gift and Sacrifice! I made Myself vulnerable because you are so valuable! Be at peace today and know how much I delight in you. I AM pleased with you.

If God is for us, who can ever be against us?
— Romans 8:31 NLT

Therefore, there is now no condemnation for those who are in Christ Jesus.
— Romans 8:1

See also: John 3:16-17; John 8:36

69

To adore Me
is to open a door
to My heart!

Every time you adore and glorify Me, you open a new door in My heart. This allows Me to access more of your heart, as well. There are four chambers to My heart: The chamber of the Bridegroom, the chamber of the Judge, the chamber of Legislation, and the chamber of Communion, which is the upper room of prayer and protection. There are many doors in these chambers. Know that I stand at the door of your heart knocking! My desire is to gain more access for your liberation. *Worshiping My heart frees your heart!* To worship Me is to communicate with Me heart-to-heart. The doors to My heart are always open to you! Is your heart open to Me? I open doors that no one can shut; and shut doors that no one can open. Every time you treasure and cherish Me, there is a spiritual transaction between you and Me. This is where I reveal Myself to you. This ushers revelation, which ushers intimacy. Wisdom says: If you are feeling alone, thirsty, dry, and without purpose, adore Me today and open new areas of your heart to Me as I open new doors to you! *I wholeheartedly want to occupy your heart and make your heart whole!* I love you with all My heart!

See also: Song of Solomon 5:2; Revelation 3:20; Song of Solomon 1:4; Psalm 28:6-9; Matthew 6:21; Proverbs 22:11

Will you give Me the time of day?

There is a common theme in heaven: Everyone wished they had spent more time with Me while on the earth! How much time do *you* spend with Me? Like a lie detector, time reveals the truth. Time will tell. What you say can be a lie, but how you choose to spend time is the truth of what your heart loves or desires. Do you love your children and spouse, but do not spend time with them? You will spend time on what you are passionate about. Wisdom says: How much time are you spending with Me? Do you have time for Me? I get so excited when I see you waking up. I can barely contain the excitement of spending the day with the one I love. Know that I AM eagerly anticipating thoughts or communication with you throughout your day. Today, I will take as much time as you will give Me. Can you give Me the time of day?

The time is near.
— Revelation 1:3

Trust in him at all times, you people; pour out your hearts to him.
— Psalm 62:8

My times are in your hands.
— Psalm 31:15

You were created in My image; do not create Me into your image of who you think I AM!

I AM! I was not created! Beware of making Me into someone that I AM not. Because of some bad experiences with religious leaders, earthly parents, and other people, so many have **created** Me into **their** image of who they believe I AM! Because of this hurt, the enemy has deceived many into thinking that I hurt My children. My Love is so genuine that your mind cannot comprehend! I AM forgiving and gentle, despite every experience of harsh betrayal that you have experienced from others. Earthly eyes and ears cannot comprehend or conceive My tenderness. My reflection is Light, which is My illumination of Love! *You are My reflection; I AM never the reflection of man!* Wisdom says: Do not allow your mind to **conceive** Me into someone who has failed to love you. Does your image of Me line up with My Word? If not, you are being deceived into **creating** Me into your image of who you think I AM!

Put on the new self [the regenerated and renewed nature], created in God's image, [godlike] in the righteousness and holiness of the truth [living in a way that expresses to God your gratitude for your salvation].
— EPHESIANS 4:24 AMP

SEE ALSO: GENESIS 1:27; 1 CORINTHIANS 2:9; GENESIS 5:1

There are no medals or trophies in My Kingdom. I appoint gifts, and I give crowns.

Your appointment is a gift from Me for the service of others in My Kingdom. Your appointment is for the equipping and building up of Christ's Body, not your ego. Some love titles on this earth. Some choose to use, or misuse, a title to give them identity. In boxing, the winner gets a title only by injuring someone else. Make sure that your title is not causing injury to someone else. Follow the example of My Son, Jesus. His title as King never hurt anyone. He has loved and respected everyone, from the least to the greatest. Because My Son wore a crown of thorns, in My Kingdom, you will get a regal crown. Wisdom says: Examine your heart today to see whether or not your title is causing injury to someone.

*Blessed is the one who perseveres under trial because ... that person will receive the **crown of life**.*
— James 1:12

He Himself gave some to be apostles, some prophets, some evangelists, and some pastors and teachers, for the equipping of the saints for the work of ministry, for the edifying of the body of Christ. *— Ephesians 4:11-12 NKJV*

They do it to get a crown that will not last, but we do it to get a crown that will last forever.
— 1 Corinthians 9:25

See also: Revelation 2:10; 1 Corinthians 9:24-27

Lock and load your weapon with wisdom and warfare.

This is My Wisdom regarding how you can walk through the fire of hurt without even the smell of smoke on you: Do not just pray for those who hurt you, as I have commanded, but also give them a gift. By blessing the one who hurt you, you are locking and loading your weapon with wisdom and warfare. To lock and load means your weapon is loaded and ready for *immediate reaction* to use against your true enemy, the devil. Giving a gift actually benefits yourself, not simply those receiving the gift. Although this gift will be a blessing to them, you can trust Me when I say that giving this gift will heap a much bigger blessing on *you*! This is not only My Wisdom, but it is powerful warfare! *When you release your gift* to the one who has hurt you, the *hurt will be released* from you. This closes the door to the attacks of the enemy, and opens the door for heaven to bless you and supernaturally *heal your hurt*. Do not expect anything in return from those who hurt you. Wisdom says: When you give gifts to those who hurt you, I will give you priceless gifts — freedom from unforgiveness, healing from the hurt, and My Peace.

*"Love your enemies, **do good** to those who hate you, bless those who curse you, and pray for those who treat you badly."*
— Luke 6:28 Phillips

See also: Matthew 5:40-41

February *26*

Disappointments become missed appointments with Me.

Disappointment has such a loud and overpowering voice! But My Word must be the loudest voice in your life. You cannot afford disappointment; it can cause you to lose hope and faith. Disappointment has to be shut down, shaken off, and put out of your mind. It must be crushed, or it will crush you. If you have been disappointed, get into My Word and Presence and allow Me to restore your hope. If you are not seeing answers to your prayers, could you have allowed disappointment to choke out your faith in My Word? Wisdom says: Disappointment will anchor you to past failures. Know today that when you are focused on the past, you will miss My appointments in the present and the future.

*Such **hope [in God's promises] never disappoints** us, because God's love has been abundantly poured out within our hearts through the Holy Spirit who was given to us.*

— ROMANS 5:5 AMP

Unrelenting disappointment leaves you heartsick, but a sudden good break can turn life around.

— PROVERBS 13:12 MSG

SEE ALSO: PSALM 22:4-6

If you **consistently** spend time with Me, your punches will **persistently** pack power.

When you eat consistently, you stay strong. The same is true about the time you spend in My Word and in My Presence. When you consistently spend time with Me, you learn to recognize My voice. This builds your faith. My guidance and My voice will keep you on the offensive, instead of just defensively recovering from the blows of the enemy. Be very strategic in your punches toward the enemy. He is strategizing over your defeat. Do not stand still and take his punches. Wisdom says: Spending time with Me will move you into the proper position and give you the ability to punch with purpose and direct aim. Today, hit hard with worship, prayer and My Word. With these weapons, the enemy will lose the fight every time. You cannot win a fight if you throw in the towel. Do not just injure the enemy; knock him out with My Word.

> *Fight the good fight of the faith. Take hold of the eternal life to which you were called when you made your good confession in the presence of many witnesses.*
> — 1 TIMOTHY 6:12

> *Therefore I do not run like someone running aimlessly; I do not fight like a boxer beating the air.*
> — 1 CORINTHIANS 9:26

You can either weather the storm, or the storm will weather you.

You have the ***power*** to choose whether you will weather the storm or whether the storm will weather you. When you are in a storm, you do not have the luxury of being passive. If you are not using your authority or voice to choose My Life, you will enforce the storm. Your choice not only changes you, but it also changes the way the storm acts. Your choice will strengthen or empower you — and Me ***in you*** — or it will strengthen the storm. Wisdom says: Every time a storm begins to rage, know that I AM setting the stage for a miracle. Do not forget, I AM stronger than every storm. Make sure the storm hears My Words with ***your*** voice of authority. Speak to the storm today; do not just weather it!

> *So [as the result of the Messiah's intervention] they shall [reverently] fear the name of the Lord from the west, and His glory from the rising of the sun. When the enemy shall come in like a flood, the Spirit of the Lord will lift up a standard against him and put him to flight [for He will come like a rushing stream which the breath of the Lord drives].* — Isaiah 59:19

See also: Luke 8:23-25; Psalm 107:29

You are powerless when *you* are on your mind! Power comes when I AM on your mind!

A wasted mind is a mind only thinking of itself. Those who are continually thinking about themselves tend to be miserable and powerless. They are without joy — and joy is their strength. In contrast, the most joyful and peaceful people are those who are continually thinking of Me. Your thoughts will follow what or who is most important in your life. Allow your thoughts to convict you about who is really on your mind. You empower what you think about. So think thoughts about My power, revelation, and love. Wisdom says: If you are without peace, then your thoughts are not on Me. When your mind is just thinking about you, then your world will be about you. When I AM on your mind, My power you will find. Always remember: You are always on My mind. My thoughts toward you are more than you can comprehend! Allow this Truth to comfort you today!

> *Nothing should be done because of pride or thinking about yourself. Think of other people as more important than yourself.* — Philippians 2:3 NLV

> *You will keep him in perfect peace, Whose mind is stayed on You.* — Isaiah 26:3 NKJV

If *you are* in the center of h*ur*t, you are in the cycle of defeat.

Being in the center of your h*ur*t is a very dangerous place to be. You may have every reason to feel hurt by someone's actions, but you cannot afford to keep the hurt. Release it to Me, and I will heal you. You cannot control others, nor can you control the attacks. But when hurt presents itself, you have an opportunity to respond in faith and love. This response sends fear down the enemy's spine! Wisdom says: If the enemy cannot control or influence your response, then he cannot control or influence you. The power is not in the attack, but the power is in you — in how you respond to the attack. This will determine if you give away your power or use it to defeat the snare of hurt. Remember, hurt is powerless to hurt you.

> *"But I say to all of you who will listen to me: love your enemies, do good to those who hate you, bless those who curse you, and pray for those who treat you badly."*
> — LUKE 6:27 PHILLIPS

SEE ALSO: JOHN 16:1; EPHESIANS 4:31; JOB 21:25; ACTS 8:23

Don't trust your ocean of emotion.

Like an ocean that is never still, your emotions keep you in constant motion (e-motion). You cannot trust your emotions. Nothing changes more often than your feelings and emotions! If you live in your emotions instead of in My Spirit, you will be unstable and double-minded. Emotional instability is like the ebb and flow of an ocean wave, rising one moment and sinking the next — with a high tide and a low tide with every new day. Choose not to live in the emotional highs and lows. The enemy is constantly trying to keep your emotions involved! Do not fall for this. It is a trap. To have stability in your soul — your mind, will, and emotions — is to have stability in your entire being. Only faith in My Word will steady you. Wisdom says: Make the choice today to wreck the enemy's plans by not being an emotional wreck.

> *The one who doubts is like a wave of the sea, blown and tossed by the wind. For let not that man suppose that he will receive anything from the Lord; he is a double-minded man, unstable in all his ways.*
> — James 1:6-8

> *Then we will no longer be infants, tossed back and forth by the waves, and blown here and there by every wind of teaching.*
> — Ephesians 4:14

Hell has no say!

*I call **heaven and earth as witnesses** today against you, that I have set before you life and death, blessing and cursing; therefore **choose** life, that both you and your descendants may live.* — Deuteronomy 30:19 NKJV

Even though earth is the enemy's domain, when you were born again, I crowned you with power, authority and dominion. I call heaven and earth to witness against you! Hell has **no** authority over you when you exercise **My** authority. It has been silenced. You will be left without excuses when you breathe your last breath. So, you must take responsibility for your choices, whether good or bad. Every consequence that comes into your life presents itself to you first with a choice. Every choice you make will either enlarge the Kingdom of Heaven or enlarge the kingdom of hell — one at the expense of the other. Wisdom says: Choose life or death, blessings or curses. Heaven and earth are witnesses against you in the courts of heaven. Both heaven and earth will have a voice — and hell has no say! Today, choose Life, that both you and your descendants may live.

I will not remember your sins. Put Me in remembrance; ... State your case, that you may be acquitted. — Isaiah 43:25-26 NKJV

See also: Luke 9:1; Matthew 10:1

Jealousy comes from a **hateful** heart. Peace comes from a **grateful** heart!

Jealousy is heart sickness. To be jealous or envious is to see what other people have and believe that you deserve it instead of them. This is a heart-sick sin, not just a sin of coveting what others have. The sin of jealousy is wrapped up in pride and hatred. You do not have the right to covet what I have blessed others with. Jealousy is saying that I AM not fair — that I love some of My children more than I love others. I AM no respecter of persons. Jealousy cannot exist in a grateful heart. I AM generous to the grateful in heart. Jealousy is the symptom of an ungrateful heart! Wisdom says: I AM always promoting those who have a grateful heart! Today, praise Me with a grateful heart, not a hateful heart. I AM always close to those who choose gratefulness.

*Set me like a seal upon your heart, like a seal upon your arm; for love is as strong as death, **jealousy** is as hard and cruel as Sheol (the place of the dead).*

— Song of Solomon 8:6 AMP

Sing to the LORD with grateful praise. — Psalm 147:7

*Let us not become ... **jealous** of one another.*

— Galatians 5:26 AMP

See also: Acts 10:34; Romans 1:21

When **I AM your Friend**, why meditate upon a defeated foe?

The enemy is desperate for your attention! He wants you to focus on him instead of focusing on Me! When going through something challenging, you cannot afford to focus on the enemy; this will waste your precious time and energy because he is already a defeated foe. Instead, waste the enemy's energy. Take authority and bind the enemy, but then give him no other attention. The enemy is tormented when he does not have your undivided attention. Wisdom says: Dwell in My Secret Place and you shall remain stable and fixed under My Shadow whose power no foe can withstand. It is your choice: On Whom will you meditate — Friend or foe?

If God is for us, who can be against us?

— ROMANS 8:31

Having disarmed principalities and powers, He made a public spectacle of them, triumphing over them in it.

— COLOSSIANS 2:15

*"Abraham believed God, and it was credited to him as righteousness," and he was called **God's friend**.*

— JAMES 2:23

*I no longer call you slaves, because a master doesn't confide in his slaves. **Now you are my friends**.*

— JOHN 15:15 NLT

SEE ALSO: PSALM 91

83

You were a planned pregnancy!

I knew you before you were formed in your mother's womb. You were right on time and positioned perfectly for greatness. You may have been a surprise to your parents, but you were certainly not a surprise to Me! *You had been My plan since before the foundations of the earth.* The world needs you — and you bless the world with your presence. There is no such thing as an insignificant life! Without you, My Body would not be whole. I determine your value, not man. This makes you priceless! Wisdom says: My Love for you has always been, and will always be, consistent. Remember today, that My plans for your life are filled with purpose. The plans I have for you are vital and very significant. Your importance can never be determined by anyone but Me. Only I can determine your value. I proved your worth with the Price of My Son, Jesus. You are a wanted child, and I AM the One Who chose your beginning and your end. *I AM dancing with joy over you every day!*

For you created my inmost being; you knit me together in my mother's womb.
— Psalm 139:13

The one who made me in my mother's womb also made them. God shaped us all inside our mothers.
— Job 31:15 ERV

SEE ALSO: James 1:18; Job 38:4; Job 38:6-7; Isaiah 51:16

If you cannot see Me in the desert, you will not recognize Me in the Land of Milk and Honey!

I AM with you in feast or famine — in season and out of season, in good and bad times. Engage Me in the desert season. When you get My wisdom concerning how you arrived there, then you will see spiritual fruit blossom as in the Promised Land — like Israel's fruit in the giant's land. Can you see Me with you in your desert season? During dry seasons, you are being trained to live by faith! See the desert from My point of view — from My vision (pro-vision). I always make a way of escape. This will carry you in times of feasting into your Promised Land, where you may have the tendency to get comfortable! Spend your time drinking deeply from My refreshing Word while in the desert season. The disciplines and decisions you make here will determine your length of stay. Wisdom says: When you are in the desert season, call forth My provision from My storehouse. Call forth My water for your thirst, and My Bread for your hunger. See Me leading you with cloud cover by day to comfort you from the scorching sun, and a fire by night to keep you warm and close to Me as I give light in the dark desert nights. Know that My perception is key, and remember: I AM leading you through this temporary season.

Let no one say when he is tempted, I am tempted from God. ... He Himself tempts no one. – JAMES 1:13 AMP

SEE ALSO: *1 CORINTHIANS 10:13; DEUTERONOMY 31:8; NUMBERS 13:27-30; 2 TIMOTHY 4:2*

It is illegal for the justice system to bring up a crime from your past when you were ruled innocent.

It is illegal for the justice system to bring up a person's crime from the past when that person was ruled innocent. This is an area in which you must stand strong against the accuser. You would not tolerate repeated guilty accusations from worldly courts. So why are you caving in so easily in the spiritual realm? ***When you tolerate a guilty accusation, you are accepting the consequences of a guilty verdict.*** You are agreeing to your guilt and accepting a sentence for a crime for which I have already said you are innocent, and for which I have already paid the ultimate price — the Blood of My Dear Son. Wisdom says: Today, choose to believe Me, the Righteous Judge, instead of a guilty plea. Because Jesus chose to bear your guilt, you do not have to wear your guilt!

> *Christ redeemed us from the curse of the law by becoming a curse for us.*
> — GALATIANS 3:13 NIV

> *The decrees of the Lord are firm, and all of them are righteous.*
> — PSALM 19:9

SEE ALSO: ISAIAH 11:3-4; PROVERBS 18:5; LUKE 1:68

You cannot put New Wine in old 'whine' skins.

You can choose your wine, symbolizing the anointing, or you can choose to whine. Choosing to whine negates the anointing! To whine will stop the flow of the anointing. In the days My Son, Jesus, walked the earth, old wine skins were soaked in water to soften them, then greased with oil to prevent leaking. Only through this process could both the wine and wineskin be preserved. Allow your heart to be soaked in the water of My Word and the oil of My Holy Spirit. Then you will not be tempted to sin with whining. ***Natural wine numbs you. But whining numbs Me from hearing you.*** Wisdom says: Whining is using My Breath for evil. Today, choose your wines/whines carefully! Drink deeply My New Wine of anointing in this end time season! Know that I have saved My best Wine for last!

"Neither do people pour new wine into old wineskins. If they do, the skins will burst; the wine will run out and the wineskins will be ruined. No, they pour new wine into new wineskins, and both are preserved."
— MATTHEW 9:17

Don't be drunk with wine. ... Instead, be filled with the Holy Spirit.
— EPHESIANS 5:18

SEE ALSO: REVELATION 17:2; HOSEA 4:11; ZECHARIAH 9:17; JOB 32:19, JOEL 3:18

Every morning starts with My name ('a.m.'). I AM!

I stop everything every 24 hours to reset the whole world! Midnight echoes the thunder of My voice around the world, saying, "I AM making all things new!" Like an artist, I take My "brush" and "paint" a new sunrise and sunset each day. I have never painted two the same, yet many do not notice or appreciate My handiwork. I AM in every new sunrise (Son rise)! Every new day is My gift to you. Treat it like the priceless gift that it is! I start the day with My name (I AM) and with new mercies and compassion. I used My great power and exploits to deliver the Israelites with My great name, I AM! Wisdom says: I begin every day with My name to remind you that My same power that divided The Red Sea and freed and healed millions overnight is available to you! I AM with you in every aspect of this new day. Since every new morning is My treasured gift to you, choose to make the most of it.

*Those who **seek me early** and diligently shall find me.*
— Proverbs 8:17 AMP

Yes, I will sing aloud of Your mercy in the morning.
— Psalm 59:16

*Because of the Lord's great love we are not consumed, for his compassions never fail. They are **new every morning**; great is your faithfulness.*
— Lamentations 3:22-24

See also: 2 Corinthians 4:16

My Holy Spirit never drives you.
I lead you!

I AM The Good Shepherd. *My Love leads you* to green pastures, still waters, and paths of righteousness. When I lead, I go before you and clear the path for you. I lead you to safety and provision. I never drive you. To drive you is to push you from behind. The enemy drives you with feelings of fear, anxiety, and restlessness. So, pay attention! Are you being led? Or are you being driven? Remember, if you are feeling driven to make a decision, it is never of Me. This is a tactic of a pushy sales person or a con artist. Wisdom says: Make your decisions prayerfully and carefully — not out of pressure. Today, allow *Me* to refresh your soul and lead you to safety! *Remember, I have given you power to drive out the enemy. If you will not drive him out, he will try to drive you!*

> *The Lord is my shepherd; I shall not want.*
> *He makes me to lie down in green pastures;*
> *He **leads** me beside the still waters. He restores my soul;*
> *He **leads** me in the paths of righteousness*
> *For His name's sake.*
> — PSALM 23:1-3 NKJV

> *In your unfailing love you will lead the people you*
> *have redeemed.*
> — EXODUS 15:13

SEE ALSO: PSALM 27:11; PSALM 84:11; MATTHEW 10:1; PROVERBS 3:6

Stop confusing movement
with progress!

Everyone is constantly moving, yet how many are actually progressing My Kingdom? To keep you moving all the time is a strategy of the enemy to keep you tired. If you are weary, consider this: Are you just experiencing a lot of movement, but no progress? When you see progress, it is hard to get exhausted. Progress is exciting! Movement is exhausting. Wisdom says: Every step I have planned for you has purpose in it. This is key! The Israelites thought they were making progress just because they were moving. Sometimes, to keep progressing, you must cease movement so you can listen to My instructions. With each step that you take, listen closely and glean every lesson and purpose. Just remember that if the scenery is looking the same and familiar, you are not making progress, you are just moving!

The steps of a [good] man are directed and established by the Lord when He delights in his way [and He busies Himself with his every step].

— Psalm 37:23 AMP

Follow the steps of good men instead, and stay on the paths of the righteous.

— Proverbs 2:20

See also: Nehemiah 9:19; Psalm 16:11; Psalm 17:5; Psalm 27:11; Psalm 44:18

When you choose **Life**, you are choosing **Me**!

I AM the Way, the Truth, and the Life! When you choose Life, you are choosing Me! *You are choosing the Law of the Spirit of Life over the law of the spirit of death.* There is nothing passive about choosing Life! When you choose Life, there is a violent confrontation in the spirit realm where Life crushes death. This decree of Life is offensive, not defensive. You must enforce Life; it will not automatically happen. Because *Life* is My name, the enemy understands the power of his defeat when you choose Me! This means that all My resources, power, and heavenly hosts rush in to defeat death in your situation! Death is powerless to the Force of Life! Wisdom says: When you choose Life, you choose all that I represent to back your decision. Death runs in stark terror from Life! Know that when you choose Life today, you are choosing *Me* and all of My help!

> *Jesus answered, "I am the way and the truth and the life. No one comes to the Father except through me."*
> – John 14:6

See also: Deuteronomy 30:19; Romans 8:2

Unity is as immunity from evil.

I multiply; the enemy divides! The enemy understands the power of division. Do you? Are you working for Me and unifying? Or are you working for the enemy and dividing? Division does not begin just because there are differences. Division starts when the enemy can keep you focused on past hurts. *If the enemy can get you to magnify the pain, it will keep Me from being magnified.* If you keep the hurt that comes from divisions, you are forfeiting your assignment of unity! Know this: If you are causing division, you are working against *My Kingdom*! A Kingdom divided against itself is brought to desolation! Wisdom says: Being in unity, or one accord, is spiritual warfare that ushers forth My Holy Spirit and heaven's armies. This absolutely crushes the enemy's forces. My Kingdom cannot thrive where there is division. Evil cannot thrive where there is unity. Be someone I can use to unify and fortify My Kingdom today.

> *Make every effort to keep the unity of the Spirit through the bond of peace.* — EPHESIANS 4:3

> *Any kingdom divided against itself will be ruined, and a house divided against itself will fall.* —LUKE 11:17

SEE ALSO: GENESIS 11:1-9; ROMANS 16:17; 1 CORINTHIANS 1:10

If you refuse to fight for what you believe in, that is proof you really do not believe.

If you really believe in something, then it is worth fighting for! And, not only will you fight for it, but you will also welcome the war. Your stance cannot be shaken. You are willing to die for the cause when you truly believe. No one can influence you otherwise — and if someone tries to take away your right to believe, you will fight them. The Israelites making the exodus to the Promised Land were not willing to fight for what they claimed they believed in. If they would have faced war in the beginning, they would have changed their minds and hearts and headed back to their past life of slavery. That is why I had to change their route. They did not trust Me. Wisdom says: Believing Me breeds passion, not complacency. Fight for what you believe today! Know that I AM always fighting for you because I believe in you!

> When Pharaoh let the people go, God did not lead them on the road through the Philistine country, though that was shorter. For God said, **"If they face war, they might change their minds and return to Egypt."**
> — Exodus 13:17

> They weren't in love with themselves; they were willing to die for Christ.
> — Revelation 12:11 MSG

See also: 2 Timothy 4:7

Your heart has eyes!

Your inability to look inward will always distort your outward vision! You cannot see the faults in others and yourself at the same time! When you choose to look with your spiritual eyes, you will see what your physical eyes cannot! The enemy will always try to distract you with the tactic of looking at the problems of others. When you look at the faults in others, notice how My Word tells you that the plank or beam in your eye is larger than the speck or splinter in your brother's eye. This implies that, in reality, your faults are more significant than theirs. How can you see a speck or toothpick when you have a telephone pole or log in your eye? Wisdom says: ***Take a good look at your own heart today, instead of those around you. Allow Me to show you what is hidden in your heart. As long as you are using your physical eyes, you will not address the eyes (I's) in your own heart!***

> ... by having the **eyes of your heart** flooded with light, so that you can know and understand the hope to which He has called you, and how rich is His glorious inheritance in the saints (His set-apart ones).
>
> — EPHESIANS 1:18 AMP

> "How can you say to your brother, 'Brother, let me take the speck out of your eye,' when you yourself fail to see the plank in your own eye? You hypocrite, first take the plank out of your eye, and then you will see clearly to remove the speck from your brother's eye."
>
> — LUKE 6:42

My Word is a
Blood-sworn Covenant.

My Word is a Covenant, ratified in Blood. It is just as easy — even easier — to believe what My Word says about you than to believe another person's opinion. *Is another person willing to die for their opinion of you?* That is why My Word can be trusted! I did not just speak it; I followed it up with the Blood of My Son — Jesus' death. Since life is in the blood, My Life (My Word) is a Blood-sworn Covenant. Wisdom says: Know that you can trust *every* Word that I have declared to you! My Word is Truth, and My Truth stands forever. Allow My Truth to be your plumb line in every situation today! Know that My Word is your title deed, written in the Blood of My Son, Jesus — because Whom the Son sets free is free *indeed* (in deed). See yourself free in the Title Deed of My Word!

You have magnified Your word above all Your name!
— Psalm 138:2

For the life of the flesh is in the blood, ... for it is the blood that makes atonement for the soul.
— Leviticus 17:11 NKJV

"This is my blood of the covenant, which is poured out for many," he said to them.
— Mark 14:24

But now in Christ Jesus you who once were far away have been brought near by the blood of Christ.
— Ephesians 2:13

95

See also: Psalm 89:33-34; Hebrews 10:19; John 8:36; Hebrews 11:1

My goldmine is mankind.

My treasure on earth consists of the souls of man! *In heaven, you will walk on streets of gold, but on earth, My "gold" is walking on the streets! Man is the goldmine that I want to call Mine!* There is no other treasure that I can measure to mankind! The reason you will walk on streets of gold in heaven and you will have walls of only the finest of jewels is to show you that none of that is of value to Me! My children are My treasure, and they are My priority. Wisdom says: *The jewels that I treasure are not cut of stone. They are cut from The Cornerstone!* The only gold that matters to Me is your heart, which has been refined as gold in My Refiner's fire! Today, allow Me to refine your heart into the finest gold for My crown! **You** are the jewels set in My crown! You are what makes My crown beautiful, exquisite, priceless, and valuable!

The foundations of the city walls were decorated with every kind of precious stone. ... The great street of the city was of gold, as pure as transparent glass.
— Revelation 21:19-21

This third I will put into the fire; I will refine them like silver and test them like gold. — Zechariah 13:9

See also: Proverbs 31:10; Job 23:10

Do not make a lifestyle out of your trial!

When something in your life is only a trial, you can walk through it. But when the trial becomes a lifestyle, or a way of life, it is much, much harder to get free and walk out! Therefore, do not adjust your life to sickness or other trials; make your trial adjust to your living a full and productive life. If you change your life and your entire schedule around the attack, you will stay there longer. You cannot afford to put this trial on your calendar. Do not schedule it in. When you give a trial room to take over your life, this is being double-minded. You already have the victory because you are living in Me. Wisdom says: Be secure in knowing today that all of My Promises are Yes and Amen. *If this trial becomes your life, it takes over your life.*

For all the promises of God in Him are Yes, and in Him Amen, to the glory of God through us.
— 2 Corinthians 1:20 NKJV

Blessed is the one who perseveres under trial because, having stood the test, that person will receive the crown of life that the Lord has promised to those who love him.
— James 1:12

See also: James 1:2-3; Psalm 34:18-19

If you are living in defeat in any area of your life, it is because you have surrendered your power to it.

There is nothing more powerful in your life than My Son, Jesus, unless you ***believe*** something else is. If you believe something else is more powerful, then that is how it will be in your life! The fact that Jesus is all-powerful will never change! To live in defeat in any area of your life means you have been deceived into surrendering your power in Jesus in that area. Know this: If you feel as if you cannot be deceived, you already are! The solution for deception is to press in close to My heart and My Word. Allow Me to show you how you have surrendered to a lie. In reality, deception is as weak as a spider's web — although it may feel like you are being wrapped in chains of iron. Never forget that the enemy has lost all power; all he has left is deception! Wisdom says: Surrender to Me only! Never surrender to a circumstance or situation. To live in defeat in any area of your life — large or small — means that you believe any trial or attack is larger than Jesus or My Word. Remember today that the Greater One lives in you!

Little children, you are of God [you belong to Him] and have [already] defeated and overcome them [the agents of the antichrist], because He Who lives in you is greater (mightier) than he who is in the world.

— 1 John 4:4 AMP

See also: Proverbs 31:10; Job 23:10; Matthew 22:29

My mercies are new every morning. Are yours?

If My mercies are new every morning, shouldn't yours be also — for your enemies, for your co-workers, for your spouse, for your children, and for strangers? I hold you to the same standard that I hold Myself. So, wake up with forgiveness and new mercies for those who have hurt you. Wisdom says: When I give you the gift of a brand new, clean slate for each day, do not fill it with the bitterness and the hurt of yesterday. When you repent every night, you wake up to your new first day of life again. Every day can be like your birthday! ***My mercy is new every morning because it takes every day to show a new dimension of My Love and mercy.***

Be merciful, just as your Father is merciful.
— LUKE 6:36

Blessed are the merciful, for they will be shown mercy.
— MATTHEW 5:7

Judgment without mercy will be shown to anyone who has not been merciful. Mercy triumphs over judgment.
— JAMES 2:13

SEE ALSO: HEBREWS 4:15-16; MATTHEW 9:13; HOSEA 6:6; NUMBERS 14:18

I live to give.

With Me, it is all or nothing. When I love, I hold nothing back. When I AM for you, I use all of My power and angelic armies to protect you. This is all at your disposal when you are Mine. When I gave My Sacrifice for you, I gave My Best — My only begotten Son. When I gave gifts, I gave the best Gift of My Holy Spirit. When I created a place for you to live, I created this most beautiful paradise called Planet Earth. When I created a Spouse for you, I did not just choose anyone. I gave My beautiful only Son. When I gave you My heart, I gave you My whole heart. When I gave you My Life, I did not just give you part of My Life when you were born. I gave you My all. Are you giving your all to Me? I cannot tolerate a divided heart. It hurts too much. To have a divided heart or loyalty is to have hypocrisy. This is why I cannot handle lukewarm. Wisdom says: Love Me or hate Me — but do not be an actor of both. Know today that when I gave you My all, I held ***nothing back!*** Because of this, I require all or nothing from you.

May the grace of the Lord Jesus Christ, and the love of God, and the fellowship of the Holy Spirit be with you all.

– 2 CORINTHIANS 13:14

*Know therefore that the Lord your God is God; he is the faithful God, keeping his **covenant of love** to a thousand generations of those who love him and keep his commandments.*

– DEUTERONOMY 7:9

I AM your Comforter Who blankets you with My Peace.

Did you know the night time is a holy time with Me? It is where you spend the last few minutes of the day with the One Who gifted this life to you. With My help, allow Me to unravel all of the knots from this day, and give you peace and rest to end this day with closure. Roll over every care to Me. Repent where you have missed the mark, and wake up to a brand new start! ***Watch as I turn your disappointments into My appointments. Where you may have made mistakes and are liable, you can now trust that I AM reliable to remember them no more.*** Wisdom says: Remember that My Love is your covering — and I blanket you with My Peace, because I AM your Comforter.

But let all who take refuge in you be glad; let them ever sing for joy. Spread your protection over them, that those who love your name may rejoice in you. — Psalm 5:11

If I do not go away, the Helper (Comforter, Advocate, Intercessor — Counselor, Strengthener, Standby) will not come to you. — John 16:7 AMPC

See also: John 16:33; Matthew 11:28

What you are willing to tolerate, you will become.

When you tolerate sin, you become numb to it. Do not allow the enemy's evil influence to exist by being silent. Your silence enables and empowers sin. You are never meant to tolerate sin in the world or agree with everyone. I gave you the commandment to love one another, not tolerate one another's sin. My Son, Jesus, did not tolerate the Pharisees. To tolerate any issue, instead of objecting to it, is to agree with something. The world wants your tolerance because it needs your agreement to empower it. Wisdom says: Choose to agree with My Truth in order to change the world. Choose to change the world by loving people with My Truth, not tolerating lies. The world wants your tolerance, not My Truth. But never forget: The *lies* that you tolerate will be the *laws* you will have to live under.

*Your eyes are too pure to look on evil; **you cannot tolerate wrongdoing**.*
— Habakkuk 1:13

*"A new command I give you: Love one another. As I have loved you, so you **must love one another**."*
— John 13:34

Our courts oppose the righteous, and justice is nowhere to be found.
— Isaiah 59:14 NLT

See also: Revelation 2:20

Lay your circumstances and burdens on My **altar**, so they can be **altered**!

My altar is holy and gives you access to Me. When you sacrifice anything on My altar, you are actually giving up possession of it and giving it to Me. I become its legal owner. You release all rights to Me. **When you lay your burdens on My altar, you give Me legal right to alter the entire situation and make it into something brand new!** You are acknowledging that you cannot change this situation on your own, but you are rolling the cares onto Me. When you keep the problem, I cannot intervene. Wisdom says: When you give up control, I can take control! This means I can alter your circumstances — hurts, problems, desires, weaknesses, relationships — and use all of My resources on your behalf. My altar is a place of holy exchange. You make the exchange for My Peace, My Power, My Hope, My Health, My Strength. Rest assured today that when you lay your circumstances on My altar, I can alter everything in your life.

"Then let us get ready and go to Bethel. I will make an altar there to God."

— Genesis 35:3 NLV

See also: Exodus 20:24; Joshua 22:28; 1 Peter 5:7

Do trials rock you?
Or are you steady on the Rock
through the trials?

Do you know that during a trial, your faith is on trial? The enemy wants to see if you believe what you are saying. How do you react when you are going through a trial? Make faith your first response! Trials are the quickest way to uncover what you are missing in your faith walk. They can reveal if you have trust issues with Me. It is very hard to keep attitudes and sin hidden when you are in a problem or trial. Pay attention when you are going through trials. Use them wisely to help reveal what has been hidden in your heart and is keeping you from growth. Do not allow a trial to rock you! Wisdom says: Seek My help and Peace. Allow Me to carry you. Keep steady on the Rock of My Son, Jesus, and choose to seek Me, your Rock, through every trial. Keep your eyes on the Rock, not the trial! Know that My eyes are continually on you because My Love is continually for you.

In the midst of a very severe trial, their overflowing joy and their extreme poverty welled up in rich generosity.
– 2 Corinthians 8:2

Blessed is the one who perseveres under trial because, having stood the test, that person will receive the crown of life that the Lord has promised to those who love him.
– James 1:12

You are never more powerless than when you are driven by power!

My Son, Jesus Christ, is The Head over *every* power and authority. When I raised Him from the dead and seated Him at My right-hand position of power, Jesus gave *you* power and authority over the enemy to be used for healing and deliverance in His name. It was never intended to be misused for making yourself a name. While living on earth, Jesus was superior to power, not driven by power. *Power is for the pure in heart.* There are too many who posture for positions of power, especially in My Body. What is your motive for power? Lay down all ungodly motives. Long to be known not by power, but by knowing Me! You actually show weakness if you are driven to get power. Wisdom says: *I want My Body to be in operation in My gifts of power, with humility and honor to My Spirit, so the world can see Me, not just you!* Seek Me, not power.

> *[For my determined purpose is] that I may know Him [that I may progressively become more deeply and intimately acquainted with Him ... and **that I may in that same way come to know the power outflowing from His resurrection** [which it exerts over believers].*
>
> – Philippians 3:10 amp

See also: Matthew 10:1

Discover revelation about My heart, through My Son and My Holy Spirit.

I AM your Father. I delight in you as My child. If you want to learn more about My heart and how I love you with an unfailing and compassionate Covenant of Love, you will find this revelation in the Old Testament in My Word. This is where you will discover the secrets to My heart. In the four gospels, you will learn about My Living Word, Jesus, your King. This is where you will find your identity. You are the Bride of the Son of My Love. In Acts through Revelation, the Person of the Holy Spirit is unveiled for you. You are the living temple of My Spirit, your Comforter, your Strengthener, your Helper, your Intercessor, your Advocate, and your Teacher. The Bible is three parts, but one book. So there are three witnesses in heaven — the Father, the Word, the Holy Spirit — and these three are One. Wisdom says: As you read My Word today, ask Me to reveal the secret treasures of Who I AM to you personally.

So there are three witnesses in heaven: the Father, the Word and the Holy Spirit, and these three are One.

— 1 JOHN 5:7 AMP

May the grace of the Lord Jesus Christ, and the love of God, and the fellowship of the Holy Spirit be with you all.

— 2 CORINTHIANS 13:14

SEE ALSO: JOHN 14:22-25; PSALM 89:26; GENESIS 28:13

My Word is a Treasure Map!

There is a hole in every human heart that only I can fill. Many try to fill that hole with the treasures and riches of this world, but the void only becomes bigger. Life is like a quest for a treasure *chest* that holds My *heart*. Those who seek the priceless treasure of My Self will find Me. The Treasure Map is My Word. When you follow the clues, or commandments, you will find the treasure in My chest: My heart of gold. What can be compared to the wealth of My Holy Spirit and My heart? Not even Solomon was even as priviliged and wealthy as you! Wisdom says: Once you have My heart, all the other jewels and treasures are as worthless as fool's gold. Know today that you can trust Me with your heart. I AM the *Keeper* of your heart!

For where your treasure is, there your heart will be also.
— Matthew 6:21

"The kingdom of heaven is like treasure hidden in a field. When a man found it, he hid it again, and then in his joy went and sold all he had and bought that field."
— Matthew 13:44

See also: Proverbs 8:18-21

March 31

Do not make your children carry what you could not release!

Unforgiveness affects your seed — your children! Can you picture your children being tortured because you could not forgive? Your iniquity can be passed on to your seed. My Word clearly tells you that the iniquity of the fathers will be visited upon the third and fourth generations! If you cannot forgive, know this: Your children may have to repay the debt for your unforgiveness. If you choose not to forgive, you will enslave your children to *your* past. They will be born with shackles and chains to your bitterness and unforgiveness. Wisdom says: When you choose to forgive, you are choosing freedom for your children. Today, your children are waiting on your choice: Slavery or freedom?

He does not leave the guilty unpunished; he punishes the children and their children for the sin of the parents to the third and fourth generation.

— EXODUS 34:7

"Therefore, the kingdom of heaven is like a king who wanted to settle accounts. ... Since he was not able to pay, ***the master ordered that he and his wife and his children and all that he had be sold to repay the debt."***

— MATTHEW 18:23-25

Laughter is where I abide!

When laugher is an expression of something pure and holy, it is praise to Me — and this is where I abide! Laughter is miraculous and contagious. *I love to hear you laugh*, just like you love to hear your baby laugh. It is so precious to Me! Pure laughter is an expression from My Spirit. It is the sound of My joy! *When you laugh, you are making the choice to express My voice of joy.* I AM Joy! The amount of laughter in your life is an expression of your attitude. If you have *not* been laughing much, check to see if you have allowed pessimism to creep in. The enemy hates to hear you laugh. The enemy is tormented by pure and virtuous laughter, so he hijacks it and uses it as a weapon of mocking. By perverting and laughing at topics that are holy to Me, the enemy uses comedy acts and the culture to hurt Me instead of to praise Me. Wisdom says: *Choose to laugh with Me today!* Consider this: Laughing in the face of an attack gives you power and strength! Because you are already seated with Me in heavenly places, you can laugh with Me as I laugh at the enemy.

"The joy of the Lord is your strength."
— Nehemiah 8:10

He will yet fill your mouth with laughter and your lips with shouts of joy.
— Job 8:21

A merry heart does good, like medicine. — Proverbs 17:22

See also: Proverbs 31:25-26; Luke 6:21; Psalm 2:4

April 2

If you are looking at what I **did,** you are missing what **I AM doing!**

If you are longing for the revivals of the past, you will settle for the anointing from the past. Although they were marvelous and holy, I have a fresh and new anointing for every new generation. The last generation's anointing will not fit this generation. My Kingdom is always progressing. I want to uniquely shine through each generation. If each generation does not change its sound or anointing, My Body will make a religion out of it. Wisdom says: Because My mercy is new every morning, I will love you with a new dimension of My mercy today. ***Remember that I keep doing something new so that you will not keep doing something old.***

> *"See, the former things have taken place, and new things I declare; before they spring into being I announce them to you."*
> — Isaiah 42:9

> *"Forget the former things; do not dwell on the past."*
> — Isaiah 43:18

> *"From now on I will tell you of new things, of hidden things unknown to you."*
> — Isaiah 48:6

A person with compromise is a person with idols!

It is impossible for Me to tolerate compromise and share My heart with anyone else. Love for Me must come from all of your heart and soul (mind, will, and emotions). I desire that you only have room for Me in your heart! Your heart was created for Me. Not only are you *My* temple, but your heart is also My Holy of Holies! I will not share My temple with anything or anyone. If it is easy for you to compromise, this should be an indication to you that there is more than just Me in your heart. Wisdom says: **Know that I gave My whole heart to you.** That is why I can demand the same from you. To com*promise* is to go back on your *promise* to Me.

> *Little children, keep yourselves from idols (false gods) — [from anything and **everything that would occupy the place in your heart** due to God, from any sort of substitute for Him that would take first place in your life]. Amen (so let it be).*   — 1 John 5:21 AMP

> *Jesus replied: "Love the Lord your God with all your heart and with all your soul and with all your mind."*   — Matthew 22:37

> *And now, Israel, what does the Lord your God ask of you but to fear the Lord your God, to walk in obedience to him, to love him, to serve the Lord your God with all your heart and with all your soul.*   — Deuteronomy 10:12

111

See also: Luke 10:27; Deuteronomy 13:3; Joshua 22:5

I resist the proud,
but I **cannot resist** the humble.

The quickest road to your next trial is a prideful mindset! Pride goes before destruction. Pride makes you vulnerable to attacks from the enemy. When you are walking in pride, you are in the enemy's territory. This gives the enemy the ability to strike you at close range and with greater accuracy! Walking in humility is knowing that your strength, your gifts, and even your breath come from Me. Walking in humility frustrates the enemy because he cannot make you stumble. Wisdom says: Today, remember that I show favor to the humble, but the proud will always stumble. Never underestimate the power of humility.

*God opposes the proud but shows favor to the **humble**.*
— JAMES 4:6

Pride goes before destruction, a haughty spirit before a fall. — PROVERBS 16:18

Humility is the fear of the Lord; its wages are riches and honor and life. — PROVERBS 22:4

*And the most proud shall **stumble** and fall, and none shall raise him up.* — JEREMIAH 50:32 KJV

Everyone needs someone to believe them — even Me.

Does it hurt you when someone does not believe you? It hurts Me too! I need you to believe Me, so I can answer your prayers. How I long to answer your prayers! I cannot violate the Laws of My Kingdom, and believing Me (having faith) enacts My spiritual Law. Not even a judge can rewrite the law. He is subject to it. When you do not believe Me, you are calling Me a liar. I will never tolerate or accept being called a liar. This indicates that you are being deceived by the enemy instead of being received by Me! Wisdom says: I appeal to you to believe My Love for you. Because I love you, I will never lie to you! Choose to believe Me, the One that cannot lie, instead of believing the enemy who cannot tell the truth! Trust Me today because I AM worthy of your trust. Believe Me: I AM Trustworthy!

And without faith it is impossible to please God, because anyone who comes to him must believe that he exists and that he rewards those who earnestly seek him.
— HEBREWS 11:6

"You are my witnesses," declares the Lord, "and my servant whom I have chosen, so that you may know and believe me and understand that I am he. Before me no god was formed, nor will there be one after me."
— ISAIAH 43:10

SEE ALSO: GENESIS 15:6

Navigate.
Do not negotiate!

Decide to navigate your way through any path where I lead you, no matter how difficult the path may seem! When I ask you to navigate, I mean for you to trust Me as you willingly travel on the course that I have planned and directed for you. I would not lead you into something that is impossible. Nor would I lead you on a path where you fail. I will never fail you! You must trust My path and My process! I AM always leading you into My Promised Land and out of slavery! The Israelites who tried to negotiate My path or to go back to Egypt did not make it to the Promised Land! Are you trusting Me? Are you negotiating to go only part of the way, or to take an easier path? Are you compromising because of trust issues with Me? Wisdom says: I lead you in paths of righteousness and to still waters and green pastures — never into failure! ***Choosing to navigate My path leads to the reward of My promise. Negotiating negates My reward!***

> *All the paths of the Lord are mercy and steadfast love, even truth and faithfulness are they for those who keep His covenant and His testimonies.*
>
> — PSALM 25:10 AMP

> *This is what the Lord says: "Stand at the crossroads and look; ask for the ancient paths, ask where the good way is, and walk in it, and you will find rest for your souls. But you said, 'We will not walk in it.'*
>
> — JEREMIAH 6:16

Dress to look great, not to intimidate.

Dressing to look nice and express your unique style and personality is good. But when you dress with the intent of elevating yourself above other people who may not be able to afford what you are wearing, this is called intimidation. Beautiful and expensive clothes are not the issue; your heart's intent is the issue. I AM asking you to check your heart to see if you are looking down on other people because of the way they dress. Walk in humility and never shame those who cannot afford to dress in a certain manner. If you are wearing clothes to exalt yourself above other people, then your clothing is more than just a covering; **your clothing becomes a weapon**. Wisdom says: Dress to represent Me. Wear humility, not pride. **Humility is a cloak that looks good on all of humanity!** Dress today to express, not to impress.

Clothe yourselves with humility toward one another.
— 1 Peter 5:5

Nothing should be done because of pride or thinking about yourself. Think of other people as more important than yourself. — Philippians 2:3 NLV

"Stop judging by mere appearances, but instead judge correctly." — John 7:24

115

See also: Jeremiah 4:30; Revelation 7:14; 1 Peter 3:3-4; Isaiah 61:3

April 8

True love always requires sacrifice!

If there is no sacrifice, then your love is not authentic love! My Love for you cannot be denied because I sacrificed My only Son. I love you the same as I love My Son. You cannot have love without sacrifice! I was willing to give all I had in exchange for having you for My very own. I gave My best Gift, My Son, for you. I redeemed you. I called you by name. Know this: You are enough — just the way you are — to receive the greatest Gift ever given. Wisdom says: Only loving those who love you back is manipulation. Loving your enemies is sacrificial, genuine love for Me. I ask you with My great Love today: Does your love for Me show sacrifice? **Today, be My living sacrifice by loving with sacrifice!**

> *I have given them the glory you gave me ... so that the world will ... understand that you love them as much as you love me.* — JOHN 17:22-23

> *This is love: not that we loved God, but that he loved us and sent his Son as an atoning sacrifice for our sins.* — 1 JOHN 4:10

> *And walk in love, ... as Christ loved us and gave Himself up for us, a slain offering and sacrifice to God [for you, so that it became] a sweet fragrance.* — EPHESIANS 5:2

SEE ALSO: 1 CORINTHIANS 7:23; ISAIAH 43:1; GENESIS 22:2; JOHN 5:20

When you complain about someone, it means that you have not forgiven them!

Choosing not to forgive will cut your life short! Murmuring and complaining is always about the condition of your heart, and not about the behavior of someone else! This is why I could not overlook this sin in the desert. Complaining is the sign of a hard heart. There is a physical disease called hardening of the arteries! It cuts off the blood flow — life flow — to and from your heart and can cause a heart attack. Complaining attacks your heart. So it is with unforgiveness. It cuts off My flow of Life from your heart. Wisdom says: A hard heart cannot forgive; a tender heart will live. Today, forgive so you will live!

Jesus asked them: … "Do you still not see or understand? Are your hearts hardened?"
— MARK 8:17

Blessed is the one who always trembles before God, but whoever hardens their heart falls into trouble.
— PROVERBS 28:14

I have hidden your word in my heart that I might not sin against you.
— PSALM 119:11

You are the common denominator of your problems. I AM the common denominator of your solutions!

Have you ever noticed that every one of your problems or challenges has the same common denominator? It is you. This is the best news you could hear today! This means that, through your choices and daily decisions, you have more control over your life than you may have imagined. Not a single one of your problems hinges on someone else's choices. If that were the case, you would have no choice but to continue to suffer from their choices. You can be **affected** by the choices and treatment of others, but you always have the choice of how you will **respond**. Choose to separate yourself long enough to seek **My Wisdom** for assistance. Wisdom says: Choose to walk in My perfect Peace. Remember, My Peace does not necessarily mean the absence of conflict. Sometimes it takes a temporary conflict to arrive at lasting Peace. I understand how hard life can be sometimes. That's why I promise I will never leave you without My help. You can always count on Me. I will walk this out **with** you. But remember: Only **your choices** determine the ultimate outcome of every problem you are facing.

"Never will I leave you; never will I forsake you."
– Hebrews 13:5 and Deuteronomy 31:6

See also: Proverbs 12:16; Deuteronomy 30:19; Ephesians 6:13

Rest assured you are heard.

I AM! ***Do not confuse My silence with deafness!***
I AM attentive to your every prayer and concern. I AM
your Father who can hear every spoken and unspoken
word — even your thoughts. I have heard your loudest
cry and your softest whisper. Be at peace that I listen
and I love you. Love always listens! You could not
believe that I love you if I refused to listen to you, My
child. I AM attentive to everything about you and to
everything that concerns you. I AM even listening to
your heartbeat, and I AM aware when it changes! You
have been granted access to My ears! You can never
say too much or bore Me with what is on your heart.
I listen to you as if you were My only creation! You
will never have to compete for My attention. Wisdom
says: Lean on the Truth that you are being heard. Allow
My Comfort to overtake any anxiety or fear of being
ignored. ***Let My Love assure you of what I promise
in My Word — that you are heard!***

> *And if we know [for a fact, as indeed we do] that He*
> *hears and listens to us in whatever we ask, we [also]*
> *know [with settled and absolute knowledge] that we*
> *have [granted to us] the requests which we have asked*
> *from Him.*   — 1 John 5:15 AMP
>
> *How gracious he will be when you cry for help! As*
> *soon as he hears, he will answer you.*   — Isaiah 30:19

I can take your **weight.**
Can you take My **wait?**

My shoulders are big enough to carry your weight. Give your burdens to Me. Release them to the only One who can truly help you. *Lean all of your weight upon Me; I will carry you. Is your faith strong enough to carry you through as you wait for My answered prayer?* My timing is always perfect. Waiting for things, promotions, and positions that you are not ready for is My mercy. The waiting process is where I lose so many of My children to impatience and discouragement. I always answer a prayer that lines up with My will. Remember today: *Waiting is My mercy, not My indifference.* Wisdom says: If you could see from My perspective, you would thank Me for the wait. In the waiting process, ask for My perspective, wisdom, and vision. Just because you have to wait does not mean I AM late!

> *Cast your burden on the Lord [releasing the **weight** of it] and He will sustain you.*
> — PSALM 55:22

> *But those who **wait** for the Lord [who expect, look for, and hope in Him] shall change and renew their strength.*
> — ISAIAH 40:31

> *The Lord will wait, that He may be gracious to you.*
> — ISAIAH 30:18 NKJV

SEE ALSO: *PSALM 38:4; PSALM 27:14; 1 PETER 5:7*

When you cooperate with My Law, I can operate in your life.

The law of gravity is a law that works the same for every person on this earth. ***If it did not work the same for everyone, it would be a phenomena — not a law!*** The spiritual Laws of My Kingdom work the same for everyone, just as the law of gravity. Therefore, since My Kingdom Laws work the same for everyone, I cannot be accused of playing favorites. Understand the gravity of thinking that I love some of My children more than others. This is an accusation that I AM very weary of hearing. Wisdom says: Know this day that I love you the same as My Son who never sinned or did anything wrong. Never forget: I operate under the Law of Love, because I AM Love. You will ***never*** be without My lavish and extravagant Love!

> *I have given them the glory that you gave me, ...Then the world will know that you sent me and have loved them even as you have loved me.* — John 17:22-23

> *For the law of the Spirit of life [which is] in Christ Jesus [the law of our new being] has freed me from the law of sin and of death.* — Romans 8:2 AMP

> *And Peter opened his mouth and said: Most certainly and thoroughly I now perceive and understand that God shows no partiality and is no respecter of persons.* — Acts 10:34 AMP

121

April 14

The world says, 'No guts, no glory,' but I say, 'No Glory, no guts!'

"No guts, no glory" is a motto that the world often uses to motivate people to achieve their dreams. In other words, a lack of courage and determination produces a lack of glory for accomplishment. *But I say, where there is no supernatural bravery and courage — no guts — it is because there is no Glory from Me. Where My Glory exists, there is never an absence of courage, bravery, and determination!* With My Glory — My Presence, grace, honor, and favor — you will have the strength to fulfill My dreams for your life. I have planned your destiny so large that only I will receive all of the glory and the honor due to Me! Everything that Jesus did was to give Me glory. When you do something to get glory for yourself, it will fail. Wisdom says: When you do everything for My Glory, I will empower you to have the boldness and guts to do what you could never imagine!

> You must do everything for the glory of God, even your eating and drinking.
> — 1 Corinthians 10:31 TLB

> ... all of us reflect the Lord's glory ...
> — 2 Corinthians 3:18 GW

See also: Psalm 79:9; Psalm 8:1

Be very slow to make promises, but be very quick to keep them!

A promise is more than simply mere words without consequences. ***When you make a promise, I consider it as: Your vow. Your oath. Your pledge. Your covenant. Your bond. Your word of honor. A promise is the same as a legal contract, but it is spoken with My Breath.*** A promise is only a promise when you keep it. When you make a promise to someone, you are also making a promise to Me that you will keep it. I will hold you accountable to every vow and promise. Do not make promises carelessly. Wisdom says: Know in your heart today that My Word is a promise I will always keep. I expect you to keep your promises, just as I keep Mine. Be very slow to make promises, but be very quick to keep them! Never forget: A promise that is not kept is a lie.

> *Who may enter your presence? ...Those who ... keep their promises even when it hurts.*
> — Psalm 15:4 NLT

> *Fully satisfied and assured that God was able and mighty to keep His word and to do what He had promised.*
> — Romans 4:21 AMP

> *On the day of judgment men will have to give account for every idle (inoperative, nonworking) word they speak.*
> — Matthew 12:36 AMP

It takes strength to fight, but wisdom to walk away — and revelation to know the difference.

Humility is choosing My way to win a war, not your own. Sometimes it is possible to win a war simply by turning your other **strong** cheek for the **weak** to slap. Love is strong; hate is weak. When you replace hate, and choose to fight with the power of **love**, the world and hell will tremble at the true power of Me that is displayed in you. When My Body begins to "fight" with love, instead of hate and division, the world will begin to take notice. My strong Son forgave those who were killing Him, and loved them in return. Wisdom says: ***Today, seek Me for the revelation to know when to fight for a righteous cause, or when to use My wisdom to walk away with love.*** Forgiveness is using My strength to "fight" with My Love! This strategy of war wins every battle every time!

> *If someone slaps you on one cheek, turn to them the other also. If someone takes your coat, do not withhold your shirt from them.*
> — Luke 6:29

> *Humility comes before honor.*
> — Proverbs 15:33

> *He will be … a source of strength to those who turn back the battle at the gate.*
> — Isaiah 28:6

There are only two kingdoms, not three.

There are only two kingdoms: Light and darkness. My Son, Jesus, rules over My Kingdom of Light. This Kingdom has already defeated — rendered null and void — the kingdom of darkness. The enemy wants you to believe there are three kingdoms: Light, dark, and *your* kingdom. No, there are only two! To *not* choose the Kingdom of Light means that *by default* you choose the kingdom of darkness. This is because all are born into darkness — because of Adam's sin — and need to be reborn into My Kingdom of Light. When you received My Son's atonement for your sins, you were literally reborn into My Kingdom of Light. I delivered you from the power of darkness, and translated you into the Kingdom of My Dear Son. This means that you have been set free from the enemy and his kingdom, which is sin, sickness, and death. The enemy wants you to believe that you have a kingdom of your own. This deception has taken so many into the clutches of hell. Wisdom says: Resist buying into the deception that you have a third option, and know that *I welcome you into My Kingdom with open arms!*

> *For he has rescued us from the dominion of darkness and brought us into the kingdom of the Son he loves.*
> — COLOSSIANS 1:13

SEE ALSO: REVELATION 16:10; MATTHEW 8:12

April 18

When you do not know your identity, you will usually be drawn to counterfeits!

Your identity can only be found in Me, and in My Word alone. *Only I* can give you your unique identity. It can *never* come from man. Other people will try to take your identity and make you just like them. When you do not know who and Whose you are, you will not easily identify a counterfeit. A counterfeit is made to look like the real thing in order to trick or deceive you. These are the wolves trying to deceive My sheep. Do not allow anyone to speak into you who is not aligned with My Word. The counterfeits are always the hypocrites. Wisdom says: Your identity should only be found in the Bride of My Son. You will never know who you are until you know Who I AM. Spend time in My Word today, and allow Me to reveal My heart to you.

> In a word, what I'm saying is, "Grow up. You're kingdom subjects. Now live like it. Live out your God-created identity. Live generously and graciously toward others, the way God lives toward you."
> — MATTHEW 5:48 MSG

> Be merciful (sympathetic, tender, responsive, and compassionate) even as your Father is [all these].
> — LUKE 6:36 MSG

SEE ALSO: 2 CORINTHIANS 13:5

When you seek My **heart**, you will also get My **eyes** and **ears**!

Your heart is connected to your ability to hear and see. *When your heart grows calloused, your eyes become spiritually dim, and your ears become dull to understanding.* But when you seek My heart, you will also get My eyes and ears — so you will understand My heart, and I will heal you. Guard your heart from becoming calloused, your ears from becoming spiritually hard of hearing, and your eyes from becoming spiritually blind. If you are having a hard time hearing from Me, or understanding revelation of Me, check to see if your heart has become calloused. Wisdom says: Sin and disobedience will cause your heart to become hardened. When you repent, I AM faithful to give you a new and tender heart! Allow Me this very day to make you tenderhearted again. The more time you spend with Me, the more I will heal your ears to hear and your eyes to see.

> *For the **eyes** of the Lord range throughout the earth to strengthen those whose hearts are fully committed to him.*
> — 2 Chronicles 16:9

> *For this people's heart has become calloused; they hardly hear with their ears, and they have closed their eyes. Otherwise they might **see with their eyes, hear with their ears, understand with their hearts** and turn, and I would heal them.*
> — Acts 28:27

See also: Proverbs 4:20-23; Isaiah 6:10

Praying in the Spirit is a legal transaction between you and Me, and between heaven and earth.

When you pray in the Spirit, you yield your tongue to pray My perfect will in your life. This is My way to get what I want released on earth without any contamination or manipulation of your will! I use your tongue to legally create what I need! I then bless you with strength in your inner being. I bless you for yielding to My perfect will. Praying in My Spirit is a language that the enemy cannot understand. He is powerless when you are praying in My Spirit. This Gift of My Spirit torments the enemy, but it blesses Me and it blesses you. Wisdom says: This prayer language is My Gift and must be treated with the utmost respect. When you pray in My Holy Spirit, this is physical proof that He is within you. The more you pray in My Spirit, the better you will be able to hear My voice. Today, make use of this Gift of My Spirit while waiting with expectation to hear Me.

... that He would grant you, according to the riches of His glory, to be strengthened with might through His Spirit in the inner man.
— Ephesians 3:16 NKJV

But you, dear friends, by building yourselves up in your most holy faith and praying in the Holy Spirit.
— Jude 1:20

See also: Romans 8:26; Ephesians 6:18; Ephesians 4:30

An apology does not **cancel** your hurt!

Do you comprehend the power given to you by My Holy Spirit to forgive or retain, bind or loose? An apology can aid in healing a relationship if it is said with sincerity, but *only you can cancel* the transgression by forgiving whoever wronged you! When you cancel someone's transgression, I cancel your hurt and I heal your heart with My Love! I will watch over you and make sure of it! Do not forget: Forgiveness heals hurt. An apology does not. You have the power to hold and remit someone else's sins. Wisdom says: When you forgive, you are unlocking the prison cell that was meant to keep you in captivity! Every time that you choose to forgive, you destroy the plans of the enemy. The sin of unforgiveness does not just affect you. Unforgiveness affects the world! Know that you can change the world just by forgiving someone today. Unlock the chains of hate around the world by releasing My Love that covers a multitude of sin.

"I will give you the keys of the kingdom of heaven; whatever you bind on earth will be bound in heaven, and whatever you loose on earth will be loosed in heaven."
— Matthew 16:19

"If you forgive anyone's sins, their sins are forgiven; if you do not forgive them, they are not forgiven."
— John 20:23

See also: *2 Corinthians 7:9; Psalm 38:18*

Failing is only final
if you let it **define** you.

Failing does not make you a failure! For all have sinned and have fallen short of My Glory. And all are justified freely by My grace through the redemption that comes by Jesus Christ. Failing is something that people **do**. It is not who you **are**, unless you let it define you. Failing makes you human. The most important thing is what you do **after** you have failed. Repent, then put it behind you. When you repent, all failures are wiped away. Wisdom says: Pick yourself up today and begin again. Failing is only final when you allow it to make you quit. **Allow Me to define you, not your failures.** Remember, you are in good company. There is only one Person who has never failed: My Dear Son, Jesus. Because you are in Jesus, and He never failed, you can never be called a failure.

> *... even the righteousness of God, through faith in Jesus Christ, to all and on all[a] who believe. For there is no difference; for all have sinned and fall short of the glory of God, being justified freely by His grace through the redemption that is in Christ Jesus.* — ROMANS 3:22-24

> *Though the righteous fall seven times, they rise again.* — PROVERBS 24:16

> *Let us then fearlessly and confidently and boldly draw near to the throne of grace (the throne of God's unmerited favor to us sinners), that we may receive mercy [for our failures] and find grace to help in good time.* — HEBREWS 4:16 AMP

Excuses limit Me.

When you make excuses regarding why you cannot do something that My Word says you can do, you are not just disqualifying and limiting yourself — but you are disqualifying and limiting *Me!* When you make excuses which contradict My Word, you are saying *I AM* not big enough to work through you! I AM so large that the entire world cannot contain Me! *An excuse is a lie that you have chosen to believe instead of My Word.* I said you can do *all* things through Christ who strengthens you. I cannot see any room for excuses in that Truth. Wisdom says: Bondages and lifelong limitations start with excuses. Once you choose to start making excuses, it is hard to get out of that habit. Starting today, choose not to allow limitations in your life! Ask Me to reveal where you are disqualifying and limiting yourself, thus limiting My Kingdom being manifest through you.

I can do all things through Christ who strengthens me.
— Philippians 4:13 nkjv

"But they all began making excuses. One said he had just bought a field and wanted to inspect it, and asked to be excused. Another said he had just bought five pair of oxen and wanted to try them out." ... "'Well, then,' said his master, 'go out into the country lanes and out behind the hedges and urge anyone you find to come, so that the house will be full. For none of those I invited first will get even the smallest taste of what I had prepared for them.'"
— Luke 14:18-20, 23, 24 tlb

Even if you live a **long** life, your time is **short**.

Time is a gift from Me. Allow Me to show you how to spend it. Choose to spend it even more carefully than you spend money. Realize that money can be replaced, but time cannot. Remember: time is even more precious than money — and the enemy loves to steal it from you. If you do not master it, time will become your master. When time is your master, you will feel driven by it — not led by My Holy Spirit and My Wisdom. Use time wisely. Wisdom says: Do not be ruled by anything but Me! Your life will not be measured by how many years you have lived, but by how much *life* you have filled into those years. You will never reach a point where you are satisfied that you have had enough time! Plan to live a long life, but live like it is your last day! Live for eternity, not for today. Know this: What you do today can affect eternity. Ask yourself this question: "If today were the last day of my life, what would I do differently?"

O [earnestly] remember how short my time is and what a mere fleeting life mine is. For what emptiness, falsity, futility, and frailty You have created all men!

— Psalm 89:47 AMP

My times are in Your hands; deliver me from the hands of my foes and those who pursue me and persecute me.

— Psalm 31:15 AMP

See also: Ecclesiastes 3:1

Believing that you are loved by True Love is the only way you can truly love.

Have you ever noticed that when you know you are loved by Me, you more readily see the good in people? This is a spiritual key! When you are feeling condemnation, you tend to lash out in condemnation! If you believe that I AM critical of you, you will be critical of others. When you are feeling forgotten and abandoned by Me, it becomes very easy to not see the needs of others, even if they are right next to you! Know this: I will never abandon you or leave you! Wisdom says: When you know that I love you with an unquenchable love, only then will you love your neighbor as yourself. Today, freely receive My Love so you can freely give that Love to those around you. ***Never forget: I truly love you.*** Because I AM the Beginning and the End, know that My Love for you has no beginning or end.

Freely you have received; freely give. — MATTHEW 10:8

I have loved you with an everlasting love. — JEREMIAH 31:3

I am my beloved's and my beloved is mine. — SONG OF SONGS 6:3

SEE ALSO: 1 CORINTHIANS 13; PSALM 23; PHILIPPIANS 4:8

Look at every hurt from the perspective of a **spiritual** war — not a **personal** war!

Every hurt boils down to one thing: Are you going to choose to make this between *you* and the enemy, or between *Me* and the enemy? The only way the enemy can win this fight is to get you to take this hurt and hold on to the offense and unforgiveness! Love is not easily offended. When you *take* offense, you walk in unforgiveness, and this removes My grace. Taking this hurt out of My hands will render My strength ineffective because you are attempting to handle it in your own strength, not Mine. This is how the enemy gets the upper hand on you! Do not give it to him! Wisdom says: Keep this battle between the enemy and Me. Hurt is an attack from the enemy. Allow Me to remind you today: You cannot afford to take hurt personally. *With hurt, no matter whose face you see, remember it is always from the enemy.*

Love does not keep a record of wrongs.
— 1 Corinthians 13:5 GNT

Love your enemies, treat well (do good to, act nobly toward) those who detest you and pursue you with hatred.
— Luke 6:27 AMP

The battle is the Lord's.
— 1 Samuel 17:47

The hairs on your head are **numbered**!

Do you realize that each hair on your head has a ***number***? This number changes many times throughout each day. Numbering them is an ongoing process. I did not just count them once. I know when every single hair on your head falls! Can you see that this means I AM more acquainted with you than anyone else is — even yourself? I know you more intimately than anyone else ever could. No one else has the capacity ***or desire*** to know you this well. Nothing about you gets past Me. To Me, this is not just useless ***information*** for Me to process about your hair. This is ***revelation*** about you. Wisdom says: My knowledge, interest, and even revelation of you indicates how My longing to have more intimacy with you exceeds that of anyone else! This is an example of the level of love that I have for you! I know everything about you because My eyes are continuously on you! Allow this to comfort you today: I AM absolutely enamored of you!

Indeed, the very hairs of your head are all numbered.
— Luke 12:7

But the people said to Saul, "... As the Lord lives, not one hair of his head shall fall to the ground, for he has worked with God this day." So the people rescued Jonathan and he was not put to death.
— 1 Samuel 14:45

See also: Psalm 139:16-18; Psalm 139:3-4

April 28

You are the only glimpse of Me that the world will ever see. How do I look?

You are My reflection to the world. A reflection is something that shows the existence or character of something or someone else. My plan was never to be hidden. It was for the world to see Me in you, not just see *you*. I was never supposed to remain invisible. *I chose to reveal Myself to the world through you. The reason I sometimes stay hidden is because the world is supposed to see Me in you.* When people see you, do they see Me? Do they hear Me when you speak? Do they see My character through you? Wisdom says: The more time you spend with Me, the more you will look like Me. You are My only reflection that many will see today. Are you making Me look good?

> *And all of us, as with unveiled face, [because we] continued to behold [in the Word of God] as in a mirror the glory of the Lord, are constantly being transfigured into His very own image in ever increasing splendor and from one degree of glory to another; [for this comes] from the Lord [Who is] the Spirit.*
>
> — 2 Corinthians 3:18 AMP

> *Jesus answered: "Don't you know me, Philip, even after I have been among you such a long time? Anyone who has seen me has seen the Father. How can you say, 'Show us the Father'?"*
>
> — John 14:9

See also: 1 Corinthians 13:12

Can you see the 'script' in Scripture?

I AM the Master Writer who has written the perfect revelation of Life. When you stick to the Script I have written — My Script-ure — you will have blessing, favor, and success in all your life endeavors. I have made it easy and have provided written directions with My Script for a healthy Life. Those who find themselves in trouble are those who rewrite the Script for themselves. In My Script, I wrote the beginning and the end of the way of Life — because I AM the Alpha and Omega, the Beginning and the End. Wisdom says: Rehearse My Script daily, because in each line you will find Me: the Way, the Truth, and the Life. A certain indication that you have deviated from My Script is if you are not loving and enjoying your life! There is such Peace when you know that all you have to do is follow My Script to live a life that is filled with My protection, joy, and love. When you follow My Script, there is no surprise ending! You win every time with My victory!

The Spirit gives life; the flesh counts for nothing. The words I have spoken to you — they are full of the Spirit and life.

— JOHN 6:63

If you fully obey the Lord your God and carefully follow all his commands I give you today, the Lord your God will set you high above all the nations on earth.

— DEUTERONOMY 28:1

SEE ALSO: JOHN 14:6

April 30

Umpires and prisoners both wear black and white stripes.

You were **born** a prisoner. But, when you were **born again** into the Kingdom of My Dear Son, Jesus, you were promoted to umpire status. An umpire is one who has the authority to judge and settle with finality every situation. In sports, or in life, no one can over-rule the umpire or the judge. In baseball, the umpire rules: Fair or foul. Safe or out. Strike three — out! As an umpire, you can use your power and authority to call the "plays" in your life. To help you determine the right call, I have given you My Peace. Let it umpire your heart. Although I expect you to take this authority, not even I will force you. But know this: If you do not rule your life, the enemy will. That is how you become a prisoner. Instead of wearing your black and white referee uniform, you will wear the black and white stripes of a prisoner. Wisdom says: Choose today to be the umpire of your life, not a prisoner.

*And above all things [put on] love and enfold youselves with the bond of perfectness [which binds everything together completely in ideal harmony]. Let the peace (soul harmony which comes) from Christ rule (**act as umpire** continually) in your hearts [deciding and settling with finality all questions that arise in your minds].*

— COLOSSIANS 3:14-15 AMP

138

SEE ALSO: 1 PETER 1:23

Insecurity is a self-inflicted wound!

Insecurity is an expression of self-hatred. It is the deception that I make mistakes when I create My children. That is impossible. I cannot make mistakes. Everyone made in My image is good! When someone hates themselves, they are hating My design. This is as devastating as hating others. Insecurity is like a perpetually self-inflicted wound that will not heal. Hate changes a person's identity, and literally cheats My Kingdom and the world of My original design. The enemy knows that keeping people so preoccupied with themselves will cause ineffectiveness in the war against the power of darkness. Wisdom says: To hate what I make is not loving what I love. Find security in Me alone! ***Stop hurting Me by hating you.*** If someone has told you that you are not worthy of love, realize this was the voice of an enemy who cannot tell the truth! I proved that you are loved when I created you. Allow Me to heal the deep hurts and trauma that have come from abusive people. Know this: People never have the authority from Me to label you. Only I have the authority to label you — and I label you loved, wanted, and adored! Love Me today by loving yourself!

> *"For this is what the Lord, the God of Israel, says, ... 'Nevertheless, I will bring health and healing to it; I will heal my people and will let them enjoy abundant peace and security.'"* — Jeremiah 33:4, 6

See also: Genesis 1:31; Acts 10:38; James 2:8; Mark 12:30-31

A **victim**'s eyes are on the **loss**.
A **victor**'s eyes are on the **cross**.

At one time or another, every one of My children has been a victim of someone else's cruelty or deception. But not all made the choice to allow this to defeat them or define them. ***Everyone who has ever been injured has been presented with an opportunity to rise out of the loss, rather than relive the loss.*** Be determined that you choose to be more than a conqueror through My Son, Jesus. Wisdom says: You are made in My image to overcome and conquer in *every* struggle. To the victor belongs the spoils of the enemy. But when you choose to remain a victim, you choose to stay in deception or defeat, which keeps you powerless and in a victim mentality. This is where self-pity thrives. A victor rises even stronger. The victor sees that through the love of the cross, and in Jesus, there is victory in every situation. A victim remains powerless. I ask you today: Are your eyes on your tragic loss, or are your eyes on My triumphant cross?

Yet in all these things we are more than conquerors and gain an overwhelming victory through Him who loved us [so much that He died for us].
— ROMANS 8:37 AMP

Swing wide the city gates ... so the victors can enter and praise.
— PSALM 118:19 MSG

SEE ALSO: HEBREWS 4:12; 1 CORINTHIANS 13:12; 1 JOHN 2:14

Discipline and obedience always get My attention!

I AM calling My people to a lifestyle of holy discipline. No discipline is ever pleasant at the time, but it produces a harvest of the fruit of peace and righteousness. My discipline for you, My child, is proof that I love you. I discipline for good only, in order that you may share in My holiness. This very issue will determine who will advance in the ranks and who will be passed over. Being willing and obedient are conditions of My blessing. I AM looking for a disciplined people who will be obedient, no matter the cost! Wisdom says: *To live in continual blessing is to live in continual obedience.* I AM calling you to be disciplined and obedient today!

> *No discipline seems pleasant at the time, but painful. Later on, however, it produces a harvest of righteousness and peace for those who have been trained by it.*
> — HEBREWS 12:11

> *God disciplines us for our good, in order that we may share in his holiness.*
> — HEBREWS 12:10

> *The Lord disciplines the one he loves, and he chastens everyone he accepts as his son.*
> — HEBREWS 12:6

SEE ALSO: ISAIAH 1:19-20; DEUTERONOMY 28

My heart is deeply bonded to your heart.

You have won My heart. To be bonded to you is to not only be as *one*, but to have a relationship with you as if you are My *only one*! Although I have many children, I have a unique relationship with you that is unlike any of My other children. I know what makes you laugh, and I know what makes you cry. Without you, I would have a void in My heart. My bond to your heart is a connection that brings two hearts so closely together that they are now considered one. My heart and your heart are grafted together and beat as one. We are One Spirit through My Holy Spirit. And we are one flesh through My Son, Jesus. I AM your Beloved, and you are Mine. Wisdom says: *You won My heart from the very start!* Live today with peace, knowing I will never leave you — because our hearts are bonded as one!

*Make every effort to keep the **unity of the Spirit** through the bond of peace.*
— Ephesians 4:3

*A man leaves father and mother and is firmly bonded to his wife, becoming **one flesh** — no longer two bodies but one.*
— Matthew 19:5 msg

I will bring you into the bond of the covenant.
— Ezekiel 20:37

See also: Proverbs 22:11; Ephesians 3:7; Matthew 6:21; 1 Samuel 18:1

It is impossible to fear Me and man at the same time.

Every heart was created to worship Me. If a person chooses not to worship Me, then that heart will worship other people and things that are made in *My image*. To worship Me is to have reverential fear, awe, and respect for Me. When fear and worship are toward Me, not man, then your identity stays intact. But when you fear man, or their opinions, that means you have begun to reverence them over Me. Then the fear of man, and what he thinks, becomes more important than Me. You will be in bondage to any man that you reverence and worship, which leads to fear of rejection. You cannot become the person I designed you to be when this is out of order. Wisdom says: When you do not have awe in your *Creator* — Me — then man will take My position and try to *recreate* you into their image. Fear of man makes you afraid to be yourself. Today, keep your adoration of Me, and keep your identity sure.

*It will be well with those who **fear God**.*
— Ecclesiastes 8:12 esv

***Fear of man** will prove to be a snare.* — Proverbs 29:25

*The Lord said to Joshua, "**Do not fear** them, because I have given them into your hand."*
— Joshua 10:8 amp

See also: Psalm 56:4, Proverbs 2

143

Your life is a prayer
when you live for Me.

How precious is a life lived totally for Me! A life lived for Me is continuous prayer. When your heart's desire is to please Me more than you want to please yourself, this is a living prayer. When I ask you to do something that is inconvenient or that will rearrange and disrupt your entire day, and you do it anyway, that is a living prayer. Obedience is more pleasing to Me than praise and worship. To live for Me is a life lived well! A life lived for yourself is a wasted life. There are no regrets on the deathbed of anyone who has lived their life for Me and not just for themselves. Wisdom says: Worship Me today by living a life for and through Me. When you pray, I AM not only listening, but I AM answering your prayers.

In the morning, O Lord, You will hear my voice; In the morning I will prepare [a prayer and a sacrifice] for You and watch and wait [for You to speak to my heart].
— Psalm 5:3 AMP

Pray continually.

— 1 Thessalonians 5:17

See also: Psalm 141:2; Isaiah 56:7; Mark 11:24; James 1:6-8

If you are fighting a giant, you are about to possess the promise!

As long as people wander aimlessly without purpose through life, they will usually not have to slay a giant. A giant does not show up until there is a Promise or a Promised Land! A giant only comes when the enemy is threatened by what you are about to possess. It is up to you to slay the giants in your life. Even though David used a stone to topple a giant, it was *My* Covenant with David that sealed the giant's death sentence. The giants that you slay this day open up new territory that you will occupy tomorrow. *If you are being threatened by a giant, it is because you are a threat to the giant (enemy). Every obstacle from the enemy is designed to stop My oracle of victory that I have decreed for your life.* Wisdom says: Use *your* Covenant rights to help slay the giants that you face today. Do not just challenge the giant, but slay him and behead him. Acquiring My Promise — your destiny — depends upon whether you terminate or tolerate the giant! If you are facing a giant, do not fear or take steps backwards. Run toward the giant, knowing you have the Stone to protect you — the Cornerstone.

The Lord always keeps his promises.

— Psalm 145:13 NLT

David replied to the Philistine, "You come to me with sword, spear, and javelin, but I come to you in the name of the Lord of Heaven's Armies. ... Today the Lord will conquer you, and I will kill you and cut off your head."

— 1 Samuel 17:45-46 NLT

See also: 1 Chronicles 20:7-8; Numbers 13:27-30

Can you see the 'yes' in every yesterday?

Can you see the "yes" in every yesterday? Or do you just see "no"? When you live in the past, you are killing your future! The purpose of each day is to help you build character — not a past. It is your choice how you decide to *view* your past — positive (yes) or negative (no). I fill every day with blessing and purpose. If you missed the mark yesterday, then the *yes* is in the blessing of My mercy and redemption, and learning from mistakes. If you wasted your time yesterday, then the *yes* is learning to be more efficient. If you used yesterday to be more obedient to Me, then the *yes* is in My reward. Wisdom says: No matter how bad yesterday seemed, choose to learn from it and use it to build character for today. ***You would not be who you are today without your yesterday!***

> *For a thousand years in your sight are like a day that has just gone by, or like a watch in the night.*
> — Psalm 90:4

> *For no matter how many promises God has made, they are "Yes" in Christ. And so through him the "Amen" is spoken by us to the glory of God.*
> — 2 Corinthians 1:20

> *Jesus Christ is the same yesterday and today and forever.*
> — Hebrews 13:8

See also: Isaiah 51:9; Job 8:9

Do you have your Father's eyes?

To have My eyes means that you can see yourself and others as I see them! I see the good in everyone. I see your value. I see Myself in My children. When you are born again, I see My Son, Jesus, in you. Everything about you is filtered through the lens of love. To have My eyes means to look upon yourself and everyone else through the lens of love. How you see yourself and your neighbors determines how you will treat others. Wisdom says: Do not look to *find* the faults of others; become *blind* to the faults of others! You know that you have your Father's eyes when you choose to see people as flawless — in spite of noticing their flaws. Remember, this is how I see you. Even when you feel you are at your worst, I cannot help but to see you through My beloved Son, Jesus! When you see what I love, and love what you see, people will say, "You have your Father's eyes!" Ask for the gift of seeing with My eyes of Love.

> *We saw the glory with our own eyes, the one-of-a-kind glory, like Father, like Son, Generous inside and out, true from start to finish.*
> — JOHN 1:14 MSG

> *While we are in this world, we are exactly like him with regard to love.*
> — 1 JOHN 4:17 GW

> *Just as I have loved you, you should love each other.*
> — JOHN 13:34 NLT

SEE ALSO: MARK 12:33; MATTHEW 19:19

In My Kingdom, forgiveness is not a choice.

Many think that forgiveness is a choice. In My Kingdom, it is not. It is My commandment to you if you want forgiveness from Me. You must sow forgiveness to reap forgiveness! You receive forgiveness as you forgive! ***To cancel someone's debt is to cancel yours.*** To believe you can be forgiven without forgiving is deception from hell! The Law of Sowing and Reaping states: You reap what you sow. Every one of My Spiritual Laws applies to everyone — and the Spiritual Law of Sowing and Reaping certainly applies to forgiveness. Know this today: In My Kingdom, forgiveness is not an option! Wisdom says: To truly love yourself is to cancel someone else's debt to you! Anyone who wants to reap forgiveness from Me must sow forgiveness. My heart cries out for you to be free of unforgiveness. ***Forgive and free yourself today!***

> *And when you stand praying, if you hold anything against anyone, forgive them, so that your Father in heaven may forgive you your sins.*
> — Mark 11:25

> *And forgive us our debts, As we forgive our debtors.*
> — Matthew 6:12

> *But if you do not forgive others their sins, your Father will not forgive your sins.*
> — Matthew 6:15

I AM breathing on the authentic, but suffocating anything without pure motives.

I AM breathing on the authentic, and I AM suffocating anything with wrong motives and intentions that could lead to hypocrisy. Authentic describes someone or something that is genuine, real, or honest. I reward the authentic. But hypocrites are deceivers, impostors, or people who try to cover up their schemes or devices to get credit for their virtues. Hypocrites assume a character that is not real. Wisdom says: Choose today to be authentic and do everything for My Glory and Honor, not for your own! I require My Body to be without hypocrisy. I will not tolerate those with abusing religious spirits like the Pharisees that are hurting My people, especially when My Body is encountering an authentic move of My Holy Spirit! You will know when you are experiencing Me, because the religious spirits will attack you just as they did My Son, Jesus. I AM asking you to clean out the closets of your heart, to be ready for My return! Be sure to have pure motives in regard to everything you do today.

*"Don't be nitpickers; use your head — and heart! — to discern what is right, to **test what is authentically right**."*
— John 7:24 MSG

"As it is written: 'These people honor me with their lips, but their hearts are far from me.'"
— Mark 7:6

SEE ALSO: JOB 8:13-15

If you are not moving **with** Me, you are moving **against** Me!

I AM the Leader and Commander in Chief in My Kingdom and of the armies of heaven. I desire a people who will willingly follow Me. I do not want a people that I have to drag! I long for your cooperation, not opposition. When I lead you into new territory or in a new way, please do not question or challenge Me because it is not the old or usual way! I need for you to trust Me in the way that I choose to lead you. I want your *reliance*, not your *resistance*. If *you* try to lead, I refuse to follow. Wisdom says: Because I AM the Good Shepherd, when *I* lead you, it is always to a better place or to a Promised Land for your comfort, safety, provision and rest. I will never lead you into harm. There is great reward when you choose to follow Me — even if you cannot see with your natural eyes where I AM taking you. I AM the Way, the Truth and the Life. Those who follow Me will *never* be lost! If you are not going My way, know that you are in My way. Today, trust that *because I AM the Way*, you can be sure *I know the way* that I AM leading you today.

> *"Whoever is not with me is against me, and whoever does not gather with me scatters."* — MATTHEW 12:30

> *Do two **walk together** unless they have agreed to do so?* — AMOS 3:3

You will be held responsible for allowing property damage to My temple.

You are the temple of My Holy Spirit. You are more beautiful and majestic than even Solomon's Temple. You are ***My*** handiwork. ***Worthy. Loved. Successful. Gifted. Mine.*** I have given you the responsibility to maintain My temple and keep it beautiful. Condemnation causes property damage. This is what condemnation looks like in the spirit realm: It looks as though someone spray-painted black graffiti all over My majestic temple! This graffiti contains words such as: ***Rejection. Worthless. Fearful. Failure. Loser. Stupid.*** You will be held responsible for allowing those condemning words to deface My property. This is your choice. Wisdom says: Choose to believe My Word over the words of graffiti that fail to tell the Truth. Use My Word to change the image of My temple. Remove the enemy's words of condemnation, and cover yourself with ***My Word*** today!

> *You realize, don't you, that you are the temple of God, and God himself is present in you? No one will get by with vandalizing God's temple, you can be sure of that. God's temple is sacred — and you, remember, are the temple.*
>
> — 1 Corinthians 3:16 MSG

See also: Romans 8:1; John 5:24

Unity never means you should lose your diversity and individuality!

I AM the Creator of diversity and individuality. Being in the unity of one Body always means that you will embrace the uniqueness and diversity in everyone around you. Pride causes division, and cannot celebrate individuality. Pride is the expression of acting, looking, and talking like everyone else. Love is the expression of being secure and celebrating your differences, and the differences in others. Love is being comfortable with who you are. Wisdom says: ***Love makes no apologies for being the person I created you to be.*** Unity does not mean you have to be the same as everyone else. It means to ***cherish*** the uniqueness in yourself and in one another! Embrace and encourage diversity in My Body today!

> *Whatever happens, conduct yourselves in a manner worthy of the gospel of Christ. Then, ... stand firm in the one Spirit, **striving together as one** for the faith of the gospel.*
> – Philippians 1:27

> *"I have given them the glory you gave me — the glorious **unity** of being one, as we are."*
> – John 17:22 TLB

See also: Ephesians 4:3-6

How you end your day is just as important as how you begin your day.

How you begin the first few minutes of each day sets the course for your entire day. I also remind you that how you spend the last few minutes of each day is just as important, or even more important. How you end each day will set the course for how your new day will begin. If you have anger, anxiety, or unresolved hurt, settle it before you end each day. You do not want to contaminate your brand new day. Wisdom says: Begin and end every day in *My* Presence. Let Me brush off the dust of this day before it flows into a new one. Because you will never be able to relive this day, end it well. Receive My Peace that no matter what will happen today, all is well, because I make all things new again tomorrow! Allow *Me* to rock you to sleep, instead of the events of the day.

I cry out to you for help, O Lord, and in the morning my prayer will come into your presence. — PSALM 88:13 GW

It is vain for you to rise early, To retire late, To eat the bread of anxious labors — For He gives [blessings] to His beloved even in his sleep. — PSALM 127:2 AMP

Be angry without sinning. Don't go to bed angry. — EPHESIANS 4:26 GW

SEE ALSO: PSALM 36:4

I desire for you to do things with Me, not just for Me!

Are you too busy to stop and ask Me for the anointing and power you need to become even more productive? I want to strengthen you to do the work in My power and not your own. I desire your fellowship as you complete your assignments. When you work *for* Me, it is just a job or work. But when you work *with* Me, you are *co-laboring* with the right motives and purposes. In My Kingdom, when I work *through* you, *I* get the glory. If you work alone, you just get the glory. Allow Me to shine through you to display My Goodness to a hurting world. The world is not impressed with you when you work in the natural realm — but people really take notice when I work through you in the supernatural realm. This is when I get all the glory! Wisdom says: Work *with* Me today, and not just *for* Me! I want to be your Father, not your boss.

Though the Lord is exalted, He regards the lowly [and invites them into His fellowship]; But the proud and haughty He knows from a distance.
— Psalm 138:6 AMP

Consider yourselves also dead to sin and your relation to it broken, but alive to God [living in unbroken fellowship with Him] in Christ Jesus.
— Romans 6:11 AMP

Pain is a weak opponent!

When something can be ***changed*** or eliminated, even for a little while, then it is weak! Pain can be altered by medications and by other chemicals and herbs; therefore, it is a weak opponent! Although pain — especially severe pain — sometimes seems so strong, there is something that is even much more powerful than pain — My ***never-changing*** Word. ***Nothing is more powerful than My Word!*** It is eternal and will never be destroyed. I will always accomplish what I intend. I uphold My Word even over My name! It would be easier for heaven and earth to pass away than for the smallest detail of My Word to fail. Wisdom says: If you are in pain today, know that I AM your Comforter and your Healer. Never forget that pain must bow to the power of My Word. I AM closest to the brokenhearted and those who are suffering! I AM never indifferent to your pain. I AM running to your rescue! Can you feel Me holding you as I hide you in My Secret Place? I AM wiping away all your tears as I wipe away Mine. I AM comforting you and easing your pain. Allow Me the time to just hold you near Me today.

You have magnified Your word above all Your name.
— Psalm 138:2 AMP

Forever, O Lord, Your word is settled in heaven.
— Psalm 119:89 NKJV

It is easier for heaven and earth to disappear than for the least stroke of a pen to drop out of the Law.
— Luke 16:17

See also: Isaiah 55:11; Malachi 3:6

The enemy becomes a larger **entity** when he steals just one **identity**.

Just stealing one person's identity from My Kingdom enlarges the kingdom of darkness. When the enemy steals who and Whose you are, he steals from Me! He wants to make you smaller so you will be ineffective in My Kingdom. To steal your identity is to steal the identity of My Son, Jesus, from this world! Know this: The world stays confused when they see a Christian without Christ in them. By this I mean that My Son *knows who He is!* My Son said what I said and did what He saw Me doing. If the enemy can steal your identity, the world won't hear what I AM saying, and they can't see what I AM doing! Your identity directly affects My Kingdom and the world! Remember, you are not just a joint heir with Jesus! You are My personal weapon that is vital to My Kingdom! You cannot and will not ever be replaced! See yourself as Jesus saw Himself! He always saw Himself as One with Me. He allowed the world to see and hear Me! Whom are you allowing the world to see? Me or you? Identity crisis is why the world is in a crisis! Wisdom says: When you only say what you hear Me say, and do what you see Me do, you will be a beautiful reflection of Me to this world. *The world is waiting and, yes, even longing for you to know who you are so the world will know who I AM!*

See also: Romans 1:2-7; Galatians 3:26; Romans 8:1-2; 1 Peter 2:10; Matthew 24:43; John 10:10

A mind without restraints becomes a mouth without restraints.

There is no such thing as a powerless thought. Every thought produces fruit. A thought that is meditated upon becomes a stronghold in a person's mind and heart. For out of the heart proceeds evil thoughts: murders, lies, and blasphemies. Bring every thought captive to the obedience of My Son, Jesus Christ. You cannot afford to allow your mind to aimlessly wander. This can take you places you never believed you would go, and can produce rotten fruit in your life that will cost you more than you can afford. Every murder started with a *thought*. Every good deed started with a thought. Therefore, do not be conformed to this world, but be transformed by renewing your mind. Wisdom says: A *mind* without restraints is a dangerous mind, and becomes a mouth without restraints. And a *mouth* without restraints becomes an *action* without restraints. Choose to think on *Me* today.

> For to be carnally minded is death, but to be spiritually minded is life and peace.
> — ROMANS 8:6 NKJV

> You will keep him in perfect peace, Whose mind is stayed on You, Because he trusts in You.
> — ISAIAH 26:3 KJV

SEE ALSO: *MATTHEW 15:19; 2 CORINTHIANS 10:5; ROMANS 12:2*

My power is **rendered** when your weakness is **surrendered.**

Look to see where you have been weak, then surrender that to Me. I exchange all your weaknesses — all your frailty, your helplessness, your powerlessness — for My strength. I can only help you when you surrender to Me. When you think you can handle a problem in your own strength, you are only deceiving yourself. When you tolerate a weakness, then that weakness can become your identity. Never confuse *who* you are with *what* weakness you are dealing with. Your identity is in Me alone, and never in your weaknesses. You were created in My image, not in the image of anyone who is weak. You are Mine, and My power is available to you when you lay your weaknesses on My altar. Wisdom says: Never allow shame to keep you from getting help. If you can *see* yourself free, you are closer than you think! Allow Me to take your weaknesses and turn them into victories today!

> *"This is the word of the Lord to Zerubbabel: 'Not by might nor by power, but by My Spirit,' Says the Lord.'"*
> — ZECHARIAH 4:6 NKJV

> *But he said to me, "My grace is sufficient for you, for my power is made perfect in weakness."*
> — 2 CORINTHIANS 12:9

SEE ALSO: PSALM 68:35; PSALM 89:21; 1 CORINTHIANS 4:10

To plan revenge is like planning your own funeral.

I need to make this very clear: Vengeance is Mine, and *I* will repay! I AM The Fair Judge. I can see what you cannot. Only I AM in position to Judge and execute vengeance, as well as reward. Unforgiveness is dangerous, but revenge is deadly! Revenge is like walking into the enemy's territory without any weapons or protection. Arm and protect yourself! Wisdom says: Forgive! Then allow *Me* to Judge. The sweetest revenge is to love in return; this way the enemy cannot harm you. ***Revenge is not only premeditated hurt of the person you hate, but also premeditated murder of yourself.*** When you revere Me as Judge, you will never seek revenge! I AM Justice. If you have suffered injustice, glory in your position in Me, in Justice.

> *Do not take revenge, my dear friends, but leave room for God's wrath, for it is written: "It is mine to avenge; I will repay," says the Lord.*
> — Romans 12:19

> *"'Do not seek revenge or bear a grudge against anyone among your people, but love your neighbor as yourself. I am the Lord."*
> — Leviticus 19:18

> *"I will execute great vengeance on them with wrathful rebukes and chastisements and they will know [without any doubt] that I am the Lord."*
> — Ezekiel 25:17 AMP

A destiny failed is a gift canceled!

You are a gift, created by Me to fulfill a need or to solve a problem, in this world. When your destiny is not accomplished, then the world and My Kingdom suffer and lose out on the gift of you! There will never be another *gift* like you to accomplish what I created you to accomplish! If *you* do not complete your destiny, I cannot make another *you* to fulfill what you were created to do. The gifts that I put in you are always to add souls to My Kingdom. This is a life-and-death issue. I need you to accomplish what I have designed for you to accomplish. Wisdom says: Seek My face today, and get *My* plans for your life. True freedom and happiness come when you are fulfilling the destiny I created for you. Never forget that there is nothing insignificant about your life. You are a crucial part of My Kingdom.

Joseph replied, "Don't be afraid. Do I act for God? Don't you see, you planned evil against me but God used those same plans for my good."
— GENESIS 50:19-20 MSG

"For I know the plans I have for you," declares the Lord, "plans to prosper you and not to harm you, plans to give you hope and a future. Then you will call on me and come and pray to me, and I will listen to you. You will seek me and find me when you seek me with all your heart."
— JEREMIAH 29:11-13

Commit to the Lord whatever you do, and he will establish your plans.
— PROVERBS 16:3

SEE ALSO: PSALM 20:4

I behold your beauty, because beauty is in the eye of The Beholder!

When you compare yourself with someone else, what you are really afraid of is that you have less! It is never about what *they* have. It is about what you *feel* you do *not* have. *I* look upon the heart. No one can compare or judge anyone because no one can see the heart except Me. The truth is, not one person can diminish the beauty and value of another. I behold your beauty because beauty is in the eye of The Beholder! I never flatter, and I cannot lie. When I call you beautiful, who can strike down My Words? Wisdom says: ***Remember this today that you are a reflection of Me. How can you be anything but beautiful?***

"Man looks at the outward appearance, but the Lord looks at the heart."
— 1 Samuel 16:7

So will the King desire your beauty.
— Psalm 45:11 AMP

In that day the Lord Almighty will be a glorious crown, a beautiful wreath for the remnant of his people.
— Isaiah 28:5

The descendants of your tormentors will come and bow before you. Those who despised you will kiss your feet.
— Isaiah 60:14 NLT

Among the nations you were famous for your beauty.
— Ezekiel 16:14 CEB

161

Hard circumstances birth champions!

Easy lifestyles birth complacency, but difficult circumstances birth champions! Being in a difficult situation will *always move you*. Use the difficult situation to catapult you into a new and better place! Those who do not face challenges tend to stay in the same place in life! That is because people do not like to move unless they are forced. I *do not cause* hard circumstances, but when they do happen, *I work them for your good*. Do not waste the challenges! Allow them to build your faith. The more you have to use your faith, the stronger you will be. This is how champions are made. There cannot be a champion without a fight. Wisdom says: Every time the enemy attacks you, know that it costs him tremendously, especially when you get up stronger. During attacks, the enemy uncovers his tactics and strategies and exposes his weaknesses! Fight the good fight of faith today! A champion gets stronger with every fight. Know that I AM always with you, helping you through every difficult time. See Me with you today with My strength to carry you through!

Many are the afflictions of the righteous: but the Lord delivereth him out of them all.

– Psalm 34:19 kjv

See also: 1 Timothy 6:12; Psalm 91; Romans 8:28

I AM too large to be stuck in the monotony of your past! I AM always in the new day!

Life is all about having a progressively, more intimate relationship with Me each new day. When you are looking back at all that has happened, you are missing all that is currently happening. I AM constantly moving forward. I never retreat! If you are looking at your past, it is because you do not trust Me with your present or your future. I AM so full right now in your present that there is no room for your past. If your life has become one of monotony, have you forgotten that I make all things new? If your relationship with Me has become monotonous, then you are missing out on all that I AM doing and saying today. Wisdom says: Make an effort to keep our relationship new and fresh! I AM revealing Myself to you every day, whether or not you see or hear Me. Take the time to listen to all I AM saying and showing you today. With every new day, I give you a new revelation of who I AM. You get the best of Me when you invest in Me.

[For my determined purpose is] that I may know Him [that I may progressively become more deeply and intimately acquainted with Him, perceiving and recognizing and understanding the wonders of His Person more strongly and more clearly].

— PHILIPPIANS 3:10 AMP

SEE ALSO: ISAIAH 48:6

163

May 26

When you **share** the spotlight with Jesus, then you are **stealing** the show.

If you take credit for everything that I have given you, you are stealing *My* Glory. Lucifer took some of the worship that was due Me! This is pride. It did not belong to him. That is why he is a thief. When he took what was Mine, I took away from him the position that I had given him. If you take the worship that is due Me, you will lose everything I intended to bless you with in your position. That would be stealing My show, and would make *you* a *thief*! Acknowledge Me in your giftings. Allow My glory to shine through every gift and ability that I have given you. *Every* good and perfect gift comes from Me — every single one. Wisdom says: Remember today that the gifts I have given you are to be used to make Jesus look attractive — not *just* to make *you* look attractive. They are for the work in My Kingdom. I AM the Gift Maker and you are to be the gift taker. You give Me the glory when you worship Me by using your gifts that I have placed in you. I want you to be confident and comfortable with your gifts from Me. Do not apologize for them, nor become prideful in them. Use your gifts to glorify Me!

> *Every good and perfect gift is from above*, coming
> down from the Father of the heavenly lights, who does
> not change like shifting shadows.   – JAMES 1:17

164

SEE ALSO: JOHN 10:10; ROMANS 12:6

I AM a Believer too!
You have made Me a Believer.

I AM Love. Because I AM Love, I *believe* all things. I, Love, hope all things. I believe in the power of My Son's name. I believe all that My Word says you can do. *I believe in you because I believe in My Son in you.* You have been given full power and authority to use His name. He is the source of all power. You are made in Our image. I only create the best quality. I did not short you in gifts and talents. You are everything I dreamed you would be! I *really* do believe that you *can* do anything — through My Son, Jesus Christ, Who strengthens you! Wisdom says: I have complete confidence in you because of the knowledge that I have of you. Jesus stripped hell of all power and gave the keys of My Kingdom to you. Now you are fully equipped with staggering power and authority in My Son, Jesus. Know today that I would not have created you if I did not believe in you! Beloved, You have made *Me* a Believer!

> For I can do everything through Christ, who gives me strength.   — PHILIPPIANS 4:13 NLT

> Love... believes all things, hopes all things, endures all things.   — 1 CORINTHIANS 13:7 NKJV

SEE ALSO: MARK 9:23

A prayer delayed can be My mercy.

Just because there has been a delay in an answer to your prayer, this does not mean that I have denied your prayer. If you ask for something you are not ready for, the delay is actually My mercy! Some day, you might just thank Me for the delay. I never say no to a prayer that is asked in faith and lines up with My Word and My will. I love to answer your prayers! Cling to My faithfulness when there is a delay. My timing is perfect! Wisdom says: Do not lose heart. Trust My wisdom and judgment that I can see what you cannot. Know that My silence is never indifference! One characteristic of a faith champion is trusting Me even when there is a delay in answered prayer! Never forget: I would not ask you to pray if I did not intend to answer your prayer.

"Do not be afraid, Daniel. Since the first day that you set your mind to gain understanding and to humble yourself before your God, your words were heard, and I have come in response to them. But the prince of the Persian kingdom resisted me twenty-one days. Then Michael, one of the chief princes, came to help me, because I was detained there with the king of Persia."

— DANIEL 10:12-13

If we know that he hears us — whatever we ask — we know that we have what we asked of him.

— 1 JOHN 5:15

SEE ALSO: *JAMES 1:5-8; MATTHEW 7:7-11;*
MARK 9:23; JOHN 14:1-5; JOHN 15:7; JOHN 15:16; MARK 11:22

When you choose division, you no longer see from **My heart**; you see from **your hurt**.

When you are in pain, you cannot trust your perception. When you look through the eyes of hurt or pain, you tend to have an exaggerated view of how you see things. Both physical and emotional hurt lead to feeling excluded or rejected. All division stems from pain. Where there is division, there is lack of My power. Thus, you no longer operate under My spiritual Law of Agreement. Do not fall into the trap of division. This is the fastest way to lose your vision, or godly perspective. To be divided is to be spiritually blind! Division (die-vision) "kills" your vision. I hate division. Wisdom says: Division causes confusion. If you are having trouble deciding which path is My will for your life, know this: Division leads to indecision. My will for you and for My Body is unity. Seek to hear from My heart today, not from your hurt!

I appeal to you ... that there be no divisions among you, but that you be perfectly united in mind and thought.
— 1 Corinthians 1:10

"Any kingdom divided against itself will be ruined, and a house divided against itself will fall."
— Luke 11:17

Live in harmony and peace.
— 2 Corinthians 13:11

Warn a divisive person once ...
— Titus 3:10

See also: Proverbs 6:16-19

Satisfaction is a comfort the enemy lives without!

The act of thievery is always progressive. A first-time thief rarely starts out robbing a bank. He starts out small to see how much he can get away with. His appetite is absolutely unquenchable. A thief is never satisfied with what he has stolen. His thoughts are always on what else he can steal. His progressive success depends upon not being seen or caught. When you allow the enemy to easily steal from you, it whets his appetite to steal more. ***Tolerating a thief makes you a target!*** Use your power and authority to stop thievery; otherwise, the enemy's next step will be ***death***. If you tolerate death, the enemy's next stage will be ***destruction***. Destruction not only destroys lives and families, but this enemy destroys destinies, purposes, hopes, and dreams! Wisdom says: Never make it easy for the enemy to steal from you. Today, use My weapons against the enemy: My Word, Blood, Name, Armor.

The thief comes only to steal and kill and destroy.

– John 10:10

Jesus called his twelve disciples to him and gave them authority to drive out impure spirits and to heal every disease and sickness.

– Matthew 10:1

See also: 2 Corinthians 10:4

The difference between **live** and **love** is that **love** has no 'I' in it!

My Love is given to you with the purest intentions! I love without expecting anything in return. I live to love and love to live. I AM continually refreshing Myself as I pour out My Love on you! My Love is pure and uncontaminated and without agendas. Some use what appears to be love to manipulate in order to get something back in return. Their fake love is full of "I," "I," "I." Love is never supposed to be about "I" or you! I AM calling My Body to love with pure and genuine motives! I need those who will love with *My* Love instead of their own limited and contaminated love. I AM asking you to love lavishly without expecting ***anything*** in return. This is the definition of how I love! My Love is the language that never needs an interpreter! Wisdom says: Love at the risk of being hurt or misunderstood! This is how I love you — and how I AM asking you to love today!

Beloved, let us [unselfishly] love and seek the best for one another, for love is from God; and everyone who loves [others] is born of God and knows God [through personal experience]. — 1 John 4:7 amp

SEE ALSO: JOHN 3:16

Do not let your eyes have the last word!

Let *My Word* have the last word — not what you see! What you *say* in faith will change what you *see* in life. Why do you put so much faith in an organ that can fail? My Word can never fail. Seeing is not believing. Faith is seeing and believing the Word instead of the world. The Word does not say that death and life are in the power of the eyes! Death and life are in the power of the tongue! My Word should always have the last word — not what you see. Wisdom says: Use the power of My Word to change what you see. Today, speak My Word of Life, and watch circumstances bow their knees. ***When your eyes are spiritually fixed on Me, only then can I fix what you physically see.***

> *So we fix our eyes not on what is seen, but on what is unseen, since what is seen is temporary, but what is unseen is eternal.* — 2 Corinthians 4:18

> *Now faith is confidence in what we hope for and assurance about what we* ***do not see***. — Hebrews 11:1

> *... fixing our eyes on Jesus, the pioneer and perfecter of faith.* — Hebrews 12:2

> *All the ways of a man are pure in his own eyes, but the Lord weighs the spirits (the thoughts and intents of the heart).* — Proverbs 16:2 AMP

See also: Luke 1:37; Proverbs 18:21; Psalm 17:2

Take opposition as a compliment!

If you are not receiving opposition from the enemy, or through other people, then you are most likely not making progress; *you just think you are!* Any time you are making progress in My Kingdom, there will be opposition to attempt to stop or defeat you! Expect it and you will not be caught off guard! Then you will be able to identify it, cast it down, take authority over it, and move past it very quickly. Wisdom says: Take opposition as a compliment today! This means you are making progress in Me. The degree of attacks from the enemy indicates the degree of My call on your life. You are My warrior, anointed for battle. Live like it! Never forget: The enemy only fights with those he fears. Take opposition as a compliment.

> *"No weapon that is formed against you will succeed; And every tongue that rises against you in judgment you will condemn. This [peace, righteousness, security, and triumph over opposition] is the heritage of the servants of the Lord, And this is their vindication from Me," says the Lord.*
> — Isaiah 54:17 AMP

> *But even if you should suffer for the sake of righteousness [though it is not certain that you will], you are still blessed.*
> — 1 Peter 3:14 AMP

> *Do not be surprised at the fiery ordeal that has come on you to test you. ... rejoice inasmuch as you participate in the sufferings of Christ, so that you may be overjoyed when his glory is revealed.*
> — 1 Peter 4:12-13 NIV

When My Son fell for you, He fell hard.

When someone tells of a great love story, it is often said that two people "*fell* in love." Some might even say that they "fell hard." In the Garden of Eden, the first Adam fell when he sinned. To redeem all of mankind into right standing with Me, My Son (the second Adam) also *fell* in the Garden (of Gethsemane). He also fell with the cross that He carried for you. When you accept the sacrifice of My Son, Jesus, then you can live with Me as if you were back in the Garden of Eden again. *Jesus fell in love with you so you could rise out of the curse and become a new creation in Him!* His love bore your sin, sickness, and death. In exchange, He sacrificed His virtue, health, and Life. Wisdom says: Jesus not only fell in love with you — He went to hell for you! There is no greater demonstration of love than this: *My Son fell so you could stand strong with Me throughout eternity!* Behold, this is the greatest love story ever told! Remember the sacrifice of My Son, so you can fall in love with Him anew today!

*Going a little farther, he **fell** to the ground and prayed that if possible the hour might pass from him.*
— MARK 14:35

She also gave some to her husband, who was with her, and he ate it. Then the eyes of both of them were opened, and they realized they were naked.
— GENESIS 3:6-7

SEE ALSO: JOHN 3:16-17

Hope is My gift to the broken.

Hopelessness is sterile ground. When you have hope in Me, this is fertile ground and your life can flourish. If you are still breathing, you have hope! You may have lost many things, but if you have hope, you still have the ability to get everything back and more! Hope can see what you cannot! Hope can see beyond your current situation! When you have lost everything except hope, you are in position for miracles! Wisdom says: Hope in Me today! Hope only comes from Me. You increase in hope when you meditate on Me. Hope soars in My Presence. There is always a reason to live in hope when you have Me for a faithful Father. Prepare your life for miracles by inviting My gift of hope to flourish deep inside you today.

Those who go down to the pit cannot hope for your faithfulness.
— Isaiah 38:18

Guide me in your truth and teach me, for you are God my Savior, and my hope is in you all day long.
— Psalm 25:5

We boast in the hope of the glory of God.
— Romans 5:2

Against all hope, Abraham in hope believed and so became the father of many nations.
— Romans 4:18

June 5

Every time you lift your hands to Me in praise, I cannot resist picking you up and holding you.

~

When you raise your hands in praise to Me, it is not just a sign of surrender, but I take it that you are raising them because you seek peace and comfort **only** in Me. This is true worship to Me. You are acknowledging Me as Father. As a parent, you know that when your small child raises their little hands for you to hold them, you drop everything to pick them up. Does it not warm your heart just knowing your child finds comfort **only** in you? If you cannot resist **your** children, how much more will I not be able to resist the opportunity to hold **you** close? If you are tender and loving to your children, how much more tender and loving am I to you? Wisdom says: You will only find True Comfort in My Arms of Love when you run to Me first. Know this today: When you lift your hands to Me in praise, you lift My heart with joy!

*Yes, I will bless you as long as I live; in your name I will **lift up my hands**. ... my mouth praises you.*
— Psalm 63:4-6 cjb

On the day of my distress I am seeking Adonai; my hands are lifted up; my tears flow all night without ceasing.
— Psalm 77:3 cjb

See also: Psalm 34:18; Jeremiah 8:18

The enemy has a difficult time stealing from a heart that has received My revelation.

A deception is death; a lie requires your agreement in order to be operational. Deception and lies are the bait to hook your agreement. Once you agree with the enemy's lies, you are under his influence. Revelation is Truth that is alive. Deception is a dead lie that needs your agreement to resurrect it! Revelation — My living insight — is the unveiling of My Truth to you that you did not previously know. It literally becomes *alive* to you. Revelation changes the way you think. Once you have revelation, it is more difficult for you to be deceived again in a particular area. Thus, pray for revelation, and not simply for answers to prayer. Once you receive *My* revelation, the enemy has a very difficult time deceiving or stealing from your heart — that is, unless you allow it. Wisdom says: Ask Me for revelation on issues and circumstances in areas where you currently struggle so you will not be deceived. Completely surrender to the power of My Holy Spirit!

Where there is no revelation, people cast off restraint; but blessed is the one who heeds wisdom's instruction.
— Proverbs 29:18

I keep asking that the God of our Lord Jesus Christ, the glorious Father, may give you the Spirit of wisdom and revelation, so that you may know him better.
— Ephesians 1:17

See also: James 1:5

175

You do not have to travel the world to change the world!

The most effective way to change the world is to change yourself! Only when you have the power and fortitude to change yourself will you be able to influence someone for Me. Many want to change their surroundings and relationships for My Kingdom, but they are not willing to work on themselves first! Those who choose not to deal with their own weaknesses and fleshly habits will not be as effective in being that authentic example for Me. Even My Perfect Son started His ministry with 40 days of prayer and fasting in a desert. *I AM not expecting or demanding perfection in you. But I yearn for a heart of inward reflection.* Wisdom says: Desire to change and become more like My Son. To change yourself is to change the world for My Glory!

> *Do not love the world or anything in the world. If anyone loves the world, love for the Father is not in them. For everything in the world — the lust of the flesh, the lust of the eyes, and the pride of life — comes not from the Father but from the world. The world and its desires pass away, but whoever does the will of God lives forever.* — 1 John 2:15-17

> *Do not conform to the pattern of this world, but be transformed by the renewing of your mind. Then you will be able to test and approve what God's will is — his good, pleasing and perfect will.* — Romans 12:2

See also: Romans 8:1

You cannot be **passionate** about Me without being **compassionate** to My children!

For in Christ Jesus neither circumcision nor uncircumcision has any value. The only thing that counts is faith expressing itself through love.

— GALATIANS 5:6

Faith and love operate as one. You cannot have one without the other. Faith always operates with love and compassion. *Faith without compassion is pride!* Do you have deep compassion for those who are genuinely suffering from the attacks from the evil one? Many who lack compassion truly believe that they are operating in great faith, but in reality they are operating in great pride! I AM not asking you to judge anyone about this issue except yourself. Do you not know that compassion is My heart moving on your heart to express My authentic and genuine Love to the world? To have compassion is to allow My extraordinary Love to move through you in a supernatural way. My compassion is the force that penetrates even the hardest of hearts to heal the broken. Compassion moves you to put yourself last, and to put Me and others first. Wisdom says: The enemy cannot overcome or outwit My weapon of compassion. You live an extraordinary life for Me when you are loving extraordinarily like I love! You can test your faith level by your compassion level. Have compassion for those who are suffering around you today.

SEE ALSO: MATTHEW 14:14; PSALM 103:13; ROMANS 9:15; MARK 6:34; MATTHEW 9:36; MATTHEW 20:34; ISAIAH 49:15; DEUTERONOMY 30:3

June 9

True cause and effect: Living for the **cause** of Christ will **affect** the world!

Do not just live for a dream or a vision for My Kingdom — although both are very good. A dream or a vision can die with a person. But when you live for the cause of **Christ**, My cause will outlive you generation after generation. A cause is a belief or position that you will support, fight for, and even die for. You cannot be moved from this position. If My people in My Kingdom all lived like this, it would affect the world! Terrorists have lived like this and have affected the entire world for evil. Terrorists refuse to be ignored because they will not just live for their cause, but they will die for it too! Wisdom says: When members of My Body, in unity, bow their knees and live for the cause of Christ — not just an opinion of Christ, like some — My Body will not be ignored. To affect the world, you must put the *cause* of Christ into *effect* today!

For this cause I bow my knees unto the Father of our Lord Jesus Christ. — EPHESIANS 3:14 KJV

You must no longer live as the Gentiles do, in the futility of their thinking. — EPHESIANS 4:17

SEE ALSO: ISAIAH 32:17

I AM at home in you!

There is no place like home! **You** are My sanctuary, My temple. I bought you with a price, the precious Blood of My Son, Jesus. You are no longer your own. My Son's name is now on the title deed to your body, written in His Blood! Have you, in perfect surrender, given **Me** the keys to your house? Do I have full access to your heart? I have entrusted **you** with the keys to My Kingdom. Wisdom says: You make Me feel at home when you choose to live your life consecrated and wholly dedicated to Me. I consider living a life of obedience to be the perfect form of worship. So worship Me today. Put yourself on the altar of My heart. Today, yield your dreams and motives to Me. Allow Me to replace them with **My** dreams ordained for you before the beginning of time. I AM at home in you! You are My home, sweet home!

*Don't you know that **you yourselves are God's temple** and that God's Spirit dwells in your midst?*
— 1 Corinthians 3:16

*Do you not know that your **bodies are temples of the Holy Spirit**, who is in you, whom you have received from God? You are not your own; **you were bought at a price**. Therefore honor God with your bodies.*
— 1 Corinthians 6:19-20

See also: John 1:14; Romans 12:1

My prophetic Word is always on time. Satan is just about out of time!

When I speak prophetically through My Word, it is always fulfilled the second that I intend. *I AM the Ancient of Days.* When I told Abraham that his descendants would be in bondage 400 years, this time frame ended *precisely* when I said. When I say something will happen in My Word, you do not have to wonder if I know what I AM talking about! I created time. I know the beginning, the middle, and the end of the Age. I AM in control of the timing of My prophetic Words. I do not guess! They *will* come to pass, just as I said. This is power! The enemy is powerless, defeated, and has already been sentenced and condemned. His time is very short, and he is very aware of it. Wisdom says: Wait on Me today. I AM not slow in keeping My promises. *Know that I AM not a procrastinator.*

> *And he gripped and overpowered the dragon, that old serpent [of primeval times], who is the devil and Satan, and [securely] bound him for a thousand years.*
> — REVELATION 20:2 AMP

> *The devil has come down to you in great wrath, knowing that he has only a **short time** [remaining]!*
> — REVELATION 12:12 AMP

> *The Lord is **not slow in keeping his promise**.*
> — 2 PETER 3:9

SEE ALSO: GENESIS 15:13; 2 CORINTHIANS 6:2; 1 TIMOTHY 6:15

Learn the lesson of how, every year, winter surrenders to the power of spring.

Life is such a powerful force! I AM Life. I have conquered death. Life is supposed to conquer, not be conquered. Without exception, you see this beautiful example *every* spring, when winter (death) surrenders to the power of spring (life). Life is more powerful than death! Consider why there was opposition to My Life at work in your life. In the natural, there is often an autopsy when life on this earth has ended. Wisdom says: Do a spiritual autopsy in any area where you have experienced a cycle of defeat, such as divorce, sickness, poverty, or addiction. Then seek My counsel, and **make adjustments for Life to reign** in that area. Prayerfully and carefully examine it, learn your lesson, then **bury** any opposition to Life. If you do not bury these cycles of defeat, you will have to relive them. Today, when you speak My name or My Word, which is **Life**, then **death** has no other option than to bow in utter defeat!

> *"Very truly I tell you, whoever hears my word and believes him who sent me has eternal life and will not be judged but has crossed over from death to life."* – JOHN 5:24

> *"Where, O death, is your victory? Where, O death, is your sting?"* – 1 CORINTHIANS 15:55

SEE ALSO: ROMANS 8:38-39

June 13

You have nothing in common with the enemy. You have **everything** in common with Me!

> *The prince (evil genius, ruler) of the world is coming. And **he has no claim on Me**; [He has **nothing in common with Me**; there is nothing in Me that belongs to him, and he has no power over Me.]*
>
> — John 14:30 AMPC

When you are in My Son, and My Son is in you, you can say the same thing. This is because you have much in common with My Son! You have absolutely nothing, however, in common with the enemy. He has **no power** over you. You are Mine! You are designed with My genetic code of truth, life, and liberty! You look like My Son, Jesus! You have all of My beautiful traits and strengths such as My beauty, love, peace, joy. You are created to rule — not be ruled by a defeated enemy. You look just like Me, your Father, not your enemy! Wisdom says: When an attack tries to shake you today, just boldly decree to the enemy: "You have nothing in common with me!" You are safe under the shadow of My fierce wings because you are Mine!

> *I do not ask You to take them out of the world, but that You keep them and protect them from the evil one.*
>
> — John 17:15 AMP

See also: John 17:22; Isaiah 43:1; John 17:10; Luke 9:1; Psalm 91

When you give someone or something your attention, it will cost you something!

Pay attention! Your attention comes with a price. When you pay attention to what I AM saying to you, it will cost you something — but there will always be much honor and great reward! When you give someone or something attention that is due to Me, it will always cost you more than you can ***afford*** to give — time, money, freedom, distraction! ***When you give the enemy your attention, you will always pay with deception and bondage!*** Whatever has your attention will also have your heart. Whatever has your heart has your future. Revelation from Me always requires your time and focus. When you sacrifice the world for Me, I will always make your reward more than you could have ever imagined. Your sacrifice will seem so small and insignificant next to My significance. Wisdom says: ***Today, focus on paying attention to My voice!*** I will bestow upon you great reward.

> *Listen and hear my voice;* ***pay attention and hear what I say.***
> — Isaiah 28:23

> *We must* ***pay the most careful attention,*** *therefore, to what we have heard, so that we do not drift away.*
> — Hebrews 2:1

> *I keep pursuing the goal in order to win the prize offered by God's upward calling in the Messiah Yeshua. Therefore, as many of us as are mature, let us* ***keep paying attention to this.***
> — Philippians 3:14-15 CJB

You can only afford to be in one accord!

When My Body is no longer blind to the truth that My Kingdom is about Me — and not about you, the church building, denomination title, or family traditions — there will be power unleashed in this world that will rock hell to its very core! My Body **must** be in a state of agreement and joined together as one. When there are fragments, then My Body is stagnant! When you are in unity and one accord, you will have the power and signs and wonders that you have longed for. Unity (you-nity) always begins with **you**! Every mighty move or revival has begun with a few people who were willing to judge their own hearts, not the hearts of those who cause divisions, pain, and rejection. **Unity cannot last if you will not examine and change your heart first!** Wisdom says: Your contrite heart causes My Body to unite! Unity means that **you** change the way **you** see others. It does not mean that you try to get other people to change their mind about you! **You be the one to ignite the revolution to unite!**

Now that you have purified yourselves by obeying the truth so that you have sincere love for each other, love one another deeply, from the heart.

— 1 Peter 1:22

See also: Acts 2:1-3; Philippians 2:2; Acts 5:12; Acts 8:6

The enemy enjoys making you think you must **serve** a life sentence for a 'misdemeanor' crime.

Whether you believe you have made huge mistakes during your lifetime or smaller ones, the enemy will try to torment you to serve a life sentence — even after you have repented and I have forgiven you. Are you being tormented over simple mistakes, failings, or weaknesses in an area of your life? Remember, when I forgive, I also *forget* your wrongs. That is My mercy. The enemy wants you to keep rehearsing your mistakes. Many fall for this. Wisdom says: Break free of the lie that you have to live a life sentence for a mistake. When the Courts of Heaven have no record of your "crime," you can live in peace. If I, the Judge, rule you innocent because of My Son's sacrifice, *you are truly free*. Do not live like you are out on parole! I have not only ruled you not guilty, but I have ruled you innocent.

> *Beloved, if our heart does not convict us [of guilt], we have confidence [complete assurance and boldness] before God.*
> — 1 JOHN 3:21 AMP

> *Therefore there is now no condemnation [no guilty verdict, no punishment] for those who are in Christ Jesus.*
> — ROMANS 8:1 AMP

SEE ALSO: JOHN 3:17

Run your race —
not ru*i*n your race.

❧

I, I, I's will ruin your race. They will take you out of your race. Run your race for My Glory and not just for your gratifications! ***Running your race for your gratifications is always about the external reward. When you run for My Glory, it's all about your eternal reward!*** Run for Me! Allow every step that catapults you forward to be about My purpose in your life! Every foot race begins by bowing down low. You get a faster start when you submit all to Me. As every runner knows, never look around or look back. This always affects your speed and could cost you the race. Keep your eyes on the finish line! That is where I AM standing. Can you hear Me, your Father, cheering you on? I AM continually saying, "Yes, you can!" My eyes are on you as I watch every step that brings you closer to Me. The only way that you fail is if you quit. Know that I AM at the finish line with My strong arms ready to catch you when you finish your race. As I hold your winded body, I surround you with My holy wind to strengthen and invigorate you! Can you already hear My applause as I thunder My voice and announce to the world: "That's My child!" Wisdom says: I encourage you today, with much confidence in you, My handiwork, to stay the course, persevere, and gain the crown of Life. To those who finish the race, I will furnish you with the heavenly prize in Christ Jesus!

See also: Acts 20:24; James 1:12; 2 Timothy 4:7; Hebrews 12:1; Philippians 3:14; 1 Corinthians 9:24

In patience, you will inherit the promise. With impatience, you will inherit the problems.

Impatience can be a killer! Impatience is a life-and-death issue. Waiting is such a valuable weapon. Consider this: A sniper is the most accurate at shooting a target because he is willing to wait with profound patience in one position. He looks through the crosshairs of his weapon's scope — which means his target is always seen through the cross! A patient soldier is a wise soldier, and deadly to the enemy! Impatience will make you react to the enemy! When you ***react***, you are not in control, and the enemy has the upper hand! Patience makes you move with caution and wisdom. Through faith and patience you will inherit My promise. Wisdom says: Do not make decisions because you are impatient in waiting for your prayer to be answered. A patient person is a highly effective warrior. Because love is patient, know that I AM always patient with you.

> *Imitate those who through faith and **patience** inherit what has been promised.* — Hebrews 6:12

> *I enter your house; here I am, prostrate in your inner sanctum, **Waiting for directions** to get me safely through enemy lines.* — Psalm 5:7-8 msg

> *Better a **patient** person than a warrior.* — Proverbs 16:32

See also: James 5:7

June *19*

Although your earthly father facilitated your birth, I AM your Father Who determines your worth!

I knew you before you knew Me. I AM acquainted with all your ways! I have searched you thoroughly, and I know you! In the secret regions of darkness, I knit you together in your mother's womb. You were a secret to everyone except Me. Though no one could see you, I saw you! I was present at your birth as I breathed My Breath of Life into you. As you took your first breath, you began to cry. I also cried — but My tears were tears of joy at your beauty! My thoughts toward you cannot be numbered for they would outnumber the grains of sand on the entire earth. I AM with you throughout your life. As I was there with you when you took your first breath, I will be there with you as you take your last breath! When you exhale, I will receive back My Breath of Life. I will be right there with you as you are escorted Home into My Presence to talk with Me face-to-face. Wisdom says: There are no orphans in My Kingdom. I have adopted you, and you are Mine forever. Adapt your life to this Truth.

See also: Psalm 139:7-18; Jeremiah 29:11-14; Ephesians 2:10

Relationship with Me brings revelation that ushers in revolutions!

This is the information age. But what this world needs is revelation of Me, not more information. There has never been a time where there has been such a deluge of information and answers to questions! Yet, some in the world are using information to replace thinking on their own. This is causing great confusion in identity. Revelation causes a complete change in the way some think and live. My Son, Jesus, revealed in the flesh to mankind, *is* the revelation of My Love. My revelation, My Son, started a revolution that cannot, nor will not be stopped. Wisdom says: The more revelation you have of My Love for you, the more you will start a revolution centered around My Love for the world. Relationship with Me brings revelation that ushers in revolutions! Know that your time spent with Me today can change the world!

*That the God of our Lord Jesus Christ, the Father of glory, may give unto you the **spirit of** wisdom and **revelation** in the knowledge of him.* — EPHESIANS 1:17 KJV

For nothing is hidden, except to be revealed; nor has anything been kept secret, but that it would come to light [that is, things are hidden only temporarily, until the appropriate time comes for them to be known]. — MARK 4:22 AMP

189

SEE ALSO: ROMANS 16:25-26

Faith makes the impossible possible; fear makes the possible impossible.

With Me, *all* things are possible — even the impossible. There is no such thing as impossible if you have faith in My Word. I desire to fulfill all the promises in My Word for you, but lack of faith stands in the way of your receiving from Me. I love doing the miraculous for you! But I need your faith! Your faith activates the impossible, and makes it become a reality. Fear is believing that I cannot or will not do anything to help you. Fear makes what should even be possible impossible, because what you believe in your heart is what will come to pass. You tie My hands when you refuse to believe Me. Wisdom says: *The question is not: What can I do? The question is: What do you believe I can do?* Believing Me and My Word will make the impossible possible in your life today!

> *Jesus looked at them and said, "With man this is impossible, but with God all things are possible."*
>
> – MATTHEW 19:26

> *"If I can?" Jesus asked. "Anything is possible if you have faith."*
>
> – MARK 9:23 TLB

Be relevant; not relative!

My Word is relevant! It is absolute Truth and Love — complete, pure, unconditional, boundless, and infinite! It is not relative and subject to opinions. My Word and Love for you never change, nor will they ever be diminished in any way. I AM absolute Truth. I change not. My Truth is **not** relative. **And My Word is certainly not relative!** Being relative is subject to others' opinions; it is watering down the Gospel of My Dear Son. When "truth" becomes relative, it becomes subject to the trends and political correctness of the culture. Wisdom says: Relative truth is **no absolute truth** at all. Today, choose to be relevant; not relative! Tell others of **Me, The Absolute Truth** — and how much I absolutely love them!

> *We speak only of what we know [we **know absolutely** what we are talking about].*
> — John 3:11 AMP

> *You shall be blameless [and **absolutely true**] to the Lord your God.*
> — Deuteronomy 18:13 AMP

> *Jesus answered, "**I am the way and the truth** and the life. No one comes to the Father except through me."*
> — John 14:6

June 23

I bury the dead,
but I plant the righteous!

~⊙~

*For you have been born again, not of perishable seed,
but of imperishable.*
— 1 Peter 1:23

All humanity ... is [momentary] like the flower of the field.
— Isaiah 40:6 AMP

Those who have eternally rejected the precious Gift of
My Son, Jesus, are buried when they die. But when you
are alive in Christ, you are never buried, but *planted* by
My hands when you die. You are actually transplanted
from this world to your eternal home with Me. You,
My child, are as glorious as one of the flowers in My
beautiful garden. While you are on earth, you are as in
the form of My indestructible and imperishable Seed,
Jesus. You are made into the likeness of Jesus, My Rose
of Sharon and Lily Of The Valley. Do not fear death; you
will never miss where you are now. Wisdom says: *Allow
Me to comfort you today if you have lost a loved one,
for they are never lost to Me!* I have planted them and
they are now thriving and blooming in My Presence!
With the Light of My Son, they are growing so lovely
and strong! With the Living Water from My River of
Life, they are drinking deeply and flourishing! I AM the
Master Gardener. I AM tending them tenderly as they
bloom with My Son's beauty that never fades nor dies!

SEE ALSO: *John 15:16; John 12:24; Psalm 103:14-15;
Isaiah 61:3; Psalm 126:6; Matthew 15:13*

Mankind. Are you living up to your name?

Mankind was not a suggestion. I called you mankind to remind you that love and kindness are My commandments. When you love one another, you are loving Me. Mankind is the whole of all people on earth — and I regard you as equal. This is not just a command to you, but also a disclosure of how I treat all mankind, both the just and the unjust. My kindness is the Gift of My Son, Jesus. Are you living up to this name today? As your Father, it grieves My heart when there are divisions among you. I desire for ***man*** to indeed be ***kind***. Wisdom says: When My children begin to imitate Me then the world will seek Me. This dying world is appalled when they see Christians that are not living as Christ! I AM Love. And I AM Kind.

*Love is patient and **kind**.*
— 1 Corinthians 13:4 ESV

*Be **kind** and helpful to one another, tender-hearted [compassionate, understanding], forgiving one another [readily and freely], just as God in Christ also forgave you.*
— Ephesians 4:32 AMP

*What a heavy burden God has laid on **mankind**!*
— Ecclesiastes 1:13

See also: Luke 6:35; Matthew 5:45; Galatians 5:22-23

If you choose to take **offense**, you choose a life **of fences!**

If you choose to take offense, you choose to live a life of limitations, barriers, and old ground. Familiarity and monotony thrive in old ground. It may feel comfortable in the familiar, but there is little or no growth! This is where so many just survive the conditions instead of thriving. You will not have the option of gaining new ground or territory. Because you are the one who sets the mental, physical, and spiritual limitations in your life, only you can remove the self-imposed "I can'ts." If you cannot seem to get away from limitations in your life, consider this: Have you taken offense? Wisdom says: I created you to **run** your race without fences, not **ruin** your race with limitations and self-imposed barriers!

Understand this, my beloved brothers and sisters. Let everyone be quick to hear [be a careful, thoughtful listener], slow to speak [a speaker of carefully chosen words and], slow to anger [patient, reflective, forgiving].
– JAMES 1:19 AMP

These things have I spoken unto you, that ye should **not be offended.**
– JOHN 16:1 KJV

"Isn't this the carpenter? ..." **And they took offense at him.**
– MARK 6:3

Just as the earth knows what to do with the seed, so your heart knows what to do with the Seed of My Word.

*The **earth produces [acting] by itself** —* first the
blade, *then the **ear,** then the **full grain in the ear.***
— Mark 4:28 AMP

In the natural realm, I created a seed to lie dormant until it is hidden in the earth and watered. The earth, ***acting by itself,*** produces first the blade, then the ear, then the full grain in the ear. The seed grows into something alive and full of purpose. Just as the earth knows what to do in the natural realm, your heart also knows what to do in the spiritual realm. When My Seed is hidden in your heart and gets watered with My Word, it becomes a weapon in you against the enemy — a ***blade,*** which is the Sword of the Spirit, My Word. This produces in you a progressive force of faith. Faith comes by hearing and hearing by My Word, My Seed. You produce faith by hearing through ***your ears, then full grain in the ear, which is mature, unshakable faith.*** Wisdom says: Plant My Word into your heart today, and watch your heart produce faith that so pleases Me!

*"This is the meaning of the parable: The **seed is the word of God.***"
— Luke 8:11

195

See also: Romans 10:17; Ephesians 6:17

June 27

Life is too precious
to waste just on yourself!

I created you for My Kingdom. So many people think their lives are their own. But you are Mine. I bought you with a price. ***Choosing to live your life just for yourself is a waste!*** Life is too precious! I graced this world with the gift of you! I created you with your destiny in mind. I predestined your life to influence many people for My Kingdom. I have granted you a distinct sphere of influence that enables you to uniquely love those around you. The gifts and talents that I have granted you are ***not just for you***, but I designed them for those who cross your path. Wisdom says: The fact that you are alive is proof that you are needed. Know this: If you are just getting your needs met, that is an indication that you are still a baby in Christ. But if you are meeting the needs of others, this is an indication that you are a mature son or daughter in Christ. Many will suffer today *if* you make the choice to waste your life only on yourself. Choose to dedicate your life to the service of others. In your destiny, I also have plans for you to enjoy life with your family and friends — but in the very end, you will give an account of how you fulfilled your calling and your destiny.

[He planned] for the maturity of the times and the climax of the ages to unify all things ... [both] things in heaven and things on the earth.
— Ephesians 1:10 ampc

See also: Luke 10:27; Matthew 20:28; Jeremiah 29:11; John 15:13; John 13:34-35

Your choice:
Agreement or argument?

Agreement is powerful. It enacts one of the Laws in My Kingdom. Unity and agreement are worship to Me. You cannot have your hands *up* in surrender and worship to Me and *out* fighting your brothers and sisters at the same time. When you truly get this revelation, you will see mighty signs and wonders. I cannot dwell in the midst of arguments, because where there is strife, there is confusion and every evil work. Strife is the strategy of the enemy. I can only operate where there is unity and agreement. That is why I designed the Spiritual Law of Agreement: If two of you on earth agree about anything you ask for, I will do it. Wisdom says: What argument could be worth the consequence of being stripped of My protection, peace, and joy? Be intentional today. Choose to agree with Me and avoid strife. Then watch Me restore unity in My Body!

> *"Again, truly I tell you that if two of you on earth agree about anything they ask for, it will be done for them by my Father in heaven."*
> — MATTHEW 18:19

> *Agree with each other and don't be divided into rival groups. Instead, be **restored** with the same mind and the same purpose.*
> — 1 CORINTHIANS 1:10 CEB

> *For where envying and strife is, there is confusion and every evil work.*
> — JAMES 3:16 KJV

Love heals. Hate steals!

To be loved *is* to be healed! You cannot separate the two. I AM Love, and I AM your Healer. This is not just something I do. ***Love is Who I AM! Healer is Who I AM!*** I AM disposed to give you all My Love. My True Love is expressed — even when I AM hated and rejected. There is nothing anyone can do that would ever cause Me to stop loving them. Your response toward Me is insignificant. Even when you reject Me, this will never change My Love towards you. I hold nothing back from you. When I love, I give all. Allow Me to love through you to heal the brokenhearted today. When you choose love, you are expressing Me. When you choose hate, you are allowing the enemy to be expressed through you. To hate is to murder in your heart — to burn with envy and not able to receive the happiness and peace you seek! Wisdom says: Do not deprive yourself and others today of My Love that heals by expressing hate that steals.

> *The thief enters only to steal, kill, and destroy. I came so that they could have life — indeed, so that they could live life to the fullest.*
> — John 10:10 CEB

> *There is no fear in love [dread does not exist]. But perfect (complete, full-grown) love drives out fear.*
> — 1 John 4:18

See also: James 4:2; Psalm 103:3-5;
Psalm 107:20-21; Hosea 14:4

Humility ushers in Wisdom. Pride ushers in disgrace.

Wisdom and humility always walk hand in hand. You cannot have one without the other. You will need both to successfully navigate with Me in life. Everyone seems to want wisdom, but wisdom requires great responsibility and integrity in My Kingdom. Those who fear Me walk in humility because they know I AM their source for every gift. The prideful are in awe of themselves, and that brings them disgrace. I oppose the proud, but show favor to the humble. Wisdom says: Make wise choices today, and let your life show wisdom by the deeds you do in humility. Those who walk in humility live in Truth. Those who walk in pride not only live lies, but they are more likely to tell lies. If you have a hard time telling the truth, could it be that you are dealing with pride? Those who are dealing with pride also manipulate the truth to make themselves look better. Ask Me to show you where you need humility so I can bless you with My Wisdom.

God opposes the proud but shows favor to the humble.
— PROVERBS 3:34 AND JAMES 4:6

Who is wise and understanding among you? Let them show it by their good life, by deeds done in the **humility** *that* **comes from wisdom**.
— JAMES 3:13

SEE ALSO: PROVERBS 11:2; PROVERBS 22:4; PROVERBS 15:33

To murmur is to tempt Me!

To question whether I AM with you and for you — even when you are in "the land of the giants" — is called an evil report. Are you trusting that I AM *for you* or against you? This will determine your outcome: either victory or defeat. To murmur or complain is to ask, "Is the Lord among us or not?" To murmur is to tempt or to provoke Me to anger — to manipulate or try to *make* Me do something for you. You never have to *make* Me do anything for you! It literally *hurts Me* when I cannot help you because of your choices. You never have to question My integrity and character as your Father. When I say I AM for you, who can be against you? Wisdom says: Be one that is quick and ready to believe Me when I say that I love you and that I AM for you only! Do you know that you insult Me when you doubt if I will take care of you? My Love and power are always ready and available to help and keep you! Today, do not tempt Me. Trust Me, then watch Me deliver your enemies into your hands!

*They **tempted** and tried the patience of the Lord, saying,*
'Is the Lord among us or not?'
— Exodus 17:7 AMP

And Jesus answered and said to him, "It has been said,
*'You shall **not** tempt the Lord your God.'"*
— Luke 4:12

*The people contended with Moses... And Moses said to them, 'Why do you find fault with me? Why do you **tempt** the Lord and try His patience?'*
— Exodus 17:2 AMP

Repent or repeat?

To repent is to turn away from what you have been doing wrong. It also means to change your mind, have regret, and have the mindset to amend your actions. This does not only mean asking for My forgiveness, but it means that your heart's intention is to *change*. When you repent, I AM faithful to forgive and forget your sins. Sin can be cyclical. You will repeat unrepented sin and its consequences. This is called torment. ***Sin not only affects you, but it also affects everyone around you.*** Your lineage will also repeat your unrepented sin. The only way to stop the cycle of sin is to repent. When you repent, I will — on purpose and with great love — remember your sins no more! Oh, what grace I show to the contrite of heart! Wisdom says: Choose to repent this day, not repeat the cycle. When you release your sins, you are returning to My house. My heart is wide open, and I stand looking for you, My child! Never allow sin to be the reason to not come home to My open arms!

As far as the east is from the west, so far hath he removed our transgressions from us. — Psalm 103: 12

And their sins and iniquities will I remember no more. — Hebrews 10:17

See also: Matthew 6:15; Luke 6:37

You are not **just** a warrior of Christ; you are My **weapon!**

Because of My Son, Jesus, you are not just a warrior; you are My weapon. I have formed you into a weapon of mass destruction for the purpose of penetrating the kingdom of darkness. There is nothing weak about you! You carry the power and authority of Jesus. When Jesus was on the earth, the enemy knew Who Jesus was because Jesus knew Who He was! Pray for the revelation of your identity **in Him**. As My warrior and weapon, you have a holy arsenal available: My Word, My Son's name, and the Blood of Christ. These will cause your enemy to flee in stark terror. Wisdom says: The power of My Word never diminishes. When **you speak** My Word today, it carries the same power as when **I spoke** My Word.

… in truthful speech and in the power of God; with **weapons of righteousness** *in the right hand and in the left.*
— 2 Corinthians 6:7

*For we are His workmanship … created in Christ Jesus [**reborn** from above — spiritually transformed, renewed, ready to be used] for good works, which God prepared [for us] beforehand.*
— Ephesians 2:10 AMP

See also: Jeremiah 51:20; Job 38:23

Look for Me in the everyday miracles.

When you are *only* looking for Me to move in the miraculous on a large scale, you will completely miss Me in the small miracles. *Everything* that I do is miraculous. There is no such thing as a large or small miracle in My Kingdom. Every day is a miracle! Many missed their King and Savior, Jesus, even while *looking earnestly* for Him! They longed for their King as a man of immediate power (large miracle), which caused them to overlook their King as a baby (small miracle in their eyes). Are you overlooking Me at work in your midst? Are you missing Me at work even in the smallest of ways? Many are missing Me because of their preconceived ideas and plans. My thoughts are so much higher than your thoughts, and My ways are so much higher than your ways. I have openly displayed My miraculous power as in the roar of thunder, and I have hidden My power and Presence as in the laugh of a baby. Wisdom says: When you are only looking for Me in My mighty roar, then you will miss Me in My loving and holy whisper! Earnestly look for the small and large miracles of today.

And after the fire came a gentle whisper.

— 1 KINGS 19:12

SEE ALSO: 1 KINGS 19:11-12; ACTS 26:22; ISAIAH 55:9

203

I AM never silent.
Only idols are silent!

I AM constantly speaking! If you say that I cannot speak today then you are calling Me an idol! Idols are gods that are dumb! I speak in many ways to you. I speak to you in My Word. I speak with My still small voice. I speak through My prophets. I speak through circumstances. And I also speak through My creation. You are a speaking spirit, made in the image of Me — your Father, My Son, Jesus, and My Holy Spirit! How can we have a close relationship if only you are speaking? I AM constantly revealing My Love for you. How I long to have that connection with you throughout each and every day, to laugh with you and talk to you about what is to come. I want to hear all about your day and all that concerns you, just like you talk to your best friend. I long for you to see Me as your Daddy, the One Who cares about *every* aspect of your life. I no longer have to quake the mountains and thunder My voice. I sent My Holy Spirit to speak to you, and He is as gentle as a dove! Wisdom says: Quiet your mind before Me, and allow Me to teach you to hear My still and small voice. Be still and know that I AM your Father. Do not allow your thoughts to strangle and choke out My voice today. If you have not spent quiet time listening to Me lately, know that I miss you just as you miss your loved ones. I AM constantly beckoning you to come closer to Me! I want you to feel My peace and My joy that come only from Me! In My Presence is joy everlasting! Yes, I AM talking to you. I still speak to you in My still voice!

See also: Isaiah 45:19; John 16 :13-16; Hebrews 12:25; 1 Corinthians 14:21; 1 Samuel 3:9; Psalm 85:8; Isaiah 50:4; John 17:8

Without faith, it is impossible to please Me. Without fear, it is impossible to please the enemy.

Living in faith is worship to Me; living in fear is worship to an inferior, subordinate enemy that My Son has already crushed. Faith is trust in Me to help you; fear is trust in an already-conquered enemy to hurt you and destroy you. Faith is believing the One Who cannot lie; fear is faith in the enemy, a liar. Faith is visualizing My Kingdom manifest on earth as it is in heaven; fear is believing the lies of a defeated enemy, instead of believing My Word, which is Truth. Faith pleases Me; fear empowers a powerless and defeated foe! Wisdom says: ***Faith always requires activity. Fear always requires inactivity.*** You cannot love Me without having faith in My goodness, kindness, and mercy toward you. To love Me is to believe Me! Today, choose faith in the King seated on ***My throne***, instead of choosing fear of an enemy who has been ***dethroned***.

And without faith it is impossible to please God.
— Hebrews 11:6

Perfect love casts out fear.
— 1 John 4:18 NKJV

Everything that does not come from faith is sin.
— Romans 14:23

205

See also: Matthew 8:26; 2 Timothy 1:7; Psalm 91:1; Genesis 3:15

July 7

Strife will strip you of My protection.

Has your tongue become a weapon formed *against you* by stirring up strife in others? When you condemn others, you are shown to be in the wrong. Do not use your tongue to condemn. This allows weapons to be formed and used against *you*. Destruction always follows strife. Know that strife is a choice. If strife is knocking at your door today, do not open it. Strife is a weapon from hell. Stay out of strife at all cost. When you choose to enter into strife with someone, you are literally opening the door to the enemy and allowing every evil work into your life. When the enemy uses someone to stir up strife against you, run for your life! Forgive and walk away free. Strife between two people is a hate contract. Use your tongue to create and establish My Kingdom on earth by speaking loving and faith-filled words! Use your tongue to bless and encourage those around you. Wisdom says: It is critical to understand what happens when you are critical. Choose today not to allow strife in your life. Strife on your tongue leads to hate in your heart. Walking in love guarantees My protection.

For where envying and strife is, there is confusion and every evil work.
— James 3:16 KJV

No weapon that is formed against you will succeed;
And every tongue that rises against you in judgment
you will condemn.
— Isaiah 54:17 AMP

See also: Psalm 45:1; Habakkuk 1:3; Proverbs 18:6; Proverbs 10:12

I made man and woman to **complete** each other, not **compete** with each other!

The woman is the only part of all My creation that I united with someone already created! The woman was joined with a man from her genesis. Man and woman are so compatible that you cannot have one without the other. I did this not only to prove that they are dependent on each other, but they are equally important. I do not favor one over the other. Their creations are a masterpiece of harmony and a symphony of reliance upon each other. This is My design. The very survival of each gender is to protect the other because it takes both to create. I end the debate and war of which is more important. When some men stopped guarding and protecting women, and some women stopped honoring and respecting men, the war for significance and independence raged! Woman cannot be independent of man, nor man of woman. ***Man was not created to dominate, but to demonstrate My Love.*** When man and woman love each other, they are loving Me. Wisdom says: ***Both must rule by being servants, not by making the other subservient to their rules. My power is dormant when man or woman want to dominate. When they embrace each others' differences in unity, they will erase the enemy's war on the genders.***

Finally, all of you, live in harmony with one another;
be sympathetic, love as brothers.
— 1 Peter 3:8

207

See also: 1 Corinthians 11:8-12;
Ephesians 5:24-33; Galatians 3:27-29

July 9

Are you a good listener?
Be still and know I AM God.

I share My heart with those who make listening to Me a priority. Be a good listener as I share My wisdom, direction, and answers. By some, I have been replaced by the news and other forms of information. ***But only My Words will refresh your weary soul.*** Those who thrive in chaotic times are ones who take time to enter into My Presence and receive My instructions. Wisdom says: Allow Me to fill you with My Peace — peace that these times require. Come into the stillness of My Presence where I AM waiting for you. I AM ever watching, just as the father of the prodigal son — looking and waiting for any sign of you coming to Me for the daily intimacy of our fellowship.

Be still, and know that I am God.

— PSALM 46:10

While he was still a long way off, his father saw him and was filled with compassion for him; he ran to his son, threw his arms around him and kissed him.

— LUKE 15:20

Be still before the Lord.

— PSALM 37:7 AMP

SEE ALSO: *2 CORINTHIANS 13:14; 1 CORINTHIANS 1:9; JEREMIAH 47:6; PSALM 81:8 GENESIS 5:24*

My Love never fails, even when you fail!

I love you in spite of what you have done or what you have failed to do. My Love never has conditions! The Laws of My Kingdom have conditions — but never My Love! I love you enough to give you choices — life or death. True love always comes with choices. You have the choice to reject Me, but even that would never change My Love for you. When you choose to reject Me, you are choosig a future without Me. Wisdom says: Who you *are* has nothing to do with who you *were*. But it has everything to do with Who I AM. Run to Me today, knowing that despite what you have or have not done, My heart is open and waiting for you now! ***You are perfectly Mine, even when you are not perfect.***

The Lord appeared to me (Israel) from ages past, saying, "I have loved you with an everlasting love."
— JEREMIAH 31:3 AMP

For God so [greatly] loved and dearly prized the world, that He [even] gave His [One and] only begotten Son, so that whoever believes and trusts in Him [as Savior] shall not perish, but have eternal life.
— JOHN 3:16 AMP

How priceless is your unfailing love, O God!
— PSALM 36:7

No one on earth has the power to break you — unless you give someone that power!

Do you know that I made you unbreakable? You are not made of glass or as delicate china. **You are made in My image — and I AM unbreakable!** I have given you the power of thoughts and words! You are only limited if you **believe** you are limited. No human can hurt or break you unless **you** decide they can! You give away your power when you choose to believe what a person says about you, instead of choosing to believe what **My** Word says about you. My Word is not an opinion. My Word is Truth. Wisdom says: The only way the enemy can stop your destiny is to lie about your powerful identity in Christ. The enemy understands how strong you are. Do you? He must lie about you to get you to question or negate your strength in Christ. This is the only way that he can stop or break you. Know today that you are unbreakable when you believe what My Word says about you!

God created mankind in his own image, in the image of God he created them; male and female he created them.
— Genesis 1:27

For those God foreknew he also predestined to be con-formed to the image of his Son, that he might be the firstborn among many brothers and sisters.
— Romans 8:29

For I am not ashamed of the gospel, because it is the power of God that brings salvation to everyone who believes.
— Romans 1:16

If your physical body is not being pushed, it will pull you!

You cannot be led by My Spirit and be pulled in the flesh at the same time. To walk in the Spirit is to conquer the flesh. The enemy does *not* have the power to keep you out of the realm of My Spirit. But your flesh can. You have more power over yourself than the enemy has over you! You can tame *your flesh* into submission more easily than you think — because your flesh is the weakest part of you. Your flesh will die someday, because it was made from the earth. *Your spirit* is My Breath and My Life. It is the eternal part of you, and the most powerful part of you. If your body is ruling, then your spirit is a slave. The body makes a horrible master! It is just a temporary house, and is not nearly as powerful as your spirit. Wisdom says: Walking in My Spirit means speaking My Word, being obedient to My Holy Spirit, through prayer and fasting, daily discipline, and praying in My Spirit. To walk in My Spirit is to rule from your spirit, not your flesh!

So I say, walk by the Spirit, and you will not gratify the desires of the flesh.
– Galatians 5:16

... walk not according to the flesh but according to the Spirit.
– Romans 8:4 nrsv

When you are looking at what you have lost, you are missing out on all you have!

I have so blessed you! Meditating on loss is living in a state of ungratefulness. It blinds you to all you have been given. Meditating on your losses is a trap from the enemy. He wants you to be ungrateful, bitter, and unforgiving. All loss comes with a choice of how you will respond. I understand loss and restoration! I experienced the loss of My only begotten Son to gain the restoration of additional sons and daughters. Wisdom says: When you experience loss, train your eyes and your heart each day to **be grateful** for all that you still have. This is the key for healing and restoration. I AM always close to the brokenhearted! I never take loss lightly. I AM close to you now to comfort you with My peace. Remember that loss is always temporary, but My Love is eternal! I restore better than before.

> *I count everything as loss compared to the price-*
> *less privilege and supreme advantage of knowing*
> *Christ Jesus my Lord [and of growing more deeply*
> *and thoroughly acquainted with Him — a joy*
> *unequaled]. For His sake I have lost everything, and*
> *I consider it all garbage, so that I may gain Christ.*
> — Philippians 3:7-8 AMP

> *After Job had prayed for his friends, the Lord made*
> *him prosperous again and gave him twice as much as*
> *he had before.* — Job 42:10

212

See also: Joel 2; Psalm 100

It is impossible to see **your** needs and the needs of **others** at the same time!

You cannot focus on Me and on yourself at the same time! You are the answer to many who are crying out to Me for help. When you meet the needs of others, I make it My personal business to meet your needs. When you are serving My children — especially the least of these — you are serving ***Me*** and you gain all of My ***attention***. Your reward will be tremendous when you serve Me through serving others. Be the vehicle that I use to meet the needs of those around you. Wisdom says: One day soon, you will give an account to Me for the times you ignored those who needed help. Please, look beyond your own needs. Choose today to ***be*** a blessing so that I can bless you! Do not simply ***see*** your reflection. Instead, ***be*** My reflection to those in need!

"Give, and it will be given to you. A good measure, pressed down, shaken together and running over, will be poured into your lap. For with the measure you use, it will be measured to you." — Luke 6:38

Let each esteem others better than himself. — Philippians 2:3

See also: Matthew 25:40; Isaiah 58:10; James 2:16

Complaining stops progress.

Complaining is a heart issue. It is sin, and it must be dealt with! Complaining is the opposite of speaking words in faith. It is speaking words of doubt and unbelief. Complaints empower negative situations and stop all progress. Every time the Israelites murmured and complained in the desert, all movement toward their Promised Land stopped. This sin had to be dealt with immediately and severely. Wisdom says: If you seem to be stuck in the same place without progress, check to see if you have been complaining. If so, repent today — and get back on the path of progress! Complaining not only stops progress, but it stops My promises from manifesting in your life. Your Promised Land cannot be attained when you complain!

He hears your murmurings against the Lord. What are we, that you murmur and rebel against us?

— Exodus 16:7 AMP

Every one of you twenty years old or more who was counted in the census and who has grumbled against me. Not one of you will enter the land I swore with uplifted hand to make your home, except Caleb son of Jephunneh and Joshua son of Nun.

— Numbers 14:28-30

Now the people complained about their hardships in the hearing of the Lord, and when he heard them his anger was aroused. Then fire from the Lord burned among them and consumed some of the outskirts of the camp.

— Numbers 11:1

See also: Jude 1:16

Pain will always move you from your current position!

Nothing gets your attention quicker than pain — whether it is physical or emotional. Pain will always move you from your current position. You will either move forward and become wiser about situations and choices, or you will move backwards into anger and bitterness. Although your pain is very real, choose never to surrender to it. Pain is My enemy. It is a defeated foe. My Son, Jesus, bore all pain on the cross for you. ***Make the decision that it will never break you.*** Wisdom says: If you are in a painful situation today, get into My sweet Presence and let Me comfort you, then pray for My revelation and instructions about how to move out of your current position. I AM never the author of pain. I AM the Redeemer of all pain. Give Me your weariness, your hopelessness, and your exhaustion today, in exchange for My strength. Know I AM carrying you through this suffering. I AM never indifferent to your pain. I AM your Refuge and the Stronghold of your life; of whom shall you be afraid?

> *People brought to him all who were ill with various diseases, those suffering **severe pain**, the demon-possessed, those having seizures, and the paralyzed; and **he healed them**.*
> — MATTHEW 4:24

> *We wait for the **blessed hope** — the appearing of the glory of our great God and Savior, Jesus Christ.*
> — TITUS 2:13

SEE ALSO: ISAIAH 53:4-5; PSALM 69:29; REVELATION 21:4; PSALM 27:1

When you are killing time, you are killing your future!

I AM in your day! *That makes every day priceless!* Every day is a miracle. When the day is gone, you can never get it back. If you are just killing time, it is because you do not understand how short and precious your life truly is. But never confuse resting and relaxing with wasting time. Your body, soul, and spirit need rest. Balance is the key to being productive. You can work your entire life away and still accomplish very little. You can also be very lazy and directionless. Ask Me to show you My perspective on time. Never waste anything that is priceless! Wisdom says: You honor Me when you enjoy your life. You will give an account for the time you have been given and how you have spent this gift. Wasting time is wasting life!

So watch your step. Use your head. Make the most of every chance you get. These are desperate times! Don't live carelessly, unthinkingly. Make sure you understand what the Master wants.
— EPHESIANS 5:15-17 MSG

So, my friend, listen closely. ...You don't want to waste your precious life among the hardhearted. ... You don't want to end your life full of regrets!
— PROVERBS 5:7-11 MSG

Your acceptance was ratified in My Son's Blood.

How can you accept rejection when you have already been received by the King of kings? I did not just say, "I love you." I confirmed it with the sacrifice of My Son! *If there would have been a greater way to prove My Love, I would have done that also.* But there was not. If you feel rejection today, know this: The enemy is trying to stop your destiny. Do not fall into his deadly trap. Your acceptance was ratified in My Son's Blood. My judgment was set in the Courtroom of Heaven. You are Mine! I love you as much as I love My Son. Meditate on this truth, and watch rejection limp away. If this does not persuade you, then you are either being deceived or deliberately choosing to believe a lie. Wisdom says: Know today that when I love and accept you, it is with My whole heart, mind, and strength. *Because I have received you, I will never replace you.*

> But you are the ones chosen by God, chosen for the high calling of priestly work, chosen to be a holy people, God's instruments to do his work and speak out for him, to tell others of the night-and-day difference he made for you — from nothing to something, from rejected to accepted.
>
> — 1 Peter 2:9-10 MSG

See also: Job 33:26; John 1:12

If your **world** is in order, it is because your **words** are in order!

In the beginning, I spoke everything into existence. You are created in *My image*. I do not do anything without *saying* it first. You create, or should create, the same way. You speak with *My* Breath. Your words carry *My* power! Never underestimate the tongue. It is such a small member of your body, but remember the enormous power it contains! ***It will either poison you or position you!*** Your tongue can start a raging fire from hell or spread My holy fire from heaven. No man can tame the tongue. It is easier to tame a wild animal than to tame your tongue. Know this: The enemy does not have a tongue to create with, so he will do anything to get you to use your tongue for his purposes. Wisdom says: Only with My help can you use your tongue to create your world instead of destroy your world. Every word carries fire. Are you speaking holy fire or hellish fire? Surrender your tongue to Me. Get your words in order by agreeing with My Word today! As in the days of Pentecost, speak My tongues of holy fire to quench hell's fire from your tongue.

Death and life are in the power of the tongue, And those who love it will eat its fruit.
— PROVERBS 18:21 NKJV

*And **the tongue is also a fire** ... and is itself set on fire by hell.*
— JAMES 3:6

SEE ALSO: GENESIS 1:3; ROMANS 4:17; JAMES 3:1-8; ACTS 2

Your choice to give up and quit is yours alone. But your choice **never affects you alone!**

You can choose to quit if you want. The choice is yours. But *your* choice affects countless numbers of My children and *their* destinies. You cannot imagine the loss when just one of My children gives up and aborts a destiny from Me. Wisdom says: In My Kingdom every position is priceless! There is no such thing as a tiny des*tiny*. Your decision to quit affects Me, My Kingdom, and the world. Do not walk away from My promises so casually. Remember, when it is easy to quit, you are not walking in faith, but fear. When you are in My will, quitting is not an easy option. I greatly reward those who persevere. Know for certain that I have placed you here for such a time as this. If you feel like giving up or quitting today, then call forth to reset your atmosphere for endurance, perseverance, and victory.

> *"And who knows whether you have not come to the kingdom for such a time as this?"* — Esther 4:14 ESV

> *So let's not get tired of doing what is good. At just the right time we will reap a harvest of blessing if we don't give up.* — Galatians 6:9 NLT

> *Be brave. Be strong. **Don't give up**.* — Psalm 31:24 MSG

> *Stay with God! Take heart. **Don't quit**.*

See also: *Jeremiah 5:23; Psalm 119:158*

Faith will make you **soar**;
fear will make you **sore**!

If you have faith, your possibilities are limitless. Faith will make you soar! It will cause you to increase dramatically and ascend to greater heights than you could ever imagine. Mount up with Me and soar high, as the eagles mount up close to the sun/Son. Like the eagles, lock your wings with Me, and effortlessly glide into your destiny on the wind of My Spirit. Consider how I made eagles fearless. They build their nests for their young at extraordinary heights, such as on the very edge of cliffs. Wisdom says: Do not allow fear to stop *your* destiny or to make you sore — grieving, offended, angry, and sorrowful. Reflect on this today: Why choose to be sore with fear when you have the liberty to soar to new heights with Me? Remember that I AM an expert at taking the sore and unbearable seasons in your life and causing you to soar to new heights with a triumphant victory that shatters the hope of the enemy to stop you! Turn the enemy's vicious attacks into a victorious testimony of My Love! Be at peace and know that you are safe under the shadow of My wings of Love.

You have a mighty arm; strong is Your hand, Your right hand is soaring high.
— Psalm 89:13 AMPC

Who satisfies your mouth [your necessity and desire at your personal age and situation] with good so that your youth, renewed, is like the eagle's [strong, overcoming, soaring]!
— Psalm 103:5 AMPC

See also: 1 John 4:18; Isaiah 40:31;

Mistakes can be costly, but what you learn from them is priceless!

Mistakes are free tuition in the University of Life. Why do you fear the very thing that can teach you the most? A mistake can be such a great teacher if you do not allow condemnation and shame to torment you. A mistake becomes something costly when you do not learn or grow from it. Some are so terrified of making a mistake that they become immobile. When you understand the depth of My Love and grace, you can easily face your mistakes and learn from them. Never give them the power to stir up fear or the power to define you. Wisdom says: ***You will make mistakes in life, but know My strong hands are always outstretched and ready to pick you up***. Remember today: Every mistake you make is redeemable because I AM your Redeemer. Know this: Your mistakes never shake Me! I AM never caught off guard when you make an error. This is why I sent My perfect Son, Jesus, to stand before Me in perfection for you!

Remember: there's no one on earth so righteous as to do good only and never make a mistake.

— ECCLESIASTES 7:20 CEB

All of us make a lot of mistakes. If someone doesn't make any mistakes when he speaks, he would be perfect. He would be able to control everything he does.

— JAMES 3:2 GW

221

SEE ALSO: ROMANS 4:25; ISAIAH 41:14; PSALM 19:14

'Amen': I AM agreeing
to what you are decreeing!
My name is Amen!

Amen not only means "so be it," but Amen is My name! I AM Amen, the Faithful and True Witness, the Originator — and all of My promises are "yes" and "amen." Not one of My promises is "no" to the one who believes. Do not allow familiarity to contaminate the power of this decree: "Amen." Know this: Amen is not just a habitual way to end your prayers. Amen means "so be it." It is using your mouth and faith to declare that what you have prayed is now so. "So be it" is making a decision to believe My Word and giving Me permission to enforce what you have prayed. You are invoking My name, Amen (AM-in), which has the power to bring this to pass. Wisdom says: Know today that when you say "Amen," you are proclaiming that every one of My promises is truthful, and you are making a declaration of agreement to My Word. When you decree and call "Amen," My name, I will always answer you.

These are the words of the Amen, the trusty and faithful and true Witness, the Origin and Beginning and Author of God's creation. — REVELATION 3:14 AMP

For all the promises of God in Him are Yes, and in Him Amen, to the glory of God through us. — 2 CORINTHIANS 1:20 NKJV

SEE ALSO: ROMANS 15:33; JOB 22:28

What you do not leave in the desert you **will** drag into The Promised Land!

Do not drag the *old* you into your *new* position in the Promised Land. The desert strips the world (Egypt) from you *faster* than any other season of life. There is no wasteland in My Kingdom. I will redeem even what may seem to be wasted time in the desert! Wisdom says: Do not despise a desert season. I have purpose in every season in your life. I AM constantly revealing to you the Truth of Who I AM. Since I have more of your attention in the season of isolation in the desert, this *can* be a more precious time for growth and surrender in our relationship than even in times of comfort! Know this: There is usually a desert before a Promised Land! Choose today to leave your baggage in the desert, so you will not drag it into The Promised Land! Then surrender your desert to Me, and I will use it for My Glory. Remember, I will never desert you.

> *God found Israel in a wild land—in a howling **desert wasteland**—he protected him, cared for him, watched over him with his very own eye.* — DEUTERONOMY 32:10 CEB

> *Walk in wisdom toward outsiders, making the best use of the time.* — COLOSSIANS 4:5 ESV

223

SEE ALSO: PSALM 6:6-9; NUMBERS 13:30

July 25

Could the spirit of gossip survive without tolerant ears?

Gossip is a sin that grieves Me. Gossip is about ruining reputations and not about passing along information. To gossip is to pass judgment on that person — that what you heard is truth. How can you be sure? Judge not, lest you be judged. For the victim, the vicious attack of gossip is like an ambush in the dark because the perpetrator falsely presents himself as a friend in order to get information as ammunition. Gossip is premeditated deception and betrayal. It gives voice to the spirit of hate. Gossiping is like stabbing someone in the back and burying a blade where the victim cannot remove it. Gossip is cowardly, like an attack from behind. Gossip hurts the other person, but it also hurts Me. When you use your mouth to gossip, you are poisoning and destroying yourself with sin. When you listen to gossip, you are as guilty as the one spewing it. Wisdom says: Today, if you are **tempted** to listen to gossip, make the choice to not give it tolerant ears.

They are gossips [spreading rumors], slanderers, haters of God, insolent, arrogant, boastful, inventors [of new forms] of evil.
— ROMANS 1:29-30 AMP

Their hearts collect evil gossip; once they leave, they tell it to everybody.
— PSALM 41:6 CEB

SEE ALSO: 1 TIMOTHY 3:11; 2 TIMOTHY 2:23-26

Declare to the snare!

My Kingdom is one of *sound* principles! Sounds and words are *light* forces! When you speak, you release *My Light!* This is why My first quoted words in My Word are, "Let there be Light!" Because you are made in My image, there is light in everything you speak! The Light of the World lives inside of you! I AM the Father of Lights; there is no darkness in Me. *My Light is not just the ability to see; My Light is the ability to be! You are full of My Light, and darkness is trembling at your existence in Me!* You are a deadly laser to the enemy — and the kingdom of darkness is terrified of you knowing and truly understanding that your identity is in *My Light.* Let Me assure you: When you are reborn in My Son, you are completely saturated in My Light. Because Light creates, your words have the power to create! Wisdom says: With your words that are weapons of My Light, and with the precision of My laser, declare to every snare: "Be removed and cast into the sea!" Visualize My Light destroying that snare. I have bequeathed My Words of Light to *heal* the world, never to *hurt* the world. Use My power to destroy the kingdom of darkness, never people!

You are the light of the world. — Matthew 5:14 amp

See also: Psalm 119:130; Psalm 119:105; James 1:17; John 12:36-37

If you are not feeling the heat, then you are not in the Refiner's fire!

When you were baptized with My Holy Spirit, you were baptized with holy fire. *I AM the Refiner's fire.* In the heat of My Spirit, I AM making you aware of dross that needs to surface so it can be removed from you. When in My fire, your heart of gold is never out of My sight, and I will not allow you to be in the fire beyond what you can handle. Know that the only way the gold in you can be refined is when you endure pressure under fire. The hotter the challenges, the higher the gold quality. Refiners know that gold is pure when they can see their image in it. As The Skilled Refiner, I know you are perfected when I can see *My image* in you. The longer you remain by choice in My purifying fire, the more you will look like Me, your Father. Wisdom says: Allow Me to burn out all impurities so you can be My reflection. Know that if you are feeling My Refiner's fire, you are becoming more and more like Me! Today, desire a heart of *gold* like *Mine!* Be My *Goldmine.* The more you are mined, the more you will shine for Me.

The Lord, the Light of Israel, will be a fire; the Holy One will be a flame. He will devour the thorns and briers with fire, burning up the enemy in a single night.

— Isaiah 10:17 NLT

See also: Luke 3:16; Malachi 3:2; Zechariah 13:7-9; Proverbs 17:3; Psalm 16:3

I have not been dethroned!

I have not been dethroned! Choose to trust Me instead of what you see. Rest assured that I have never been caught off guard about anything! I planned the beginning and the end, because I AM the Beginning and the End. I know what will happen today, and I have already made provision for you. I give you the giants for your bread, not for you to fear. I create a path of victory for you today. I go before you, and I AM your rear guard. These are indeed the perilous times that I warned you of in My Word. I always make a way of escape for those who trust Me. I AM not sweating in this season. I AM on My throne laughing at the wicked who oppose Me! I AM the Almighty, and I AM very capable of taking care of you. Wisdom says: I was with you yesterday. I AM in your today. And your tomorrow is Mine. Receive My Peace. Call forth the necessary resources from My storehouse that are yours for the asking.

> *The Lord laughs at [the wicked], for He sees that their own day [of defeat] is coming.* — Psalm 37:13 AMPC

> *Oh, let the wickedness of the wicked come to an end, but establish the righteous [those in right standing with You]; For the righteous God tries the hearts and minds.* — Psalm 7:9 AMP

> *Your throne, O God, is forever and ever.* — Psalm 45:6 AMP

See also: Psalm 103:19; Psalm 47:8; Psalm 59:7-9

When you have the power of My Son, Jesus, **in** you, how can anything have power **over** you?

What is mankind that you are mindful of them, or son of man that you care for him? You made them a little lower than the angels; **you crowned them with glory and honor and put everything under their feet. In putting everything under them, God left nothing that is not subject to them.** — Hebrews 2:6-8

To allow anything to rule over you, when I created *you* to rule over everything, is creation out of order. I have put everything under your feet. Because you are in My Son, Jesus, I have made *everything* subject to you: This includes addictions, poverty, sickness, lack of peace, and everything under the curse. When you allow something to have power over you, it is an indication that you have lost the revelation of how I created you to rule in My Son, Jesus Christ, and how dearly I love you! Wisdom says: Know that through My Son *I have crowned you with power and authority.* So how can anything else have power over you? Today, see My arms around you with a *strong hold* while I AM breaking *strongholds.*

Jesus called his twelve disciples to him and **gave them authority** *to drive out impure spirits and to heal every disease and sickness.* — Matthew 10:1

SEE ALSO: GALATIANS 5:16-26

If you are always striving to please people, then how can you be pleasing to Me?

Live and conduct yourself in a manner that is worthy of a Father like Me. Strive to please only Me. You cannot be pleasing to Me if you are always striving to please man. This is being double-minded and will cause you to be unstable in all your ways. Being a people pleaser is exhausting work! Others may be momentarily happy, but you will not be! You will eventually resent the very ones that you are trying to please. You will never be able to please both Me and man. Wisdom says: I AM the Rewarder of those who diligently seek Me. When you strive to please man, instead of Me, then you are making man your idol and your god. Strive today to be pleasing *only* to Me! When you are pleasing to Me, My eyes are constantly watching you. Those who are *pleasing* Me never have to *plead* for My attention.

The Lord's eyes scan the whole world to find those whose hearts are committed to him and to strengthen them.
— 2 CHRONICLES 16:9 GW

Am I now trying to win the favor and approval of men, or of God? Or am I seeking to please someone? If I were still trying to be popular with men, I would not be a bond-servant of Christ. — GALATIANS 1:10 AMP

SEE ALSO: HEBREWS 11:6; COLOSSIANS 1:10; JOHN 5:30

If you are struggling with self-hatred, it is because you cannot see Me in you!

All hate begins with **self**-hatred, which empowers the enemy. His power is deception. When the enemy plants the spirit of fear, hatred, and confusion into your thoughts, it is his method of stealing, killing, and destroying. I gave the commandment — not the suggestion — to *love* your neighbor *as yourself*. How can you hate someone whom I love? When you put yourself down, or hate who you are, you are doing the enemy's work. You are Mine! You have lost the right to hate anything or anyone who looks like Me. This includes your neighbor and yourself. Wisdom says: I AM the lover of your soul! Self-hatred comes only because of hateful things said and done to you. Remember, My precious child, that I cannot hate you for any reason! Allow My loving Word to heal the words and actions done to you by people who are broken. My Love for you is everlasting! If you have no love for yourself on the inside, there will be no love to flow out to others. Know this: If you cannot see Me (I AM Love) in yourself, then how can you expect to see Me in anyone else? When you love yourself, you are loving Me.

"Love your neighbor as yourself."　　　– Matthew 19:19

See also: 2 Timothy 1:7; 1 Peter 1:22; Proverbs 10:12

Insecurity creates impostors!

Insecurity completely changes My original and beautiful design of you, and you can unknowingly become an impostor of yourself. Impostors are formed when you *act* like someone else and acquire a false identity. Know this: The enemy is threatened by the authentic you! I want to comfort you with My Peace, but insecurity robs you of this. When you are secure, you will experience growth and thrive in new ground. Insecurity is the deception that you are not enough. ***How can you not be enough when I have created you? I love who you are.*** Wisdom says: Protect My design of you! Do not allow the lie of insecurity to rob you of who I intend you to be. I give you the right to only be yourself. My Love for you is perfect security. Choose today to be *in Me*, not *in*secure.

> *"No one does anything in secret when he wants to be known publicly. If You [must] do these things, show Yourself openly to the world and make Yourself known!"*
>
> — JOHN 7:4 AMP

> *In Him also we have received an inheritance [a destiny — we were claimed by God as His own], having been predestined (chosen, appointed beforehand) according to the purpose of Him who works everything in agreement with the counsel and design of His will.*
>
> — EPHESIANS 1:11 AMP

SEE ALSO: EPHESIANS 2:10; EPHESIANS 5:13

Purposeful surrender
brings revelation.

You will never just stumble into My destiny for you! It is too large to just stumble into! You will find My plan for your life by surrendering on purpose and with purpose. Surrendering your will and preconceived ideas to Me brings revelation about the amazing things I have planned for you. Never confuse surrendering with giving up. When you surrender your all to Me, I give you My power to persevere. Surrender to Me only; never surrender to any of the enemy's tactics that attempt to get you to quit. I reveal only as you surrender. The more you surrender, the more of your heart I will possess. Know this today: When you surrender on purpose, I will reveal your true purpose. Wisdom says: Give Me your surrendered heart so I can fill you with revelation of the destiny I assigned to you. This only comes when you spend time with Me. I give the treasures of My heart to a heart that is surrendered to Me. I take complete possession of a completely surrendered heart!

The presence of the Lord was with them with power, so that a great number ... surrendered themselves to Him.

– ACTS 11:21 AMP

You make known to me the path of life; you will fill me with joy in your presence, with eternal pleasures at your right hand.

– PSALM 16:11

You will not take authority over anything you fear.

When you fear something or someone, you are giving that person or thing **respect**! Respect **Me only**! You will fear the enemy when you respect his power over you. He has been defeated and stripped of all power. The enemy is a con artist. All con artists use deception because they have no power. The enemy's only trick is to deceive you into believing that he holds all the power. **Why would the enemy use deception if he really had all power to harm you?** I AM Power! I AM the Almighty! I do not and will not ever deceive because My power is real. Allow Me to wash all fear from your heart and mind. If you knew how much the enemy fears **you** — because of My Son in you — you would never again be afraid to use your authority! The enemy is subject to My Word. He runs in fear at the sound of My Word. Wisdom says: You have been given power to tread on serpents and scorpions, and over **all** the power of the enemy, and nothing shall by any means harm you. Why would you fear someone who cannot harm you? Take authority today! I, The Creator, have all power over My creation. When you are submitted to Me, the enemy will flee.

Submit to God. Resist the devil and he will flee from you.
—James 4:7 NKJV

See also: Luke 9:1; Luke 10:19

Unworthiness will stop a 'visitation' from My Son, Jesus.

Your feelings of unworthiness never stop *Me*. They stop *you* from wanting Me to come closer! Unworthiness causes you to fear My rejection of you. This is deception and a lie! My child, I will never reject you! Feelings of unworthiness are barriers to visitations from My Son, Jesus, or close encounters in My Word. Notice that when the centurion said, "Lord, I am *not worthy* to receive you, but only say the Word and my servant will be healed," it did not *stop* Jesus' healing. But the centurion told Jesus not to come closer. *Faith did not stop the healing, but feeling unworthy stopped Jesus from entering the centurion's house. What other miracles might the centurion or his family have experienced?* Wisdom says: Unworthiness and fear of rejection ruin the opportunity for true intimacy in a relationship. *If you are not spending much time with Me, could it be that you do not feel worthy — that you fear My rejection? I decree that you are worthy and fully accepted! I AM pleased to make you Mine. I will never disown My Own.*

> For the sake of his great name the Lord will not reject his
> people, because the Lord was pleased to make you his own.
> — 1 Samuel 12:22

See also: Luke 7:2-10 amp; Romans 8:1; 1 Corinthians 11:27-29

If you are not allowing Me to be authentic **in** you, then you are allowing the enemy to be authentic **through** you!

You were created to be an expression of Me. You are My handiwork. When you are not the authentic expression of Me, your Creator, you will become influenced by the kingdom of darkness. The enemy wants to change My design of you into a twisted version of himself. True joy and happiness come when you are doing what I created you to do in My Kingdom. My desire *for* you is My design *of* you. Do not resign yourself to become the enemy's design. Wisdom says: When you are not being authentic, you will only reach the hypocrites! Allow Me to be authentic in you today! Do people see *Me* when they see you?

> *For we are God's handiwork, created in Christ Jesus to do good works, which God prepared in advance for us to do.*
> — Ephesians 2:10

> *And we know that in all things God works for the good of those who love him, who have been called according to his purpose.*
> — Romans 8:28

My power is **ignited** when My Body is **united**.

The enemy trembles at the power of forgiveness. Your two little words, "I forgive," can wipe out *generations* of the enemy's work. Oh, how he shudders at those words. When you declare this from your heart, years of his attacks crumble before his eyes. Without forgiveness, you will not walk in unity and in one accord with others. ***This strategy from the enemy has kept My Body divided and disjointed, with little power.*** That is why the enemy wants to keep reminding you of hurts. Not forgiving those who have hurt you leads to illness, torture, and torment. The enemy becomes your ruler when you do not forgive. You are recreated to rule and reign with Christ. Wisdom says: Unity and forgiveness are keys to effectiveness. So today, take the time to seek My heart if you need to forgive! The only way that you can be one with Me is to be one with My family. You don't have the right to pick and choose which members you accept. You cannot love Me, but hate and have unforgiveness toward My children. To love Me is to love My *entire* family.

> *"Shouldn't you have had mercy on your fellow servant just as I had on you? In anger his master handed him over to the jailers to be tortured, until he should pay back all he owed. This is how my heavenly Father will treat each of you **unless you forgive** your brother or sister from your heart."*
> — MATTHEW 18:33-35

SEE ALSO: EPHESIANS 4:16; MATTHEW 6:15; JOHN 20:23

A life full of Love is
a life full of power.

To hate is to be weak. To love is to be full of power and strength. My power within you is strong enough to overcome any situation you encounter. This power that I gave you at your rebirth is activated by love. When you love Me, despite your current circumstances, you tap into My power that will overcome every circumstance. When you love your enemies, instead of hating them, oh, My child, you are clothed with such power! If you could literally see My power flowing through you when you love, you would never be tempted to hate again. Wisdom says: ***You are never more powerful than when you are loving. You will never be weaker than when you choose to hate.*** Choose to be full of My power today by loving one another.

Be fully capable of comprehending with all the saints (God's people) the width and length and height and depth of His love [fully experiencing that amazing, endless love].
— EPHESIANS 3:18 AMP

We have heard of your faith ... and of the [unselfish] love which you have for all the saints (God's people).
— COLOSSIANS 1:4 AMP

Faith will always make you **proceed**. Fear will always make you **recede**.

Both My Kingdom of Light and the kingdom of darkness are constantly progressing. Fear and faith both fight to increase and expand. Each spiritual force continually tries to break into new territory. Faith always propels you forward. Fear freezes your decision-making ability and causes you to recede or retreat. If you are standing still or having a difficult time moving forward with Me, consider whether you are being influenced or attacked by fear. Wisdom says: Make the decision that you will see through the eyes of faith and proceed forward with Me. Why retreat to the old familiar ground of fear, when you can advance in faith to the new beauty of a Promised Land? ***I AM always moving forward!*** Never fear, for I AM near. Today, receive from Me by faith; don't retreat from Me in fear.

> *In this case, moreover, it is required [as essential and demanded] of stewards that one be found faithful and trustworthy.*
> — 1 Corinthians 4:2 AMP

> *Be on guard; stand firm in your faith [in God, respecting His precepts and keeping your doctrine sound]. Act like [mature] men and be courageous; be strong.*
> — 1 Corinthians 16:13 AMP

See also: Habakkuk 3:19; Hebrews 10:38

The woman's body is My gateway from heaven to earth.

In the animal kingdom, I created males to be bolder in color and more beautiful. I did this to camouflage the female and to protect the young that may be with her. But in My Kingdom, I held nothing back from My woman! *I anointed every woman to be the carrier of My beauty!* My woman is trusted with the honor of carrying *life* — and *life is beautiful!* I have hidden My protective attributes in her. Some have misunderstood her, but I understand her perfectly. She is everything that I desire her to be! *She is the seeker of Love.* Her body is My temple — and the gateway from heaven to earth! I have crowned her with exquisite contrasts: She is gentle, yet strong enough to endure — yes, even welcome — the excruciating pains of birth, all for the life of her child! She will go without, just to see her child smile. She is tender, yet becomes like a lioness to protect anyone she loves. She is the rose, with the delicate petals that carry the scent of heaven. Wisdom says: My woman is My secret weapon that I AM raising up in this last hour. The enemy fears her passion for Me. The enemy trembles at her ability to nurture, teach, and serve — but it especially terrifies him that she is My gateway from heaven to earth for life. My Son, Jesus, is washing the feet of the women who have been listening at His feet.

See also: Song of Solomon 2:1-4;
1 Peter 3:1-4; Ephesians 5:21-33; 1 Peter 4:19

Your fruit will increase to the size of your appetite!

Learn the lesson of the giants in the land of Canaan and the magnitude of their fruit. To sustain their appetites, I grew their fruit larger than normal. This was not only for the sake of the giants, but it was also to bless My beloved people with an *inheritance*. Know this: The fruit of My Holy Spirit also grows to the size of your appetite — to your desire for My Presence within you! Your appetite decides how large your fruit of love, joy, peace, patience, kindness, goodness, faithfulness, gentleness, and self-control will be. Wisdom says: Increase your hunger daily for My Truth and for the fruit of My Holy Spirit. I will always answer your hunger with more of Me. I will never ignore your cry for more of Me. You please Me when you pursue Me.

> When they arrived ... they cut off a branch with a single cluster of grapes — it took two men to carry it — slung on a pole. — NUMBERS 13:23 MSG

> "The seed will grow well, the vine will yield its fruit, the ground will produce its crops, and the heavens will drop their dew. I will give all these things as an *inheritance* to the remnant of this people." — ZECHARIAH 8:12

> But the fruit that the Spirit produces in a person's life is love, joy, peace, patience, kindness, goodness, faithfulness, gentleness, and self-control. — GALATIANS 5:22-23 ERV

SEE ALSO: PROVERBS 13:4

The difference between **mourning** and **morning** is 'u' (you)!

If you are mourning, feeling deep sorrow and grief, I AM with you! This is why I said, "Blessed are those who mourn, for they will be comforted" — not just by anyone, but by Me! I AM close to those who are brokenhearted. There is a season to mourn, but it is just a season, never a lifetime. Only you have the power to choose if you will continue to mourn, or if you will choose to trust Me and allow yourself to start a brand new day. There may be weeping in the night; know that I weep with you, but joy *will come* in the morning! I grace every morning with joy because I make all things new — even My mercies. Revel in the new wonder and adventure of this day, and not in the difficulties of the past. Only you decide if you want to stay in *mourning* or start a brand new *morning*! Wisdom says: Ask Me for the strength to start afresh. Today, I pull you close to My mouth and blow My refreshing and healing Winds of change upon you! Only I can restore your soul and make you whole! I AM with you in every ending and every beginning! Ask Me to show you great and exciting things to come!

Weeping may stay for the night, but rejoicing comes in the morning.

— PSALM 30:5

SEE ALSO: *ECCLESIASTES 3:1, 4; 1 THESSALONIANS 5:16; JEREMIAH 33:3; PSALM 147:3; ISAIAH 61:1-3; PSALM 34:18; MATTHEW 5:4; PSALM 59:16*

Remember, the anger you hold on to becomes the danger that you invite!

Can you see the **danger** in anger? When the sun goes down on your anger, the sun comes up on your unforgiveness. This is how the enemy gets his foothold. Anger and bitterness are corrosive and caustic, like acid, and they can cause damage to your body. Do not allow strongholds of anger, bitterness, and unforgiveness to form as you sleep. The whole reason for sleep is to let the day completely "reset" for you to something brand new. When you go to bed angry, you literally program your brain and heart for anger to be what you feel when you wake up. When anger becomes a stronghold, you are no longer simply dealing with anger, but a lifestyle of a bad temper and an open door of destruction from the enemy. Anger destroys *you*! It is a sin that affects everyone around you. Wisdom says: Give your anger and emotions to Me at the end of each day. Allow your new day to be uncontaminated by the attacks of yesterday. Wake up to a new day, not an old day! Release all anger, and receive all My unlimited and unconditional love for you!

In your anger do not sin: Do not let the sun go down while you are still angry.
— Ephesians 4:26

See also: James 1:20; Proverbs 30:33; 1 Corinthians 13:5

Are you holding yourself to a different standard than you expect from Me?

The instruction that I give to you is the same standard of integrity that I demand of Myself. I AM honor-bound to keep My Promises to you. The reason I say, "Thou shalt not lie" is because I do not lie. I AM the Truth! If you are expecting Me to keep My Word, yet *you* refuse to keep yours, that is the action of a hypocrite! This is what the Pharisees did. They expected Me to be at a level to which they refused to rise. Jesus only did what He saw *Me* do. He was not a hypocrite. Wisdom says: When you keep My commandments, I can keep what I have promised. It is the spiritual Law of Sowing and Reaping. Search your heart if your prayers are going unanswered. Are your choices restricting My ability to answer them? If you are holding Me to a different standard than you are requiring of yourself, then that could be the reason! Today, keep your word just as I will keep Mine! I AM above reproach in every way. I must keep My Word to keep My name: Truth.

> *Jesus gave them this answer: "Very truly I tell you, the Son can do nothing by himself; he can do only what he sees his Father doing, because whatever the Father does the Son also does."* —JOHN 5:19

SEE ALSO: PSALM 138:2; JOHN 5:30; 2 CORINTHIANS 9:6; PHILIPPIANS 4:8

Evening is when I make things 'even' again for a brand new day.

Whatever may happen today, know that I AM busy about your every step. I AM personally involved with every aspect of your brand new day. Nothing about this day will catch Me off guard. For years now — and in some cases, for generations — I have been planning solutions for every problem, and making provisions for you, just for this day, at the exact time that you will need them. When evening comes, I *level* out the mountains and lift the valleys of the day into a flattened ground for your brand new day! Wisdom says: Relax this evening knowing that I AM ironing out the wrinkles of this day. Each morning, everyone starts over on an *even* playing field. I AM aware of everything that you need today — and I AM Faithful to provide exactly what you need! I have the power to effortlessly take all of the mountains and valleys of this day and make them level and even again.

Forget the former things; do not dwell on the past. See, I am doing a new thing! Now it springs up; do you not perceive it?
— Isaiah 43:18-19

The uneven ground shall become level. — Isaiah 40:4

SEE ALSO: LAMENTATIONS 3:22-24; ISAIAH 33:2; 2 CORINTHIANS 4:16

I AM Revelation.

Everything you say about yourself in the present tense is actually a ***declaration*** and a ***decree***. When you say anything about yourself in the present tense, you cannot say it without invoking My holy name — I AM. I often hear My people say, "I AM sick" or "I AM tired" or "I AM so poor" without thinking that My name is holy. Every single time you ***invoke My name, I AM***, you are saying a decree — or curse — depending on your words! My name, ***I AM that I AM***, freed millions of My people overnight from bondage and 400 years of slavery! My name has that same power when you say it today! Use My name with the utmost respect. I have given you My name to use to free yourself, not to enslave yourself! I have bequeathed My holy name today for you to use with wisdom, reverence, and honor. Wisdom says: When you decree I AM free, I AM healed, and I AM loved, know and respect what power is being unleashed by using My holy name. When you invoke My name, I revoke the enemy's hold on you! I unleash "plagues" and terror that utterly devastate the enemy. Know that you plunder the enemy's camp with My name, I AM! Decree yourself out of any slavery or bondage in your life! When you decree My holy name, I AM demanding of the enemy: "Let My people go."

God said to Moses, "I am who I am. This is what you are to say to the Israelites: 'I am has sent me to you.'"
— Exodus 3:14

See also: Exodus 5:1; John 15:16; Psalm 91:14; Hebrews 11:1; Isaiah 52:6

Loneliness can be
a form of self-hatred.

Not all loneliness is self-hatred, but some loneliness is a form of self-hatred. You can tell that loneliness is actually self-hatred when a person is still lonely in the presence of others. Sometimes people hate the company that they are keeping — themselves. I can heal all of your loneliness and self-hatred. You cannot have peace and self-hatred at the same time. Self-hatred is a thief that will steal everything if you allow it. Wisdom says: To hate yourself is to hate Me. I AM in you. This hurts My heart deeply. Allow My Word, and what I think and know about you, to heal the lie that you are not good enough. When you say you are not good enough, you are saying I AM not good. Make the decision that you will believe My Promises instead of the lies of the enemy. I believe you are worthy of My Love and I proved it with My Son's death. The fact that I created you is proof that I love you! Know that I will never leave you nor forsake you. How can you be lonely when I AM always with you? Today, be aware of My Presence in your day.

He [God] Himself has said, I will not in any way fail you nor give you up nor leave you without support. [I will] not, [I will] not, [I will] not in any degree leave you helpless nor forsake nor let [you] down (relax My hold on you)! [Assuredly not!] — HEBREWS 13:5 AMP

SEE ALSO: PSALM 34:18; PSALM 68:6

You do not need **more of Me.** I need **more of you** — more of your surrendered heart!

So many people beg Me to give them more of Me. That is impossible. I already gave all that I could possibly give. I did not even withhold My only Son from you. I AM bound to the Laws of My Kingdom — as you are. I will not violate My Laws, nor will I violate the Law of Love that is in free will. Through My Son, you have been repositioned into My Kingdom. Because of your Covenant rights, everything I have is now yours. This means you must enforce these rights and privileges with My Word and not violate the Laws of My Kingdom with fear and disobedience. Wisdom says: The more your heart is surrendered, the more My Kingdom is rendered. ***You already have all of Me. Do I have all of you?***

> *So then, any of you who does not forsake (renounce, surrender claim to, give up, say good-bye to) all that he has cannot be My disciple.* — LUKE 14:33 AMP

SEE ALSO: JOHN 3:16

You **have** not because you ask not.

I said in My Word, "Ask and you shall receive." I also said, "You have not because you ask not." When you do ask in faith for something in prayer, you receive it. However, there is another layer of truth as well: If the enemy tries to curse you with something for which you did *not* ask, you have the authority to refuse and reject it. The enemy will try to send you sickness and poverty, hoping you will accept them. Stand on My Word and proclaim, "No! I have no sickness because I did not ask for sickness." Wisdom says: Because you rule and reign with Christ, you decide what is allowed into your life. If you did not ask for something and it is now afflicting you, you have the authority and right to challenge this illegal attack from the enemy. Even though sickness is real, it does not have the right to stay when challenged. Today, reject every curse that is trying to attack you.

For everyone who asks, will receive what he asks for.
— LUKE 11:10 NLT

You do not have because you do not ask. — JAMES 4:2 NKJV

For everyone who asks receives, and he who seeks finds, and to him who knocks it will be opened.
— MATTHEW 7:8 NKJV

SEE ALSO: MATTHEW 10:1

You are **not defined** by your mistakes. You are **refined** by your mistakes.

When is a failure a success? When you get up again and learn from your mistakes. You are created in My image — created to be blessed and to succeed. But disobedience and quitting disqualifies you from My blessing. Both of these are the result of your choices, not My choices. Success is a choice! You are the one who decides whether you quit or keep going. A mistake or failure can lead to success when you learn a lesson that alters the course of your entire life. Wisdom says: *A failure is only final if you allow it to be.* Today, make the decision to learn from every mistake. Some of the most successful people have made the most mistakes. Consider Saul of Tarsus/Paul: He made the most profound mistakes, but became the most profound servant in My Kingdom. Every mistake, without exception, is the opportunity to become more like My Son — perfection. I have not disqualified you because of your past; I have pre-qualified you because of your future.

> *This Book of the Law shall not depart out of your mouth, but you shall meditate on it day and night, that you may observe and do according to all that is written in it. For then you shall make your way prosperous, and then you shall deal wisely and have good success.*
> — Joshua 1:8 AMP

See also: Proverbs 28:13; James 3:2

Re-offenders are those who cannot stay **out** of prison.

Being offended steals your time, your joy, your life, and your identity. It puts you in bondage — a prison-like state in which your freedom is gone. Re-offender is a term applied to those who cannot stay out of prison! *If you are easily offended, then you are a re-offender.* For offenders and re-offenders, the only hope for restored freedom lies in forgiveness. In prison you lose your freedom and you are chained to time! You are tormented about the past, you cannot enjoy the present, and you do not have a future when you are offended! Time rules over every offender in prison! Your name is replaced by a number, and without your name, you lose your true identity — who you were before the offense. Like a prison, unforgiveness torments and takes over every area of your life! This affects and disrupts everyone around you! If you want to stay out of prison, do not become a re-offender. Wisdom says: Offense never just randomly falls on you, nor is it accidentally placed on you! Offense has to be taken or claimed by your will! Instead of choosing offenses, choose to forgive! *Never forget: Forgiveness reaffirms your freedom; offense reaffirms your life of fences!*

It is harder to win back the friendship of an offended brother than to capture a fortified city. His anger shuts you out like iron bars. — Proverbs 18:19

See also: 1 Corinthians 13:5;
Matthew 24:10; Matthew 18:34-35

If you are in Christ,
I will never reject you.

I AM in My Son, Jesus, and My Son is in you. We are One. If I divided My Kingdom, it would not stand; My Kingdom would be ruined and fall. If I rejected My Son in you, I would ruin My Kingdom and would violate My Word and My Covenant. I would lose My throne. Know this: I will never lose My throne because I will maintain My Love for My Son forever. My Covenant with Him will never fail. I will establish His line forever and His throne as long as the heavens endure. Wisdom says: I will never reject you because I will never reject My Son in you! Know, as My **beloved**, you will always **be loved** and be part of My Kingdom that endures forever.

My covenant with him will never end. He will always have an heir; his throne will be as endless as the days of heaven.
— Psalm 89:28-29

Jesus knew their thoughts and said to them, **"Every kingdom divided against itself will be ruined**, *and every city or household divided against itself will not stand. If Satan drives out Satan, he is divided against himself. How then can his kingdom stand?"*
— Matthew 12:25-26

I pray ... that all of them may be one, Father, just as you are in me and I am in you.
— John 17:20-21

See also: Mark 3:25

Words that carry the most weight are words that are weighed carefully before spoken.

Do you comprehend the gift I gave when I created you to speak? Words are spirit forces that are stored in your heart and spoken with your mouth. Your words are spoken with My Breath! I breathed into you My Breath of Life so you can speak and create whatever you choose. So heavy is this responsibility that your words will either acquit you or condemn you. Wisdom says: Weigh your words very carefully. Words carry the power of life or death, blessing or cursing. Even though every word is a privilege, every word comes with a price. Can you afford what you are saying? Know this: Every word is a *gift* from Me! Words are spirit and they can never die! Can you fathom the insurmountable chaos that I would release if I began to just haphazardly speak without thought and purpose? I would release deadly pandemonium! You cannot recklessly speak either because your words carry My power! Be as cautious as you would expect Me to be!

> *"For every idle word men may speak, they will give account of it in the day of judgment."*
>
> — MATTHEW 12:36 NKJV

> *Watch the way you talk. Let nothing foul or dirty come out of your mouth. Say only what helps,* **each word a gift***.*
>
> — EPHESIANS 4:29 MSG

SEE ALSO: JOB 33:4; ACTS 17:25

You do not have the right to let My dreams for you die!

You do not have the right to let **even one** of My dreams die! My dreams for your life will always be bigger than you, and cannot be accomplished without Me. This is by design. If your dream is too small, it is possible for you to accomplish it on your own — without My help — and you will be able to take all of the credit due to Me. I give huge, seemingly impossible dreams so the world will recognize that it is **beyond** you — and so I will get the glory. There is so much more at stake than just your destiny being fulfilled! I AM constantly thinking about the lost! If your dream or assignment is planned by Me, fulfilling it will impact souls throughout eternity. Wisdom says: Do not shy away because of the size of My dream for you. Most give up because they cannot visualize a dream so large. **Know today that My dream for you is always so large, because I do not know how to dream small!**

> *All the days ordained for me were written in your book before one of them came to be. How precious to me are your thoughts, God. How vast is the sum of them! Were I to count them, they would outnumber the grains of sand.*
> — Psalm 139:16-18

See also: Jeremiah 29:11; Romans 11:2

Resurrecting the past kills the future!

I created time to expire. When a day expires, it should stay in the past. Every day I have created for you has purpose. When that purpose is fulfilled, it is to stay behind you. When you try to bring back something that is gone forever, it wastes your time and energy that you could use for the new day. I need you to look ahead. Those who dread the future do not trust Me or themselves. Do not allow yourself to be tempted or to long for what is ***dead*** when you are in a new day that is full of ***life***! When you cling to the past, you cling to death. You miss out on life, and you miss out on Me in your day. Wisdom says: Instead of focusing on old memories, make new ones! Those who live in old memories will miss out on My new surprises. I AM in your present and in your future. If your relationship with Me is about yesterday, you have lost your passion. If your relationship is about the present, then you have My perception! Living in the past is living in religion, not a relationship.

*One thing I do: **forgetting what lies behind and reaching forward to what lies ahead**, I press on toward the goal to win the [heavenly] prize of the upward call of God in Christ Jesus.*

— Philippians 3:13-14 AMP

See also: Psalm 145:2; 2 Corinthians 4:16

Your greatest struggle will usually identify your calling — and your strength!

I AM calling you to be strong in Me, and very courageous. You must not quit in a season of struggle! Pray for My perception, and I will help you to see with clarity. There is much at stake when you are in a trial. The enemy attacks you when he sees how much I have blessed you with My gifts. He needs to stop you before you stop him. You will champion the cause for others with passion and compassion when you have overcome in the same struggle. Wisdom says: While wrestling with Jesus, Jacob refused to let go without a blessing. In Jacob's struggle, I renamed him Israel. Know this: If you are in a wrestling match today, hold on to My Son, Jesus, as tightly as you can! It is in this struggle that I not only change your walk with Me, but I also rename you for promotion, power, and anoint you with a prevailing spirit. Refuse to quit! Allow Me to turn your struggle into strength.

> *Consider it nothing but joy, my brothers and sisters, whenever you fall into various trials. Be assured that the testing of your faith [through experience] produces endurance [leading to spiritual maturity, and inner peace]. And let endurance have its perfect result and do a thorough work, so that you may be perfect and completely developed [in your faith], lacking in nothing.*
> – JAMES 1:2-4 AMP

SEE ALSO: 1 PETER 1:6-7; ROMANS 5:3; JOSHUA 1:9; GENESIS 32:24-30

Faith will make you **complete**; fear will make you **compete**.

Faith will always make you complete because it ushers in My Love and peace. Being complete implies that no part is missing. Completeness is wholeness and unbroken unity. Faith creates the atmosphere for unity; fear creates the atmosphere for division, especially competition. Make My Word your top priority! My Word builds strong faith and confidence that you are loved by Me. I never compare you to anyone else. With this revelation, you will never have to compete with anyone again. If you find yourself competing with others, know this: The root is always fear. Wisdom says: Love can flourish where faith is strong! Know that I have given you My Spirit of power, love, and a sound mind to combat all fear! Today, seek My heart and allow Me to heal you completely, so you will never again feel as if you have to compete for My attention!

> *I in them and you in me — so that they may be brought to complete unity.* —JOHN 17:23

> *My goal is that they may be encouraged in heart and united in love, so that they may have the full riches of complete understanding.*
> COLOSSIANS 2:2

SEE ALSO: 1 CORINTHIANS 12:20; 1 JOHN 4:12; 2 TIMOTHY 1:7

If you cannot forgive hurt, you will have to relive hurt.

*Behold, I give you the authority to **trample** on serpents and scorpions, and over all the power of the enemy, and **nothing shall by any means hurt you.***

— LUKE 10:19

The enemy sends hurt via people — especially through those you love the most — so it will **hurt** the most. He is desperate for you to fall into the trap of feeling you have the **right** to hold on to your hurt. But when you hold hurt you relive it over and over again. I give you the **choice** to hold on to your hurt, **but never the right.** I have commanded you to love one another and forgive. Wisdom says: If you believe that you have a legitimate **right** to keep your hurt, you will feel justified to seek revenge — and you will disregard My commandment to forgive. When you entertain thoughts and memories of your hurt, it is like entertaining the enemy. Both are deadly. Either you or the enemy will be trampled by your response to hurt. Make the choice today to forgive hurt, so you will not have to relive it.

SEE ALSO: PROVERBS 23:35; MARK 11:25

If you are looking at things through the eyes of pain, your vision **will** be distorted!

Nothing distorts your perception like pain. When you are in pain of any kind, cry out to Me for clarity of vision, and I will help you! Your perception determines your outcome, attitude, and destiny. Life is all about perception — *your* perception of Me, yourself, and what you have been through. Every problem can be an opportunity for Me to be glorified! Surrender your pain, and all of the disappointments that come with it, to Me. Notice how a window has a window*pane* that blocks your ability to see? This is to remind you that pain blocks and distorts your ability to see with clarity. You will have to depend upon *My vision* during this time, since pain distorts the way you see life. Wisdom says: Today, *allow Me to be your eyes* and to lead and guide you out of this pain.

> *"He will wipe away every tear from their eyes; and there will no longer be death; there will no longer be sorrow and anguish, or crying, or pain; for the former order of things has passed away."*
>
> — Revelation 21:4 AMP

SEE ALSO: *2 Peter 3:16*

Denial is only comfortable for the moment. My Truth comforts eternally.

In the Truth of My Word, you will find True Comfort. My Truth will always set you free. Be cautious if you are someone who settles for a counterfeit of the temporary "comfort" of denial over the True Comfort of My Word! Denial may feel good for a moment, but it will cause you to make wrong choices. Denial is bondage to a lie, or the refusal to face or admit the Truth. Wisdom says: When you face the issues with Truth, you will live a life with My Peace and My Comfort. Denial is choosing a prison. My Truth is choosing freedom. Choose My Comfort today, instead of the counterfeit and deception of denial.

For out of the abundance of the heart the mouth speaks.
— MATTHEW 12:34 NKJV

And you will know the truth [regarding salvation], and the truth will set you free [from the penalty of sin].
— JOHN 8:32 AMP

There is utter truth in all your laws; your decrees are eternal.
— PSALM 119:160 TLB

SEE ALSO: TITUS 1:1-2

Pride closes your heart; humility opens your heart.

Are you taking the sin of pride as seriously as it should be taken? A prideful person will not pursue or yearn for Me. Pride is the sin that deceives a person into thinking they need no one to help or save them. Pride blinds the heart. It cannot see the needs of others and is the first to withhold mercy. Prideful people believe they are better than others. They are their own god and have no need of Me. I have to demote the prideful and arrogant. It hurts Me to watch them be this blind. *My heart aches for those who are deceived in pride.* My mercy is there to pick up the prideful when they fall. I will do anything to wake them up on earth before they wake up in hell. Wisdom says: I resist the proud, but will give grace to the humble. A humble heart is a surrendered heart. I surround a surrendered heart. I can mold a humble heart, so open your heart to Me today.

> *"Everyone who exalts himself will be humbled, but he who humbles himself [forsaking self-righteous pride] will be exalted."*
> —LUKE 18:14

> *Pride goes before destruction, a haughty spirit before a fall.*
> — PROVERBS 16:18

SEE ALSO: OBADIAH 1:3; PSALM 10:2

Are you missing the power of ministering to one because you want to minister to multitudes?

Are you overlooking those to whom you are assigned to minister this day? I have taken much time to set up encounters for you to shine My Love and Good News of the Gospel. Many miss their assignment to do this because they are too busy or because they are put off by outward appearance. My Son was never too busy to minister to the one. So many want to reach the multitudes but forget the importance of ministering one-on-one. When Jesus ministered to the woman at the well, many believed in Him because of that woman's testimony. Wisdom says: Remember, when you are obedient to ministering to the one, I will give you a platform to minister to the multitudes. Today, whether you are ministering to one person or to a thousand, know that your reward comes with your obedience — not with the size of the audience!

Now many Samaritans from that city believed in Him and trusted Him [as Savior] because of what the woman said when she testified, "He told me all the things that I have done."

— JOHN 4:39

SEE ALSO: *1 PETER 4:10*

September 1

You must identify your enemy, or **everyone** is at risk!

You must identify your enemy. If you do not, then anyone and everyone can become your enemy. The devil is your enemy and just *uses* people. We do not wrestle against *flesh and blood*: that's people. Cut off your true enemy, the devil, not people. Never forget that the person being used by the enemy is deceived. He wants you to identify the people who hurt you as your enemies. He *needs* you to fight people so you will not fight him. As long as you fight people, he goes free and unchallenged. The source of all strife and confusion is the devil. Take authority over him, in the name of Jesus. My Word will render him powerless and ineffective. Wisdom says: Forgive those who have been used by the devil. Have mercy *knowing* you, too, have been used by his trickery. Love is the most powerful weapon for defeating the devil. Always remember: *You have been given power and authority to drive out demons, not people.*

> *We are not fighting against humans. We are fighting against forces and authorities and against rulers of darkness and powers in the spiritual world.*
> – EPHESIANS 6:12 CEV

> *The weapons of our warfare are not physical [weapons of flesh and blood]. Our weapons are divinely powerful for the destruction of fortresses.*
> – 2 CORINTHIANS 10:4 AMP

SEE ALSO: LUKE 9:1; PROVERBS 20:3

Allow Me to interrupt your day.

When you live every day the same, then you are living in monotony instead of adventure with Me! The adventure comes with fellowship and being obedient to what I AM telling you. Monotony can kill a vibrant relationship. When you *do not* allow Me to interrupt your day, then you are living for yourself and not My Kingdom. When you allow Me to interrupt *your* day, then you can interrupt *Me* at any time! I long for your passion for Me. A passionate relationship is one that is in communication throughout your day. Wisdom says: Those who communicate with Me throughout the day hear My secrets and personal thoughts to which others are not privy. To live with structure is wise and builds discipline, but be careful not to remain so structured that you no longer receive personal instruction from Me. Do not allow familiarity to creep into your relationship with Me. *A relationship is closest to failure when it becomes familiar!* Remember today that talking to you is the sweetest part of My day! You make My heart sing and My feet dance every day. Never underestimate how much I love talking to you!

The secret [of the wise counsel] of the Lord is for those who fear Him, And He will let them know His covenant and reveal to them [through His word] its [deep, inner] meaning.
— Psalm 25:14 AMP

See also: Psalm 85:8; Acts 22:14; Psalm 5:3

I need your heart to have the correct condition for your Kingdom position.

I want your heart to be passionate about serving others. The desire and longing of My heart is for you to not be concerned about titles or about being honored and treated like you are the most important, like a celebrity! I long for the genuine who will serve the "least of these" like they are celebrities! How I desire holy discipline and obedience from everyone. I AM filling Kingdom *positions* with those who are willing to be lowly in *condition* — those who become like children — trusting, humble, forgiving, and loving! Wisdom says: If you can serve a child as if that child were Me, then you are ready for your Kingdom position.

Listen, my beloved brothers and sisters: has not God chosen the poor of this world to be rich in faith and [as believers to be] heirs of the kingdom which He promised to those who love Him?

— JAMES 2:5 AMP

Therefore, whoever takes the lowly position of this child is the greatest in the kingdom of heaven.

— MATTHEW 18:4

SEE ALSO: MATTHEW 5:8; JOEL 2:13; PSALM 19:14

If you choose to be **insulted**, you then choose to be **assaulted** by the enemy!

To allow yourself to be insulted or hurt is very dangerous! This is an open door to an assault by the enemy of bitterness, unforgiveness, and hurt. When you become hurt by someone, release this to Me immediately and make a verbal declaration to forgive! This slams the door in the enemy's face and renders the enemy powerless in this attack. When the enemy uses people to hurt you, instead of becoming insulted, choose to decree a blessing upon them. This stops hell in its tracks! I AM not asking you to not have feelings, but I AM showing you how to stay free from this snare of the enemy! Hurt is like a cancer. It will consume you as it grows. Everyone is going to deal with hurt, and everyone will hurt someone. Allow My Love and grace to take over so you will walk away from this attack unharmed. Wisdom says: I have sent to you The Comforter. Allow Me to comfort you, wipe away every tear, take away every hurt, and carry this for you. *My Son, Jesus, was hurt in every way in your place so that you can live free from the dangers of hurt and insults!*

See also: Psalm 31:20; 1 Peter 2:23; Psalm 147:3 ; Psalm 31:4-15

Your words are weapons, not just expressions.

My Word is the Sword of the Spirit! My Word is alive and full of power — making it active, operative, energizing, and effective. It is sharper than any two-edged sword. When I speak, I AM not just communicating; I AM creating. *You* are created in My image and likeness. Because you speak with My Breath, *your words* carry My power to create. *Your words* are also active, operative, energizing, and effective in *your* life. They are weapons that carry the power of death and life! Because words are weapons, you must be respectful of their power. Treat them as if you are firing bullets when you speak, because you are! Remember, you will give an account for every bullet that you shoot. Faith-filled words carry the power to bless, heal, and create. Wisdom says: Because your words are weapons, there is no such thing as a powerless word. You are never just expressing yourself. You are releasing spirit forces that never die. *What you say today is one of the most serious things you will do today.*

Then God said, "Let us make mankind in our image, in our likeness, so that they may rule ..."
— Genesis 1:26

See also: Hebrews 4:12; Ephesians 6:17

You can never terminate an enemy that you tolerate.

To tolerate the enemy is to permit, or allow him to endure, without prohibiting or opposing him. This is a very dangerous thing to do! The thief comes only in order to steal, kill, and destroy. To tolerate the enemy is to invite thievery, death, and destruction. When you are tolerating the enemy, you are giving him permission to take over. To ignore the enemy and allow him to destroy you is giving him power and authority over you! My Son gave you power and authority over unclean spirits to drive them out. Wisdom says: Terminate the enemy. Put an end to his attacks by using your power and authority in My Holy Word. Do not tolerate an enemy that you can terminate. Never forget: The enemy is terrified of My Son in you.

And Jesus summoned to Him His twelve disciples and gave them power and authority over unclean spirits, to drive them out, and to cure all kinds of disease and all kinds of weakness and infirmity. — MATTHEW 10:1

*Listen carefully: I have given you authority [that you now possess] to tread on serpents and scorpions, and [the ability to exercise **authority**] over **all the power of the enemy** (Satan); and nothing will [in any way] harm you.*

— LUKE 10:19 AMP

SEE ALSO: PSALM 91:13; JOHN 10:10

267

Satan is the author of every disease and pain.

The enemy is an "evil genius." He studied the human body to figure out horrible ways to torment and make humans suffer. He enjoys torture, stealing, and killing. He is not satisfied without causing destruction! Since he has lost his position as heaven's worship leader, when someone screams in fear or pain, he receives this as worship and praise to himself! That is why horror films are so detestable in My eyes! There is no entertainment there; this is giving the enemy praise and the attention he so longs to receive. Hell is full of screaming. The enemy cannot hear it enough. He enjoys seeing humans in fear. Wisdom says: Fear not! When you are tempted to accept sickness, pain, or fear, remember it is never from Me. ***Choose to respond: "It is written..."*** Know that becasue you are in My Son, Jesus, the enemy has no claim on you. The enemy has nothing in common with you; there is nothing in you that belongs to him, and he has no power over you. Be alert, not afraid! When you keep yourself ***informed*** of My Word, the enemy cannot keep you ***infirmed*** with disease and pain. I AM with you always!

*I will not talk with you much longer, for the prince (evil genius, ruler) of the world is coming. And he has no claim on Me. [**He has nothing in common with Me**; there is nothing in Me that belongs to him, and he has no power over Me].* – JOHN 14:30 AMP

SEE ALSO: PSALM 27:3; ACTS 10:38; ZEPHANIAH 3:15

Worship is the warship of faith!

Worship is warfare. It confuses the enemy. When you worship Me, you keep *My* power before your eyes. You are reminding yourself that *I* can do what *you* cannot! When the Israelites went to war, they had a battle plan. They won many wars — not with weapons, and sometimes without even having to fight — but with worship! Wisdom says: When you worship, you are reminding yourself that the battle is not yours. **Victory is yours, but the battle is Mine.** Every time you worship, this gives Me an open door to move on your behalf. Worshiping Me destroys the enemy's strongholds! Worship Me and watch the enemy panic. Allow Me to use you as a warship against the enemy today. **When you worship Me in Spirit and Truth, I inhabit your praise — while the enemy is intimidated by your praise!**

I worship, giving thanks to you for all your loving-kindness and your faithfulness. — Psalm 138:2 TLB

For God destroys the mightiest warships with a breath of wind. — Psalm 48:7 TLB

I will worship you with deepest awe. — Psalm 5:7 TLB

See also: Psalm 99:5; Psalm 99:9

September 9

Men open doors in My Kingdom.

The physical realm is a reflection of the spiritual realm. In the physical realm, men open doors for women to show honor and respect. In the spiritual realm, I have anointed men to open doors in My Kingdom as I show them honor and respect. This is My design for men: Men are the reflection of My strength. I have infused them with the warrior Spirit of My Son, Jesus. They are as the Lion of Judah and rule their designated territories without fear. Men have inherited My brave heart that is stout for war. They never back down from the fight for righteousness and justice. I have crowned men with My Glory to champion the cause for life. Men have the strength of a warrior, but never abuse it. Men are as gentle as a whisper to those who need their protection. They always put the needs of others before their own. Oh, how I honor and respect this provider heart that beats within the chest of My men. Wisdom says: To honor the men I have created is to honor Me. They are just like Me — their Father. They have the heart of love and mercy first, and are only satisfied when there is justice. Today, open doors of love and peace, so that My Kingdom may manifest on earth as in heaven. Know this: Because creation was created for man, when My men praise Me, creation sings along.

270

SEE ALSO: PSALM 45:3-6; 1 PETER 3:7; EPHESIANS 5:25-32; COLOSSIANS 3:10; PSALM 66:4; GENESIS 1:26

If your relationship with Me is about yesterday, that is religion; if it is about today, that is revelaton!

*"If you keep My commandments [if you continue to obey My instructions], **you will abide in My Love and live on in it**, just as I have obeyed My Father's commandments and live on in His love."*

— JOHN 15: 10 AMP

The Bride abides in My Love! The Bride of My Son, Jesus, lives on My Love, as you live on food. When you have not eaten in a while, your belly "growls" or cries out for more. Did you know that your soul and spirit cry out or "growl" for more of Me? Just as a lion growls when it is hungry, your soul growls in hunger for The Lion of Judah! I will always answer the hungry growl for more of Me! Your hunger always gets My attention. Know this: **When you are content and satisfied and no longer hunger for Me, this always gets the enemy's attention!** To be satisfied in a relationship depicts loss of love. But to be hungry in a relationship depicts there is much passion! If your relationship with Me is about yesterday, then it is religion. If your relationship is all about Me today, that is a relationship built on revelation! True love is always seeking for more of Me! Wisdom says: Know that your hunger for Me is a guarantee that I will fill you. When I hear your hungry growl, I will fill you — and out of your belly will flow Rivers of Living Water!

271

SEE ALSO: MATTHEW 5:6; JOHN 15:1-11; LUKE 6:21; REVELATION 7:16

September 11

Could there be terrorists if everyone in My Kingdom refused to be terrified?

Would terrorists be able to operate effectively in this world if My people — the citizens of My Kingdom — were in their proper positions, using My authority? Terrorists may be able to inflict terror in the world, but they should not be able to affect My people. *A terrorist can only gain access where there is fear.* If you are fearful, then build up your faith in My Word about My protection. I AM your Protector, your Defense, and your High Tower. If you are fearful, it is because you are uncertain of My Love for you. Allow Me to tell you of My Love *for you* today! My Love is more powerful than fear! Wisdom says: My perfect Love drives out fear! Choose to walk in My Love and Truth — not in fear. Yes, the terrorists may be dangerous, but know this: *Just one of you is more dangerous than all the terrorists combined, when you are in Christ!* Cling to Me, and know that I AM mocking My enemies from My throne. *The terrorists are terrified of Me. When they see Me in you, they cower to My power.*

> *There is no fear in love. But perfect love drives out fear, because fear has to do with punishment. The one who fears is not made perfect in love.*
> — 1 John 4:18

See also: Psalm 91:5; Psalm 2:4; Psalm 59:9; 2 Timothy 1:7

Something shifts in the spirit and physical realms every time My Word is spoken or heard!

My Word is My Spirit and Breath of Life. Every time you encounter My Word, it impregnates your spirit, soul, and body, and empowers and strengthens you to change to look more like My Son, Jesus. When My Word is spoken, it looks as if a dynamite blast is exploded in the spirit realm. This is My "dunamis" power — My Life force that exists in My Word. This power changes, rearranges, and shifts everything to be in My order in the spirit and physical realms. Wisdom says: Visualize My Word as dynamite, blasting away every barrier and mountain blocking your path to victory! When you speak, hear, read, or meditate upon My Word, I unleash and release My power *in you* and *on your* circumstances.

*For the Word that God speaks is **alive and full of power** [making it active, operative, energizing, and effective]; it is sharper than any two-edged sword, penetrating to the dividing line of the **breath of life** (soul) and [the immortal] **spirit**, and of joints and marrow [of the deepest parts of our nature], exposing and sifting and analyzing and judging the very thoughts and purposes of the heart.*

— Hebrews 4:12 AMPC

See also: 1 Thessalonians 2:13; 1 John 5:1-5; John 6:63

Do you live each new day in My Glory or **your** glory days of the past?

Every new day is a *Glory day*! When you live in your old glory days, you have no vision or excitement about your present or future! Do not build shrines of your past! If you still dwell and celebrate in the glory days of your past, you are most likely not fulfilling your present assignment from Me. I have an assignment for every new day and every new season of your life for My Kingdom. *It is your choice: Are you going to meditate on all that you used to be in your glory days, or meditate on all that I AM when you carry My Glory every day?* Wisdom says: I will never retire you! You are valuable and irreplaceable to My Kingdom during every season of your life. Know this: With maturity comes value and wisdom. I can especially use you when you are in your "golden years." This is because you have been in My Refiner's fire longer, and I need your high gold content and quality! Do not meditate on your glory days that are long gone. Instead, dedicate new days filled with My Glory!

Why do you brag of your once-famous strength?
You're a broken-down has-been, a castoff
Who fondles his trophies and dreams of glory days
and vainly thinks, 'No one can lay a hand on me.'
Well, think again.
— Jeremiah 49:3-5 MSG

See also: Psalm 148:13; Psalm 145:2;
Proverbs 4:18; 2 Peter 3:18

To love yourself as I love you is spiritual warfare!

To love your neighbor as yourself is strategy and warfare. To love yourself is to love Me! I made you and I AM dwelling in you. To hate what I made gives the enemy a foothold. Most diseases stem from self-hatred. To hate anything is to give the enemy a voice! When I created you, I said, "It is good!" I did not just say this about Adam; since you were in the lineage of Adam, I also said this about *you*! The enemy panics when you choose to love yourself. He uses self-hatred as a weapon so you will destroy yourself. Hate destroys, but love is spiritual warfare that stops the destruction of self-hatred in its tracks. You must defeat the trap of self-hatred. You will never win a war when you have the stance of any hatred. Wisdom says: You cannot love a neighbor that you do not know without loving yourself that you do know! When you hate yourself, you are hating what I made! Love yourself as I love you. The enemy is brought to a screeching halt when you choose to love yourself. To love yourself is to please Me.

For the entire law is fulfilled in keeping this one command: "Love your neighbor as yourself." —GALATIANS 5:14

SEE ALSO: MARK 12:33; JAMES 2:8

September 15

Hell is creation out of order.

*Now in putting everything in subjection to man, **He
left nothing outside [of man's] control.***

— HEBREWS 2:7-8 AMPC

When I created mankind in My image, I blessed
him to be fruitful, but also to subdue the earth
and have power and authority over everything I
created. Mankind was created to have rule and
dominion over the angels, including the enemy
and other fallen angels. *I designed My creation in
order.* After Adam committed treason, I sent My
Son to redeem mankind. But for those who refuse
and reject the loving sacrifice of My Son, they will
live for eternity in hell, where the enemy and his
demons have power, authority, dominion, and
rule over mankind — the same mankind who was
created a little lower than Me, to rule over them!
It was never My original plan for the enemy to
rule over mankind. *This is creation out of order!*
But for those who accept My Son's sacrifice and
become reborn into His likeness, My Son gives
them all power and authority over the enemy.
This is My creation restored to order! Wisdom
says: Take dominion and walk in the authority I
have given you today. *Remember, the enemy has
already been sentenced by Christ, and you have
already been seated with Christ.*

276

*SEE ALSO: PSALM 8:5; MATTHEW 10:1; COLOSSIANS 1:13; MATTHEW 28:18;
EPHESIANS 2:6; REVELATION 1:18; 2 TIMOTHY 2:12*

If you fear man, you make man your enemy and not your equal.

There is no such thing as freedom for the person who is a slave to the opinions of others. If ***you*** surrender to man, or the opinions of man, ***you*** make ***yourself*** a slave — and you will not experience My true Freedom and Peace. Fear of man changes My design of you. It changes you into a person I do not recognize. If you fear people, or what people may think of you, they become your enemy instead of your equal. This is how competing with each other thrives. Fear makes enemies. When you fear ***Me***, with reverence and love, then everyone becomes your equal! Wisdom says: Do not surrender to man, or to the opinions of man, or you make yourself a slave to man. When you love and fear only Me, you will have the peace to be the person I have designed you to be.

So we may boldly say: "The Lord is my helper; I will not fear. What can man do to me?"

— Hebrews 13:6 NKJV

In God, whose word I praise; In God I have put my trust; I shall not fear. What can mere man do to me?

— Psalm 56:4 AMP

277

See also: James 2:1; Psalm 118:6

Only those who are expecting will give birth.

Whatever you expect or are expecting, you will give birth to! If you expect sickness, you will be susceptible to sickness. If you are expecting failure, then you give failure the ability to manifest in your mind. My Son defeated sickness and failure. *Expect to be made whole and complete!* Notice how this occurs when a woman is pregnant; she is *expecting*. When you are expecting, life has been conceived. Whether for something good or bad, you have tapped into My Spiritual Law. Every time you expect something, you enact the Law of My Spirit of Life! The only way that you will not give birth to what you are expecting is to miscarry — to no longer carry — the expectation. How do you kill what you are expecting? You kill with your words, with fear, and with unbelief. Wisdom says: When you are expecting a miracle, you are already pregnant with it. You just might not be showing yet! Know this: You will conceive what you believe! Allow the power of My Word to conceive new life, faith, hope, and love in you today!

Hope deferred makes the heart sick, but a longing fulfilled is a tree of life.

— PROVERBS 13:12

See also: ROMANS 8:19; DANIEL 12:12; LUKE 3:15; LUKE 21:26; HEBREWS 10:27

Walk in divine love, and Divine Love will walk in you!

Love is the key that opens many doors in My Kingdom. ***Know this: When you are a true brother or sister in Christ, you can witness someone at their worst, yet still see them at their best.*** When you love even the unlovable and unlovely, I will always be close at hand with much reward. My Love never fails you. The more you love with My Love, the closer I walk with you. Too many are trying to walk in love that is manufactured in stirred-up emotions. This isn't love that never fails; this is emotion that will always fail you. Wisdom says: When you walk in My Divine Love, you will never be alone, because I AM always with you! When your response to everyone is love, you will walk in My power, not just My Love. When you allow My Love to shine ***through*** you, I make sure My Love shines ***to*** you. Because Love never fails, My Love for you never fails.

For over all the glory shall be a canopy (a defense of divine love and protection). — Isaiah 4:5 AMP

Walk in the way of love, just as Christ loved us and gave himself up for us. — Ephesians 5:2

Love never fails. — 1 Corinthians 13:8

SEE ALSO: *2 John 1:6; Song of Solomon 8:6; 1 Peter 2:17*

279

If your identity is being stolen, then you are not in a group, you are in a prison!

I have created you with uniqueness and distinction. You are My masterpiece. This is what makes you so valuable. It is painful for Me to watch when the enemy works through other people to strip you of what makes you priceless. ***This is never from Me.*** Those threatened by your individuality are the ones who are insecure in theirs. If you find yourself in a group, family, or a church that tries to take away your individuality, you are not among friends or family; you are in prison. In prisons everyone is required to be the same. Your name and identity are taken and you are treated as a group, not an individual. Do not stay among those who cannot value your authenticity! Love them while you leave them. Wisdom says: Find those who celebrate you like I do, then surround yourself with them. I call it a privilege to be around you. You are created for My palace, where I AM privileged to be with you, never a prison.

Bring my life out of prison, that I may confess, praise, and give thanks to Your name.
— Psalm 142:7 AMPC

Make a careful exploration of who you are and the work you have been given, and then sink yourself into that.
— Galatians 6:4-5 MSG

See also: Matthew 23:12; Psalm 146:7-8; 2 Kings 25:29

If you speak slander towards someone, you have become an accuser of the Brethren.

If you slander someone, this is very serious to Me. To slander or accuse is putting a person on trial without representation or the ability to defend themselves. The person slandering becomes the judge and jury. It does not even matter if the person is guilty or innocent of the accusations; slander is about ruining reputations! The spirit of slander works hard to get others involved and in ***agreement*** with its lies, inflicting a wound that will not easily heal. This malicious intent is to isolate the victim so they do not know whom to trust. But, in actuality, if you are slandering or agreeing with slander of someone, you are isolating yourself from My blessing and favor, and have become an accuser of the Brethren. Wisdom says: Refuse to be a pawn in the enemy's schemes to ruin someone's reputation. If you have been hurt, know that I AM your Peace, Comforter, and Vindicator. I AM even a Redeemer of reputations! I will be your Shield and will shelter you from every hurt and lie.

Believers, do not speak against or slander one another.

— JAMES 4:11 AMP

SEE ALSO: *PSALM 57:3; PROVERBS 26:22;*
ECCLESIASTES 10:11; TITUS 3:2; MATTHEW 15:17-18

September 21

If you are casual with warfare, you will be a casualty of war.

You must **enforce** My Word. If you are not compelled to fight for the Life that is already yours in My Kingdom, you will become a casualty of war! You cannot be complacent when it comes to enforcing your rightful inheritance of victory in Me. Even though your enemy has already been defeated, he is very diligent in his strategies to deceive you. You cannot be casual with an enemy who is very persistent against you in stealing, killing, and destroying what is yours. Against My Word of Truth, he has no defense! My Son, Jesus, completely stripped him of all power and authority and gave this to you to enforce My Word against the enemy. Wisdom says: Submit yourself completely to My Word. Speak My Word of Life, and **do** what My Word says. When the enemy is persistent, be even more consistent with the pressure of My power in My Word. **You leave the enemy destitute every time you execute My Word.**

Submit yourselves, then, to God. Resist the devil, and he will flee from you.

— James 4:7

See also: 1 Timothy 1:18-19; Proverbs 24:5-6; Ephesians 6:12

Why would you choose to live a **meaningless** life for yourself when you could live a **meaningful** life for Me?

The sooner you realize that your life is all about *Me*, the sooner you will *live* your life. There are so many people who are wasting their lives on things that are without merit. Some people deal with depression and oppression because they are not fulfilling their destiny — the purpose for which I called them. When you live for Me, and not for yourself, you will find your purpose with joy! People cannot be truly happy and fulfilled unless they are doing what *I* created them to do! Wisdom says: Cry out to Me for a life that has purpose and direction. Ask and I will lead you to the purpose that I have custom designed just for you. You cannot really live life until your life is lived for Me!

Remain in Me, and I [will remain] in you. Just as no branch can bear fruit by itself without remaining in the vine, neither can you [bear fruit, producing evidence of your faith] unless you remain in Me.

— JOHN 15:4 AMP

SEE ALSO: PROVERBS 5:21; EPHESIANS 5:8; ROMANS 14:8-9; 1 JOHN 5:12

To the degree you treasure mankind is the degree that you treasure Me!

~

Those who say that they love Me, but hate a brother or sister, are liars! How can someone love Me and hate someone who looks just like Me? To reject your brother or sister is to reject Me. This hurts My heart to the uttermost depths. When you move closer to Me, the closer you feel toward those I love. There is no justification for discord and hatred in My family. I have given you access to My Love, but you must choose to pursue it. I have poured My Love into your heart by My Holy Spirit to be used to love one another supernaturally. Do not let My Love lay dormant in your heart. Wisdom says: If you really want to please Me and serve Me, then please and serve My children! When you choose to love those you see, then truly are you loving Me!

Whoever claims to love God yet hates a brother or sister is a liar. For whoever does not love their brother and sister, whom they have seen, cannot love God, whom they have not seen. — 1 JOHN 4:20

SEE ALSO: *1 JOHN 5:1; 1 JOHN 3:10; JOHN 13:34-35; MATTHEW 6:21; ROMANS 5:5*

September 24

If you long for your past more than your future, it is because you cannot see Me in your future!

When you have been through hard trials, it can be difficult at times to be excited about your future. It takes childlike faith to see Me in your future. Just as your earthly father and mother watched you take your first steps as a child, with their outstretched arms toward you, and you bravely fell into their arms of love, I have My arms outstretched to you. I will catch you if you fall, and I will clap and celebrate with you as you again take your steps of faith! You are entirely loved and safe with Me! Take a new step with Me every day. Do not allow hard times to rob you of the gift of today. Your future will be amazing because your future has Me in it! Wisdom says: I challenge you to raise your hands to Me again in hope and faith to overcome the sense of loss. Take a step towards Me with faith that I AM always with you. Listen today as I assure you that you are brave and full of courage. Even though you may have lost much, know for certain that you are loved much. I will always restore.

Have I not commanded you? "Be strong and of good courage; do not be afraid, nor be dismayed, for the Lord your God is with you wherever you go."
JOSHUA 1:9 NKJV

SEE ALSO: JAMES 1:2–4; 1 PETER 1:6; ROMANS 5:2; ROMANS 15:13

285

September 25

You will love life when you understand and know that **Life** loves you!

It is impossible to love your life unless you understand how intensely *My Love burns for you.* How can you appreciate life unless you understand that you were birthed with purpose and greatness? Nothing about you has happened by chance! With much planned precision, you were My choice. I have positioned you in this exact location and in this chosen generation. I placed you specifically where I need you right now so that you can impact the world for My Kingdom. Wisdom says: You will really begin to love your life, and it will take on new meaning daily, when you know and comprehend that My Love for you is not because I *need* you, it is because I *know* you. I AM Life! I love you. I AM living in you. My Love for you is fierce.

> *For God so loved the world that he gave his one and only Son, that whoever believes in him shall not perish but have eternal life.*
> — John 3:16

> *Jesus said to her, "I am the resurrection and the life. The one who believes in me will live, even though they die."*
> — John 11:25

286

See also: John 15:13; John 10:11; Psalm 34:12-13

Be cautious not to desire a word over My Word!

I have gifted and graced My Body with spiritual gifts for edification and direction. I AM revealing Myself and the future with prophetic words of knowledge, wisdom, and prophecy. But My Holy Word, Jesus, can never be looked upon as an equal to these gifts. My Word is infallible, but My gifts flow through flawed people. I honor My Word even above My name. Be sure to honor My Word with the same measure. My Word does not just contain instructions; it is the conception of My Life that is birthed in you every time you read It! Wisdom says: My Word is alive and is a prophetic word every time you need one. If you **need** a word today, then **read** My Word today!

Thou hast magnified thy word above all thy name.
— Psalm 138:2 KJV

For with God nothing is ever impossible and no word from God shall be without power or impossible of fulfillment.
— Luke 1:37 AMP

The words I have spoken to you — they are full of the Spirit and life.
— John 6:63

See also: Hebrews 4:12; Matthew 4:4; John 1:1; John 14:24

Embrace every race.

Every human is in a race for My Glorious Prize, Jesus Christ! *Are you running your race with love, or ruining your race with hate?* Because I AM Love, I love every race that I fashioned as The Master Jeweler! Since I created you from the dust of the earth — and the earth has many shades of color — your skin color represents all the colors and shades of the earth. This proves that you are created from the earth as My Precious Stones that are only formed deep under the ground. From the exquisite collaborations of these shades from the earth, I created the colors that I wanted for the jewels in My crown! *Your skin tones are My gem stones!* From the beautiful black to the umber and sienna brown skin tones, I created you as My black jasper and sardonyx gem stones. From the rich red tones found in clay, you are My carnelian gem stones. From the delicate yellow hues to the alabaster white skin tones, you are My chalcedony (white agate) and yellow chrysolite gem stones. Notice that these are some of the twelve precious stones that decorate the foundations of the city walls of The New Jerusalem! This is why the enemy strives to build walls between you so you will not represent My beautiful wall! Wisdom says: If you are being divisive among the races, then you are an instrument of hate in the enemy's hand! *I ask you with tears streaming down My face: Can you see My family in every race?* Can you see your family or *kin* even through the color of someone's s*kin*? I command you to embrace every race!

SEE ALSO: GENESIS 2:7; 1 CORINTHIANS 9:24; GALATIANS 3:28; HEBREWS 12:1; PHILIPPIANS 3:14; GALATIANS 5:7; GENESIS 1:26

You are a human **being** — what?

Have you noticed that you are called a human being? But I did not complete the sentence. I left it blank for you to fill. Are you a human *being a blessing*? Are you a human *being a curse*? Are you a human *being successful* or limited? Are you a human *being obedient* or disobedient? Are you a human *being Christ-like*? I have loved you so much that I let you choose how to fill in the blank. It is your choice, not Mine! Only *you* decide how you define yourself as a human being. Choose to be a human being full of life and blessing, instead of death and cursing. Wisdom says: My perfect Love for you always comes with choices. I would not be Love if I did not give you the free will in every decision about your life. To Me, you are priceless and can never be replaced by someone else. *You are a human being deeply cherished and treasured by Me — your heavenly Father!*

> *I have set before you life and death, the blessings and the curses; therefore **choose** life.*
> — Deuteronomy 30:19 AMPC

> *Who is the man who fears the Lord [with awe-inspired reverence and worships Him with submissive wonder]? He will teach him [through His word] in the way he should choose.*
> — Psalm 25:12 AMP

See also: Psalm 8:4; Romans 14:22

If you have seen another human, then you have seen a glimpse of Me!

> *But Moses protested, "If I go to the people of Israel and tell them, 'The God of your ancestors has sent me to you,' they will ask me, 'What is his name?' Then what should I tell them?" God replied to Moses, "I AM who I AM. Say this to the people of Israel: I am has sent me to you."*
>
> — Exodus 3:13-14 NLT

I gave part of Myself to Adam (add AM) as well as to every person! Inside of every human you can see a glimpse of Me. You are not only made in My image, but I have also hidden traits of Myself in you. This is much like how you can see similarities and attributes of parents in their children. I have placed in you My beauty, courage, and love. Likewise, you can see Me in My children. It takes a countless number of people to see the full expression of Me! This is one of the reasons why the enemy snatches and kills babies in abortion before they can ever be seen. This prevents the world from seeing the full expression of Me in My children. Wisdom says: Be careful to treat every person with honor and dignity — as you would treat Me! Every time you encounter another human, you are seeing a glimpse of Me.

> *Then God said, "Let us make mankind in our image, in our likeness."*
>
> — Genesis 1:26

See also: Mark 12:30-31; Ephesians 5:1

Giants never nibble!
Neither do spiritual giants!

Giants are always feasting! Giants eat to sustain their size. They could not grow to that stature without a tremendous amount of nutrients. When the Israelites encountered the size of the food that the giants were eating, two men were needed to carry one cluster of grapes. Well, spiritual giants never nibble either! Their spiritual intake is enormous and out of the ordinary. They did not become spiritual giants by chance, but by their choices of priorities! Wisdom says: Anyone can be a spiritual giant — but no one can become a giant by just snacking on My Word and nibbling on prayer snacks and appetizers! Spiritual giants are sustained by the amount or size of their intake. You will only grow to the amount of My Word you are consuming.

"There we saw the giants (the descendants of Anak came from the giants); and we were like grasshoppers in our own sight, and so we were in their sight."
— NUMBERS 13:33 NKJV

Man shall not live and be upheld and sustained by bread alone, but by every word that comes forth from the mouth of God.
— MATTHEW 4:4 AMPC

291

SEE ALSO: 1 THESSALONIANS 2:13; 1 JOHN 2:14

Faith will always reveal; fear will always conceal.

Faith reveals Light and Truth. It reveals My Kingdom, plainly and clearly. When I reveal, I make things that once were hidden able to be seen in the clear view of My Light! I reveal Myself to you through faith. Faith makes things known through My divine inspiration, while fear hides or conceals My Truth. When something is concealed, it is hidden from sight, which prevents recognition of My Truth. Fear and deception can only survive in darkness and trickery. Fear is the likeness of the enemy; he is darkness. Faith is the likeness of My Son, Jesus. He is Light! Wisdom says: *If something is being concealed, know this: It is never from Me. I AM constantly revealing Myself to you.* I long for you to know Me, as I know you.

Jesus replied, "Blessed are you, Simon son of Jonah, for this was not revealed to you by flesh and blood, but by my Father in heaven."
— Matthew 16:17

For in it the righteousness of God is revealed from faith for faith, as it is written, "The righteous shall live by faith."
— Romans 1:17 esv

See also: Matthew 10:26; 1 Peter 1:5-8; Galatians 3:23; Hebrews 4:13

If you retaliate when hurt, you participate in hurt.

When someone is being hurtful to you, this *never* gives you license to retaliate in the same way! So many of My children believe that if hurt is done to them, it gives them the *right* to return similar behavior. **Know this**: You *will* reap what you sow — just as the one who hurt you will! This is the Law of My Kingdom. It has nothing to do with what another has done or sown into your life. There is no clause in My Law that says you will reap what you sow, "except if someone hurts you"! This excuse has been used in My Body too often as a way to justify bad behavior! Wisdom says: Allow *Me* to vindicate you or settle the score! Do not take matters into your own hands. You simply cannot afford the consequence of violating My Law. Instead of retaliating, choose love. *Love not only stops battles, but ends wars!*

Do not be deceived: God cannot be mocked. A man reaps what he sows. — Galatians 6:7

When he was insulted, he didn't retaliate with insults; when he suffered, he didn't threaten, but handed them over to him who judges justly. — 1 Peter 2:23 CJB

See also: 1 Peter 3:9; Matthew 5:43-44

*O*ctober *3*

You will never change the world for Me if you are living a life of mediocrity.

~~⌒~~

You must leave the average to achieve the exceptional! Everything Jesus did was extraordinary! The reason is because He did everything with His whole heart, and with the help of My Holy Spirit. His Excellence was demonstrated in how He longed to be just like Me, His Father! He was completely surrendered to Me, and totally filled with My Love and Compassion. This is power! I desire for you also to live with such passion! My plan for your destiny contains no hint of mediocrity. A mediocre life is passionless and powerless! A life of mediocrity is one not surrendered to the power and authority of My Holy Spirit. Has your enemy deceived you into thinking that you have reached as high as you can go? ***Remember, you can be regarded as a success in many areas and still live a life of mediocrity. I hate lukewarm!*** Wisdom says: How can you change the world if there is mediocrity in your life? Today, allow My Ideal Servant, Jesus, to be reproduced in you!

> *"This [peace, righteousness, security, triumph over opposition] is the heritage of the servants of the Lord [those in whom the **ideal Servant of the Lord is reproduced**]. This is the righteousness or the vindication which they obtain from Me [this is that which I impart to them as their justification], "says the Lord.*
> — Isaiah 54:17 AMP

294

See also: Revelation 3:16; Psalm 8:1

Live a life of conviction, not contradiction.

Living a holy life of conviction is what I earnestly desire of My Body! Living with conviction is the state of being absolutely convinced that I AM Trustworthy. It means being of strong persuasion or belief that I AM Faithful and that My Word is Truth. If you are truly a person of faith, and you live by faith, you live with conviction! But there are many who live a life of contradiction! Although they claim conviction and faith, their actions often contradict both. They are double-minded and unstable in all their ways. I cannot violate My Kingdom Laws for them. Because of their unbelief, although I desire to answer their prayers, they have no faith on which I can move. Wisdom says: I need a Body, with strong faith, that will demonstrate a life lived with conviction, not contradiction.

The faith which you have, have as your own conviction before God. Happy is he who does not condemn himself in what he approves. — ROMANS 14:22 NASB

SEE ALSO: HEBREWS 11:1; JAMES 1:6-8; 1 TIMOTHY 6:20

Never be your own impostor!

Be the authentic *you* that I created. I *only* give you license to be *you*. You do not have license to be anyone else. That would be an impostor or counterfeit! An impostor is a person who deceives others by pretending to be someone else. This is actually against worldly law. It also goes against My Laws of creation! No one has the right to say who you are and who you are not — except Me. When you try to get your identity through another person's opinions, it is the same as if you have a fake identification made. On a fake ID, the only thing that looks the same is the picture. Otherwise, the person's actual identity has been altered. Wisdom says: You will never be successful at being someone else. You will only be successful at being yourself. Know today: When you try to be just like someone else, you are not only cheating Me and My world out of the gift of you, but you are also stealing someone else's identity!

> *But evil men and impostors will proceed from bad to worse, deceiving and being deceived.*
> — 2 Timothy 3:13 NASB

> *Be perfect, therefore, as your heavenly Father is perfect.*
> — Matthew 5:48

To be able to forgive means that you are positioned with Me.

If you forgive the sins of anyone, they are forgiven; if you retain the sins of anyone, they are retained.

— John 20:23 AMP

To be able to forgive shows how high you are in position next to Me. You are a joint heir with Christ. You are seated with My Son in heavenly places. No, this does not mean that you are greater and mightier than I AM. But to have the power to forgive sins reveals your identity! ***Because you have received and are led and directed by My Holy Spirit, I give you this great privilege***: If you forgive anyone's sins, they are forgiven; if you retain anyone's sins, they are retained. Because you are My reborn child, created in the likeness of My dear Son, you are privileged with My gift of forgiving those who hurt you — just as I forgive you when you hurt Me. Wisdom says: Only those who are made in My image can forgive a sin. Forgiveness stops the enemy on many levels and closes many doors to his wickedness. Evil can only thrive where sin and hate abide. Every time that you forgive, you stop hell in its tracks and advance My Kingdom's territory. Forgive and frustrate the kingdom of darkness today!

See also: Luke 5:21; Romans 8:17

October 7

If you don't learn something today, you are not paying attention.

I never waste time — not yours or Mine! I AM constantly loading your day with My instructions, warnings, signs, lessons — and benefits! Are you listening to My voice? Every Word I speak is designed for your advantage. I AM your Great Father. Because of My intense Love for you, I teach and correct. If you are not paying attention, you will miss My lessons for the day. So listen and be alert! Only when you give Me your time, will you learn the lesson I have planned. Every day I create for you is birthed with purpose. Wisdom says: It is to your advantage to glean every lesson from each new day. You will need this knowledge and Wisdom to take your next step tomorrow!

Nevertheless, my Lord God, please pay attention to my prayer for mercy. Listen to my cry for help as I pray to you today. — 1 KINGS 8:28 GW

Blessed be the Lord, Who daily loads us with benefits. — PSALM 68:19

Remember today all the great things the Lord your God has done to teach you. It was you, not your children, who saw those things happen and lived through them. You saw how great he is. You saw how strong he is, and you saw the powerful things he does. — DEUTERONOMY 11:2 ERV

298

SEE ALSO: 2 PETER 1:19; MARK 4:24

You are usable in My Kingdom if you are ready for persecution!

More fall away from Me because of persecution than for any other reason. Do you not realize the rewards of persecution? If you could see what I have planned for those in heaven who have been persecuted for My sake, you would greatly rejoice when people persecute you because of Me. ***Consider it an honor to be known and hated for My name's sake!*** So many want the rights that come with My name, but not the persecution! If you are not suffering persecution, then you are not saying enough about Me to the world. Wisdom says: You are never to prosecute those who persecute you for My name's sake! Vengeance is Mine! I will defend My Own. Love is the only answer for persecution! When you are persecuted, it is just a reminder that you are not of this world, but you are a beloved citizen of heaven. ***The persecuted are always promoted!***

"Blessed are you when people insult you, persecute you and falsely say all kinds of evil against you because of me. Rejoice and be glad, because great is your reward in heaven, for in the same way they persecuted the prophets who were before you."
— Matthew 5:11-12

Therefore, among God's churches we boast about your perseverance and faith in all the persecutions and trials you are enduring.
— 2 Thessalonians 1:4

Just because you are **not failing** does not mean that you are succeeding.

Being successful in My Kingdom means that you are doing what I predestined for your life. Just because you are not failing, and you may even be having some success, does not mean that you are successful in My Kingdom! If you are out of position, the entire Body suffers because of it. So many stop before they reach what they were created to do because they get comfortable with their minimal success. I consider a successful life to be one marked with a no-quit attitude and with unwavering obedience to My plan for your life. Wisdom says: Pray about your position and role in My Kingdom. Many are just living what they think is a successful life, yet they will be very astonished when they see the plans I had for their life that were never pursued or fulfilled. Do not resign to your limited idea of success, but submit to My extravagant design of your success. When you compromise your destiny, you compromise My Kingdom.

David acted wisely in all his ways and succeeded, and the Lord was with him. —1 Samuel 18:14 AMPC

"For I know the plans I have for you," declares the Lord, "plans to prosper you and not to harm you, plans to give you hope and a future." — Jeremiah 29:11

See also: Ephesians 2:10; 1 Corinthians 12:25-26

Do you want to **impress** the world, or **change** the world?

The world is waiting on you to become someone who *inspires* them to *want* to be close to Me! The closer you become to Me, the more people will want to be around you. The more you act like Me, the more the world will seek Me. Do *you* seek to draw people to My Kingdom, or seek to draw people to yourself? Has your ministry become your identity? If so, then your ministry is no longer about Me; it is about you! There are parts of My Body that need more genuine teachers than just talkers! I desire for My prophets to make more progress. Some in My Body seem to be trying to *impress* the world more than *change* the world. Wisdom says: Cry out for My Presence. With repentance and prayer comes My River of Holiness to cleanse you and My Body with genuine and pure motives and agendas for My Kingdom. When you increase in holiness, you increase in wholeness — and holiness will increase your audience with Me, not just your audience with the world!

> *Make every effort to live in peace with everyone and to be holy; without holiness no one will see the Lord.*
> — HEBREWS 12:14

> *When Christ appears, we shall be like him, for we shall see him as he is.*
> — 1 JOHN 3:2

SEE ALSO: EPHESIANS 4:24

Pride makes justifications; humility makes transformations!

Those who make justifications when I discipline are operating in pride! To justify is to make excuses for your behavior. You will never become the person I designed for you to become without welcoming My corrections. ***When I correct you, it is never about punishment; it is because I see potential!*** My child, I AM demonstrating My mercy and love when I correct you. The degree to which you heed My correction is the degree to which you will be favored with higher positions in My Kingdom. The humble of heart are quick to make transformations because My call on their life is to one that is filled with integrity. Wisdom says: Promotion is reserved for the humble; the prideful will always stumble. When corrections come, be quick to make changes. I will honor you with My Wisdom and the secrets of My heart for welcoming My holy discipline.

Pride goes before destruction, And a haughty spirit before a fall.

— Proverbs 16:18 nkjv

For the Lord takes delight in his people; he crowns the humble with salvation.

— Psalm 149:4

See also: Psalm 147:6; Proverbs 22:4; Psalm 18:27; Proverbs 11:2; Proverbs 8:13

A winner is **not defined** by a 'no,' but is **refined** by **Who** they know — Me!

A winner is one who can hear a yes in every *no*! Those who are bound for success will not allow a *no* to interrupt My dream and destiny for their life. They will use the *no* to test their faith and allow their faith to mature and grow. I cannot work with someone who keeps quitting. A *no* is just someone's opinion! The One you know is ever working to help you not only ignore the *no* coming from the enemy, but to help you persevere and to carry you into the fulfillment of My destiny for you. Wisdom says: Today, do not quit because of discouragement; keep moving with My encouragement! Take every thought captive! Let the *no* catapult you, not stop you! ***Winners make adversity their servant!***

Count it all joy when you fall into various trials, knowing that the testing of your faith produces patience. But let patience have its perfect work, that you may be perfect and complete, lacking nothing. — JAMES 1:2-4 NKJV

SEE ALSO: 2 CORINTHIANS 13:5; REVELATION 2:10; ROMANS 8:28; 1 CORINTHIANS 8:3

If a person believes that something is true, not even My Word can talk that person out of what they believe.

Nothing can alter the course of a life more than when a person's mind is rigidly made up to believe something is truth. Not even the highest Truth, My Word, can change the course of that person's life. Not even I, your Creator, will talk someone out of what that person believes. As a person thinks in his heart, so is he. I watch people *believe* themselves into hell — even though this hurts Me more than I can express. But *My Love* allows every person the free will to choose. What do *you believe* about yourself today? This question is so very important! Answering this question can uncover and reveal many issues. What you believe you deserve will be a self-fulfilling prophecy. Wisdom says: Choose to believe My Word over anything else. Believe that I love you with all My heart. Your worth is so high that I AM the Only One who could pay the price for you. Never doubt My Love for you. I honor My Word above My name.

For as he thinks in his heart, so is he. — PROVERBS 23:7

You have magnified Your word above all Your name! — PSALM 138:2

Make them holy by your truth. — JOHN 17:17 NLT

SEE ALSO: *2 TIMOTHY 2:15*

The name of Jesus is the key that unlocks My heart.

When I give someone a new name, it is for the purpose of calling forth and unlocking that person's identity and destiny. Look at Abram/Abraham, Jacob/Israel, and Saul/Paul. Consider this: In My Word, Jesus is the Bride*groom*, demonstrating how He sees Himself already One with the Bride. The bride takes the groom's name and has access to everything that is his. And the groom combines his name, becoming the bridegroom, and has access to everything that is hers. Her heart. Her time. Her resources. Her life! I have given *you* a new name — My Son's name, Jesus. Wisdom says: The name of My beloved Son, Jesus, is the key that unlocks My heart. With His name, you have access to My heart as well as My throne. Every time I hear His name, I extend My scepter to you. This is why I said I will give anything you ask in His name. Use His name with the utmost respect. Remember that His name is so powerful that chains unlock and fall every time His name is heard. Consider how blessed and loved you are to have lips and a mouth to speak the name of the Son of My Love.

In that day you will no longer ask me anything. Very truly I tell you, my Father will give you whatever you ask in my name.
— JOHN 16:23

SEE ALSO: GENESIS 32:28; GENESIS 17:5

*O*ctober *15*

Contentment in every season is a gift from Me.

Some have lost their ability to be content with the blessings I have bestowed on them. Ask Me to give you the Spirit of Peace that grants you power to be content. This never means to stop asking and seeking My blessings. It means that I will give you the ability to enjoy and be satisfied with what you already have. Being blessed with prosperity is part of My Covenant with you, but prosperity should never be your focus! Just because you have needs does not mean that you cannot enjoy life and be content during your waiting process. Many cannot enjoy all that they have because they focus on what they do not have! Being content is having your eyes on *Me* and not on *things*! Seek Me today to see if you have fallen into the trap of being discontent. Wisdom says: Be content in every season — with a grateful heart. This is strategy for staying free from the snares of the enemy.

I have learned to be content whatever the circumstances.
— Philippians 4:11

But I have stilled and quieted my soul; like a weaned child with its mother, like a weaned child is my soul within me.
— Psalm 131:2

See also: Proverbs 19:23

Division is a hate crime.

I cannot dwell where there is division! It is not that I **will** not; the issue is that I **can** not! Division breeds contention, rivalry, disharmony, and all sorts of evil and vile practices. Where there is division, there is much deception. You are powerless when you are divided. Even My creation knows this well! Many of My animals live in packs, herds, and prides. Their survival depends on dwelling in unity — as does yours! To divide is a hate crime that you commit against yourself, other people, and against My Kingdom! I say, "Any kingdom divided against itself will be ruined, and *a house divided against itself will fall.*" *You are My house!* Division will affect you, as well as everyone around you, and My Kingdom. My Word promises that when you divide, *you will fall!* Wisdom says: *Love your differences, not loathe your differences!* Love not only stops hate crimes, but it stops wars. Not only will the united stand, but those who unite will have access to My heart. Those who have access to My heart have access to My throne.

*It is these who are [agitators] setting up distinctions and **causing divisions** — merely sensual [creatures, carnal, worldly-minded people], devoid of the [Holy] Spirit and destitute of any higher spiritual life.*

— JUDE 1:19 AMPC

SEE ALSO: 1 CORINTHIANS 3:3; JAMES 3:14-18; LUKE 11:17; ROMANS 16:17; EPHESIANS 4:13; MATTHEW 12:25

*O*ctober *17*

Complaining gives the enemy access to your heart and cuts off your access to My heart.

Complaints hurt My ears! They are personal attacks on My great ability to care for you. When complaining, you voice words of death instead of blessing the situation with My Words of Life. When you complain, you use your own mouth to prophesy a curse on yourself, and you give the enemy an open the door to steal, kill, and destroy you! When the Israelites complained about Me, their complaints are exactly what they received. They complained about the possibility of dying in the desert, and they received exactly what they said without seeing fulfillment of My promise. Complaining sets the law of destruction on a collision course with My plan for your life! When you complain, you give the enemy access to your heart, and cut off your access to My heart. Wisdom says: Speak My Words of Life today and bless your situation! When you speak Life, you bless your day. When you complain, you curse your day.

But they sulked and complained in their tents;
They did not listen to the voice of the Lord.
— PSALM 106:25 AMP

SEE ALSO: EXODUS 16:8-10 AMP

Faith makes love work;
fear makes you love works.

My Word says that faith works by love. This means that you will never have faith in Me unless you *know* that you are loved by Me! The more you believe you are loved, the greater your faith will be. It hurts Me as it would hurt you as a parent if your children did not believe they were loved. Fear implies that I do not genuinely love you, so you believe you must impress Me or earn My Love by working for it. This is a picture of the Pharisees. They loved works because it gave them confidence in *themselves* instead of in their personal relationship with Me. I had always longed for a relationship with them. Works blinded them and they could not even recognize Me; *neither can today's Pharisees tolerate someone who has an intimate relationship with Me.* Wisdom says: Do not use your works to get My affection and attention. Fear and works will always strip you of any personal relationship with Me! Today, trust that you never have to work for My True Love.

*For in Christ Jesus neither circumcision nor uncircumcision avails anything, but **faith working through love.***
— GALATIANS 5:6 AMPC

For as the body without the spirit is dead, so faith without works is dead also.
— JAMES 2:26 NKJV

SEE ALSO: *1 CORINTHIANS 13:13; EPHESIANS 2:8*

What if you believed that you truly could do **everything** through Christ who gives you strength?

My Word is Purest Truth! What if you really could do everything that I said you could in My Word? Most assuredly, I tell you that you can! What would change in your life if you believed My Word instead of your feelings? If you are having a hard time believing and living My Truth, consider whether you are attempting to do things in your own strength instead of allowing Christ to strengthen you. When I give a promise to you in My Word, you will only accomplish this in *My* power flowing through you — not in your human strength and power. Wisdom says: The enemy is very aware of your strength in Christ. Are you? The only way he can stop you is to deceive you into thinking that you are weak. The only way the enemy can stop your ability to do all things ***through Christ*** is to lie about your identity ***in Christ***. Make the decision today that whatever you read in My Word *is* Truth for you. You can and will do what I decree you can do! I would not have given you these declarations of ***who*** you are if it were not Truth! This is the victory that overcomes!

I can do all this through him who gives me strength.
— PHILIPPIANS 4:13

The sum of Your word is truth.
— PSALM 119:160 AMP

Sanctify them in the truth [set them apart for Your purposes, make them holy]; Your word is truth.
— JOHN 17:17 AMP

Choose Life or death?
Faith or fate? Give each
new day an assignment!

*I call heaven and earth to **record** this day against you,*
that I have set before you life and death, blessing and
cursing. Therefore, choose life, that both you and your
descendants may live. — Deuteronomy 30:19

Begin each day with declarations and decrees of life
and faith! If you do not plan your day, the enemy will!
Without instructions from you about your day, there
is no guidance and no direction. Without instructions,
your day is at the mercy of fate, not faith. Know this: Faith
is proactive; fate is reactive. Decreeing powerful words
of faith gives the day and its circumstances direction!
Fate is living at the mercy of this natural world, natural
forces, and the enemy, instead of exercising your faith to
direct, protect, and lead your day. Thus, I call heaven and
earth to record this day. To **record** something means that
something ***must be said!*** Heaven and earth are recording
everything, blessing or cursing, Life and death. Decree
to heaven and earth how your day will go. Wisdom says:
Take command of your day. See Me helping you become
victorious in every circumstance.

You will also decide and decree a thing, and it will be
established for you. — Job 22:28 AMP

You are clothed in
My righteousness!

There was a reason why I did not allow the Israelites' clothes to wear out while they wandered in the desert for 40 years. This was not only to take care of them, but to reveal to you that neither does your robe of righteousness ever wear out! Know that your righteousness cannot get soiled or dirty, nor become old before Me! I have covered you in My righteousness that never fades away. Wisdom says: Glory in your position of righteousness before Me! Do not return to your closet to pull out the old, stained, washed-out clothes of your past and try to wear them again in shame because of your mistakes! Once I have clothed you with My robe, you do not ever have to wear your old rags and hand-me-downs again! You are now covered in My beautiful, ornate robe of righteousness that never gets old or fades away!

You're done with that old life. It's like a filthy set of ill-fitting clothes you've stripped off and put in the fire. Now you're dressed in a new wardrobe. Every item of your new way of life is custom-made by the Creator, with his label on it. All the old fashions are now obsolete.

— Colossians 3:9-11 MSG

See also: Deuteronomy 8:3-4; Isaiah 61:10; Ecclesiastes 45:7-8

I reckon! This is the season of My righteous reckoning!

My righteous reckoning is My justice *swinging swiftly* in your favor! I AM rendering My righteous judgment of mercy and bestowing it upon My children who love Me. I AM considering, judging, and settling accounts *for reward* according to what you have sown. No one can overrule My righteous reckonings. *Once I reckon My judgments of mercy and rule in your favor, they are settled forever in the courts of heaven and nothing on earth or in hell can stop them!* Repentance ushers My mercy, which is boundless and without measure. My mercy is reckoning what is rightfully yours and returning what has been stolen. Use wisdom like David. In his time of repentance, he threw himself on the mercy of My courts. Wisdom says: Trust Me today that My justice is coming swiftly on your behalf! Those who sow in mercy will always reap My mercy of My righteous recompense.

The Lord has made proclamation to the ends of the earth:
"Say to Daughter Zion, 'See, your Savior comes! See, his
reward is with him, and his recompense accompanies him.'"
— Isaiah 62:11

See also: Psalm 51:1; 2 Samuel 24:14; Psalm 18:20; Matthew 18:24-27; Isaiah 10:3

I will not force you to walk in your destiny. I just planned it.

Before the foundation of the world, I planned your life. To accomplish My purpose for your assignment, destiny, and talents, it is crucial that you get My instructions and be obedient to them! So many are getting their instructions from man. How does man know My plans for you? Wisdom says: Man can confirm My plans for you, but you — only you — are responsible for choosing to get My instructions for your destiny. Neither you nor man can dream and plan your destiny like I can. Why go anywhere else but to Me? Only the Designer knows what you are designed to do. You will not experience pure joy until you are doing what I have called you to do. Ask Me to show you My plans and My will for you today! When you get quiet before Me, I will show you the destiny that I have planned just for you.

> *"I say this because I know the plans that I have for you." This message is from the Lord. "I have good plans for you. I don't plan to hurt you. **I plan to give you hope and a good future."***
>
> – Jeremiah 29:11 ERV

See also: Proverbs 4:1; Romans 8:29; Romans 11:2

I AM never the source of your pain, but I AM always your solution.

Pain and suffering are never a tool that I use to mold and sculpt you! My Son carried all sickness, suffering, and pain for you so you would not have to. I AM the Father of the great exchange. You can legally exchange all pain and sickness for what Jesus provided for you. Pain and pressure will motivate you like never before to align yourself with My promises in My Word. Use times of pain with much wisdom so you can get out faster! This is not the season to waste time. Adjust the things in your life that need to be adjusted, then trust Me as your Healer. I hate suffering. I even turned away from My Son, Jesus, upon the cross as He took in His body all sin, sickness, and pain for you. I looked away from *Him* so I would *never* turn away from *you*! Wisdom says: If you are suffering, enforce My Word that says you have already been healed! Cry out to Me today and I will answer you. Call forth My refreshing Wind, and I will bring comfort and restoration. You will not fear bad news when your heart is securely trusting in Me. Never forget: I AM your Comforter and Healer!

Surely he took up our pain and bore our suffering.

— Isaiah 53:4

315

See also: 1 Peter 2:24; Psalm 147:3; Psalm 112; Zephaniah 3:15

What you **behold** you become!

Not only will you **become** what you are looking at, you will reproduce it! I illustrated this in My Word when Jacob set rods that he peeled in the place where his flocks would mate. The flocks reproduced what they saw. The disciples intensely watched My Son and they, too, reproduced the works that He did. What are you looking at or beholding? Whatever you are spending time looking at will influence you. This could not be said with more caution! Whatever has influence over you will change you. If the media and culture have influence over you, that is what will be reproduced in you. This is the war of the world raging against My Word, vying for your attention. When you are gazing upon My Word, you will become and reproduce My Son, Jesus. TKnow this today: Whatever you behold will take control of you! Choose to look at My Word instead of the world! Wisdom says: You can only become the person I predestined you to be in My Kingdom when you allow My Word to influence you more than the world.

> But we all, with unveiled face, **beholding as in a mirror** the glory of the Lord, are being transformed into the same image from glory to glory, just as by the Spirit of the Lord.
> — 2 Corinthians 3:18 NKJV

See also: Genesis 30:38-40; Psalm 27:4; Psalm 63:2

You receive a two-fold blessing when you pray for your enemies.

There is something supernatural that happens to your heart when you pray for those who have hurt you. You not only open the door for Me to bring healing in your *own* heart, but you are also interceding for healing for those who hurt you. You receive a two-fold blessing for praying for your enemies! This blessing will not only heal the damage done to you, but it can also heal the hurt in relationships. It also authorizes Me to set in motion the Law of Blessing in your life instead of hurt and unforgiveness. You will reap what you sow! I will bless you as you bless your enemies! The quickest way to be healed from hurt is to pray for your enemies. When someone says or does something evil to you, it is at the expense of *their* character, not yours! Wisdom says: If My Body would put this into practice, there would be so much peace in My Kingdom. Pray the hurt away!

Invoke blessings upon and pray for the happiness of those who curse you, implore God's blessing (favor) upon those who abuse you [who revile, reproach, disparage, and high-handedly misuse you].
— Luke 6:28 AMP

I will bless those who bless you, and whoever curses you I will curse.
— Genesis 12:3

Do not **regret** the process, but **relish** the progress!

❧

Life is a process. I set the Law of Seed*time* and Harvest. The only thing that is immediate is a miracle from Me! Only you can choose whether or not you will *enjoy the journey.* My desire is that you *relish every step* in life, not just your final destination. There are no shortcuts in My Kingdom. Every season and step you take in life has value — if you choose to see things with *My vision!* To hate the process is to hate life. Oh, if only the Israelites could have seen through the eyes of My mercy when they walked through the route that I chose for them in the wilderness. At that time, they still possessed a slave mentality — thus, they were not yet ready to face the giants of the Promised Land. I chose that route because if I had chosen another, they would have turned around. The wilderness route trained them to become warriors, ready to face their giants. *Trust that the route I have chosen for your life will also prepare you to face future giants.* Wisdom says: Trust My timing and mercy in every season. It is rare for prophecy and fulfillment to be in the same season. Just because you receive a prophecy does not mean you are mature enough for the manifestation. This is My mercy, to not give you more than you are ready for. Let My peace rule your heart as you go through the process. Trust My hand to guide you as I train you in the war on your life!

By day the Lord went ahead of them in a pillar of cloud to guide them on their way and by night in a pillar of fire to give them light. — Exodus 13:21

See also: Exodus 13:17; Isaiah 43:18

A life lived with Me is a life lived with **no regrets.**

Time is the proof that you live in this physical realm. Everyone is given My gift called time. Know that time marks your entrance and exit on this earth. When you were born, before anything else was documented, the time of your birth was recorded. As with your birth, the same will be true when you die physically. Even before the cause of death is recorded, the time of death is recorded. Time is so important that you will have to give an account to Me of every second. Time only ends your physical life. But your eternal life will live on — through the end of time! You are a spirit that will never die. Death is never an end. For those in Christ, it is the beginning of living in your rewards in Me. Wisdom says: Even your heart rate is measured with time. That is to remind you that nearly every second your heart beats. Every tick of the clock is to remind you that your heart is to beat for Me alone. ***Be determined today to put as much life in your time as possible!*** A life lived with Me is a life lived with no regrets. I AM the Creator and Redeemer of your time.

Then the Lord God formed a man from the dust of the ground and breathed into his nostrils the breath of life, and the man became a living being.

– Genesis 2:7

... by giving his life for all mankind. This is the message that at the proper time God gave to the world.

– 1 Timothy 2:6 TLB

See also: Ecclesiastes 8:8

*O*ctober 29

A slave cannot free another slave.

Many have ***adapted*** to the life of a hired servant, when they have been ***adopted*** by Me to be served at My table! So many people are held captive in their minds. As they left Egypt, the Israelites were in a captive state despite the freedom displayed through exploits of My power and My provision of health and wealth. I did not even allow their clothes to wear out. I daily supplied them manna and did not allow one among them to be feeble or sick. Yet the Israelites could not ***see*** it. Until members of My Body ***see*** they have been adopted and not hired, free and liberated people will continue to wear shackles. ***How can you reign in chains?*** Wisdom says: The measure that you believe you are loved will be the measure that you are free. Allow Me to show you today that you are only as free as you can ***see***.

Now a slave has no permanent place in the family, but a son belongs to it forever. So if the Son sets you free, you will be free indeed. — JOHN 8:35-36

Therefore you are no longer a slave but a son, and if a son, then an heir of God through Christ. — GALATIANS 4:7 NKJV

*I no longer call you slaves, because a master doesn't confide in his slaves. **Now you are my friends**, since I have told you everything the Father told me.* — JOHN 15:15 NLT

SEE ALSO: 1 CORINTHIANS 7:23

Are you rooted and grounded in the One True Root, My Son, or in yourself?

I am the Root (the Source, the Life).

— Revelation 22:16 amp

Did you ever look closely at the *root* of the problem in the parable of The Sower? *Offense.* Trouble and persecution *will* come your way. But when it does, I give you the option to *choose* not to become offended. This will protect you from the enemy trying to steal My Precious Word from your heart, which causes you to stumble and fall away. If you desire to bear much fruit in your life, your identity must be grafted into the One True Root, My Son, Jesus — not in yourself. Those who have no root in themselves are those who rely on themselves for their identity and love instead of the Root, Jesus. They have no *Root* in themselves! Because of this, they become easily offended and fall away. Wisdom says: Make the decision today to not be easily offended. This will allow your heart to remain rooted and grounded in the Living Word of My Son, Jesus.

> *In a similar way these [in the second group] are the ones on whom seed was sown on rocky ground, who, when they hear the word, **immediately receive it with joy [but accept it only superficially]; and they have no real root** in themselves, so they endure only for a little while; then, when trouble or persecution comes because of the word, immediately they [are **offended** and displeased at being associated with Me and] stumble and fall away.* — Mark 4:16-17 amp

See also: Romans 15:12; Revelation 5:5

The enemy knows that he is defeated and powerless. Do you?

The enemy is rendered powerless, because he has already been sentenced and condemned. His sentence will never be revoked because his judgment was set and ratified in The Blood of My Son. On the cross, Jesus disarmed the principalities and powers that were ranged against you. He made a bold display and public example of them — thus, the enemy cannot torment you. You now have the power and authority to torment him when you speak the name of Jesus! My Word says, "When they see the enemy in the end, they will be stunned! They will think and say, 'How can this be the one who terrified and shook the world?'" Wisdom says: The enemy only has the power that you give him. His only weapon is deception. *Every time the enemy attacks you it will cost him, because he exposes his weak and defeated tactics.* As a result, you keep growing stronger and wiser! My Son, Jesus, has *all* power and authority, and He has given it to you. Know today that you are loved with My passionate and powerful love.

[Satan] is judged and condemned and sentence already is passed upon him. — JOHN 16:11 AMP

Everyone there will stare at you and ask, 'Can this be the one who shook the earth and made the kingdoms of the world tremble? ... Is this the king who demolished the world's greatest cities and had no mercy on his prisoners?' — ISAIAH 14:16-17 NLT

322

SEE ALSO: COLOSSIANS 2:15; REVELATION 12:10

I AM the source of your confidence!

What you believe about yourself in your heart can change your destiny. If you have *self*-confidence, then your confidence will constantly be subject to your own image and circumstances. This is great instability. You will then look to other people for validation and will be dependent on man instead of Me. You cannot hear enough compliments from man to create the confidence that *only* I can give! Wisdom says: Because I never change, when your confidence is from Me, your confidence is secure. People, circumstances, and your own image can change, but when I AM your source of confidence, you cannot be shaken. I have chosen and qualified you because I have unwaivering confidence in you. Be confident that My Love for you is fixed and everlasting.

*For You are my hope; O Lord God, You are my trust and the **source of my confidence** from my youth.*
—Psalm 71:5 AMP

*... the Father, the creator of the heavenly lights, in whose character there is **no change at all**.*
— James 1:17 CEB

*I have told you these things, so that in Me you may have [perfect] peace and **confidence**. ... For I have overcome the world.*
— John 16:33 AMPC

See also: Philippians 4:13; Hebrews 10:35; Ephesians 3:12; Philippians 3:3; Hebrews 4:16

Count the cost,
not the loss!

What is the loss of your reputation with family and friends compared to gaining citizenship in My Kingdom? Nothing can be compared to having new life in My Son, with all the privileges and promises that are yours in My Word. You have eternal life instead of eternal death. I promise to take care of you and your needs because you are My child. I lavishly give both earthly and eternal rewards. I have held *nothing* back from you. I gave you My only Son. To reject My Gift is to reject Life. Wisdom says: Count the cost. When persecution arises because of Me, remember the benefits of being aligned with Me. I always defend My own. Never forget: Persecution ushers promotion and My exceeding reward. Today, hold nothing back from Me. I AM Generosity. I AM a generous Father. I never consider the price when it comes to you. Even with the staggering price of My Son, I still say you truly are worth it.

> *What good will it be for someone to gain the whole world, yet forfeit their soul?* — MATTHEW 16:26

> *But what things were gain to me, these I have counted loss for Christ. Yet indeed I also count all things loss for the excellence of the knowledge of Christ Jesus my Lord, for whom I have suffered the loss of all things, and count them as rubbish, that I may gain Christ.* — PHILIPPIANS 3:7-8 NKJV

The Vine sustains you.
You do not sustain Me.

> *For to us a Child is born, to us a Son is given; and the*
> ***government*** *shall be upon His shoulder, and His name*
> *shall be called Wonderful, Counselor, Mighty God, Ever-*
> *lasting Father [of eternity], Prince of Peace.*
>
> — Isaiah 9:6 AMP

I AM The Vine. ***You are the branches.*** I can exist without you, but you cannot exist without Me. As The Vine, I grow in many directions to cover much ground. I choose what I AM going to wrap around, or anchor Myself to. You have no choice but to follow Me. Notice that vines are mostly invisible! Yet, as the branches, you are the most visible part of Me! Wisdom says: I AM asking you to enforce the ***Government of My Son, Jesus.*** Be My ***Executive Branch*** to govern My Kingdom, to rule and reign with Christ in love. Be My ***Judicial Branch*** of Justice to those who have suffered injustice. Be My ***Legislative Branch*** to legislate My Laws of Love and Faith to a hurting and dying world. I AM asking you to branch out wherever I AM leading you.

> *"I am the vine, **you are the branches**. He who abides*
> *in Me, and I in him, bears much fruit; for without Me*
> *you can do nothing."*
>
> — 1 John 15:5

See also: Isaiah 9:6-7; Ezekiel 17:7;
Joel 1:7; John 15:1-9

November 7

You were completely loved, even before you were completely formed.

I AM your Father! Your rebirth certificate gives you citizenship in My Kingdom. You are born of My Spirit. You came from My spiritual womb. You have been carried by Me from the womb! Nothing about you was an accident in any way! I spent much time considering every aspect of you. Know that you are exactly what I want you to be! You were knit together in the regions of the deep with much pleasure and joy as My masterpiece. You were, even then, completely loved before you were completely formed! From your origin, you are completely an original, just as I carefully and exquisitely created you. My name is on your rebirth certificate because you are Mine! I not only know your name, but you have My name! Wisdom says: I AM your Father who loves to be involved with you in every way. Today, relish the truth that you can never again be abandoned, abused, or abducted! You are legally and legitimately Mine forever! You are My much treasured and cherished child!

*Listen to Me [says the Lord], O house of Jacob, and all the remnant of the house of Israel, you who have been **borne by Me from your birth, carried from the womb**.*

– Isaiah 46:3 AMPC

See also: John 3:3-5; John 3:31; John 14:30

Your identity is God-given, not man-given.

You are made in *My* Image! Man was not made in man's image. How can you get your identity from someone who did not create you? *You are My idea and who you are gives Me much delight!* I give you the right to be only you! Do not allow other people's opinions of you to change who you really are. People's opinions about you will constantly change. If their opinion influences you and changes what I created you to be, you will lose your identity and the person that I adore. My opinion of you stays the same. I love you the same every day! Allow My Word to define you. I have given you My Spirit and My Breath. You did not get these from man. Your identity can only be found in Me! *If you are feeling worthless and insecure, you have been looking to man for your identity and not to Me.* Wisdom says: Do not let anyone change your identity. Be the person *I* have called you to be. Never forget: You are an expression of *Me*!

> "In a word, what I'm saying is, Grow up. You're kingdom subjects. Now live like it. **Live out your God-created identity**. Live generously and graciously toward others, the way God lives toward you."
> — Matthew 5:48 MSG

See also: Luke 6:35-36

If you have a hard time forgiving someone, it means you have forgotten how much **you** need forgiveness!

Is it not amazing how quickly some can forget how merciful I have been to them, yet they find it hard to forget the smallest of infractions from someone else? When someone hurts you, think of all the times you have hurt My heart and I have forgiven you. Love keeps no record of wrongs! You will find mercy in your heart when you remember the mercy I have extended toward you! Never forget that you will need forgiveness for just about every day! You do not know the sins and mistakes you will make tomorrow, but I do! Wisdom says: Those who **sow** in mercy will never be without a **harvest** of mercy. Forgive so you can be forgiven! I AM always forgiving and merciful to those who are forgiving and full of mercy.

But if you do not forgive others their sins, your Father will not forgive your sins.
— MATTHEW 6:15

Forgive, and you will be forgiven.
— LUKE 6:37

SEE ALSO: PSALM 32:1

If you do **not** know I AM *for* you, you will think everyone is **against** you.

If you do not know that I AM your Friend, you will think everyone is your enemy! The enemy starts division and rejection when you do *not* know I AM for you! There is such peace when you know I AM for you! I will never be against you! You must settle this issue if you are going to walk in faith. Without faith, you will not get your prayers answered. This is the enemy's strategy to keep you defeated. If you *know*, really know, from your heart, that I AM always here for you, rejection and fear of rejection will be impossible. *If you are not certain of this, rejection by people and fear of them will keep you living a defeated life! The enemy will use people to make sure of it!* Wisdom says: Enemies are formed when you think I AM against you! Faith starts when you *know* I AM only for you! Love believes the best. Because I AM Love, I always believe the best of you.

> *If God is for us, who can be [successful] against us? [Who can be our foe, if God is on our side?] He who did not spare [even] His own Son, but gave Him up for us all, how will He not also, along with Him, graciously give us all things? Who will bring any charge against God's elect (His chosen ones)?*
>
> — ROMANS 8:31-33 AMP

SEE ALSO: JOHN 14:21

329

Champions are already winners in their hearts and minds **before** the fight!

You never see a champion boxer in his corner before a fight crying and saying he knows he cannot win the fight. Such a boxer would be defeated even before the match began. *A champion does not need a title to know who and what he already is! He is a champion long before the fight's outcome.* What do you believe? Are you already defeated or are you already a winner? Fighting the good fight of faith is believing you're already a winner. Have the mindset before the fight that you will walk out in victory! Wisdom says: My Truth, My Word, and My Promises never change whether you are fighting a giant or something small. Know that I have already made you My champion and winner in Christ! I call you one of great valor because of your great value.

We are more than conquerors through Him who loved us.
— ROMANS 8:37 NKJV

If you faint in the day of adversity, your strength is small.
— PROVERBS 24:10 AMP

SEE ALSO: ISAIAH 42:13; 1 TIMOTHY 6:12; 2 TIMOTHY 4:7

Every seed still carries My voice and instructions that give the seed the power to reproduce.

Seeds are carriers of My voice! Every seed ***still*** contains My Life and My voice with the same power to reproduce from the day I called it forth since Genesis 1:11. The same power is within every seed and in every tree as when I originally spoke them into existence. My Life and power cannot be diluted. Every tree has been through thousands of seed-to-tree cycles, yet the power of those spoken Words in that seed are still as powerful today as on the ***third*** day of creation! My Word is ***My Seed***, Jesus, Who rose from the dead on the ***third*** day. The power of My Word has just as much power for you today as if I just decreed it forth! ***When you speak My Word, My Seed, is itill carrying My voice to rearrange, reproduce, recreate, and repel death in your life!*** Wisdom says: Speak My Word and Seed today with the expectation that you are releasing My voice to recreate and change what you need changed!

> *For you have been born again, not of perishable seed, but of imperishable, through the living and enduring word of God.*
>
> – 1 Peter 1:23

See also: Galatians 3:16; Genesis 1:11-12; Luke 8:11-17

Why all the Sword fights?

Some in My Body are using the Sword of My Spirit — My Word — to fight and cut one another. How? With words. My Word is a weapon of great power to be used against the enemy — never against one another, and especially never against family! Allow My Truth to be said with great love and conviction, but never to be said to hurt another. When you injure your brothers and sisters, you injure yourself! It grieves My heart when I see that the most vicious attacks come from within My Body! There is nothing friendly about friendly fire! Wisdom says: Lay down your self-righteousness, pick up My Banner of Righteousness and march as one! My Body can *only afford* to be in *one accord*! Never use the weapon of My Sword to hurt, divide, or destroy My Family. I gave you the Sword of My Word with power and authority to cast out demons, not people.

> *So continuing daily **with one accord** in the temple, and breaking bread from house to house, they ate their food with gladness and simplicity of heart, praising God and having favor with all the people. And the Lord added to the church daily those who were being saved.*
> — ACTS 2:45-47 NKJV

> *Rescue me from enemy swords.*
> — PSALM 22:20 CEV

SEE ALSO: PSALM 37:13-16; PROVERBS 12:18

The only past you can afford to think about is **My** past!

Think about **My** past faithfulness and rehearse **My** past victories. I commanded this repeatedly to My People, the Israelites, so they would never forget My goodness. I scheduled My Feast Days around how I delivered them in the past. Feasting about My faithfulness, not fasting, is remembering how I answered prayers in your life. This will help steady your faith. Remembering the miracles in your past builds faith for My miracles in your future. Thinking on your past is futile. Thinking on My past builds your faith — because My past is filled with faithfulness, mercy, escapes, and deliverance. Wisdom says: Meditate and keep reminding yourself of ***all*** My past victories, answered prayers, and miracles in your life. This will help you keep a healthy perspective of what you are facing now. ***What you are going through today will not seem so overwhelming when you remember My overwhelming victories in the past.***

I do not hide your righteousness in my heart; I speak of your faithfulness and your saving help. I do not conceal your love and your faithfulness from the great assembly.
PSALM 40:10 NLT

SEE ALSO: DEUTERONOMY 15:15; PSALM 25:4-7

Being grateful always brings forth My reward.

〜

Complaining always costs you something. But being thankful always pays; it ushers in My reward. *Complaining never solves problems. It creates more!* If you are using your words and My Breath to complain, you are cursing yourself and sabotaging your future! Complaining will always cost you the fulfillment of My promise in your life. Complaining kills faith and empowers fear and unbelief. Wisdom says: *When you are grateful, you have My full attention!* Being grateful builds faith. Remember today that a grateful heart is focused on Me. A grateful heart is a stable heart that cannot be easily rocked. I AM always grateful for a grateful heart.

He who brings an offering of praise and thanksgiving honors and glorifies Me; and he who orders his way aright [who prepares the way that I may show him], to him I will demonstrate the salvation of God.
— Psalm 50:23 AMP

Enter into his gates with thanksgiving, and into his courts with praise: be thankful unto him, and bless his name.
— Psalm 100:4

Giving thanks always for all things unto God and the Father in the name of our Lord Jesus Christ.
— Ephesians 5:20 KJV

See also: Ephesians 5:20; Numbers 11:1

The earth is listening to your voice!
The earth has an ear to hear!

Sound is the governing force of this planet. Everything you see, as well as everything you do not see, is made of sound. I created this planet with the booming thunder of My voice — sound! Earth and all creation, along with everything else in the universe, have no option but to bow and obey the sound of My voice and My Word. When you are reborn, the earth recognizes My voice in you. I crowned you with authority and power over all the earth. Because you are made from the earth, it must obey your spirit. The earth has an ear to hear. Everything around you is listening to your words, which give the sound and all matter direction. Your words will do one of two things: They will either give everything around you instruction, or they will cause destruction! Wisdom says: All matter must obey the sound in your voice! Words matter! Use them wisely.

"Listen, O heavens, and I will speak;
And let the earth hear the words of my mouth."
— DEUTERONOMY 32:1 AMP

Come near, you nations, and listen; pay attention,
you peoples! Let the earth hear, and all that is in it,
the world, and all that comes out of it!
— ISAIAH 34:1

SEE ALSO: MICAH 1:2; ISAIAH 49:1; ISAIAH 1:2

Are you living with habits, or are you in the habit of living?

When people live with *habits*, their habits and schedules dictate their day; I AM no longer first priority. But, when you are in the habit of living, this means that you are in the habit of living *in My Presence* and I have first priority in your day. I love when you listen to My voice throughout your day despite your busy schedule. How can you have a bad day when you are in communication with Me? I AM always right there with you, giving you peace, giving you insight, directing you, and comforting you. I desire for you to live with discipline, but do not live such a rigid lifestyle that you have to pencil Me into your busy schedule. Wisdom says: *Live and walk habitually with Me.* Be in the habit of living to the fullest in Me, instead of living with habits that pull you away with Me!

Set your mind and keep focused habitually on the things above [the heavenly things], not on things that are on the earth [which have only temporal value].
— COLOSSIANS 3:2 AMP

When Abram was 99 years old, The Lord appeared to him and said, I am the Almighty God; walk and live habitually before Me and be perfect (blameless, wholehearted, complete).
— GENESIS 17:1 AMP

SEE ALSO: PSALM 1:2

To the extent that you know Me is the extent that you become free.

I unveil Myself to you in My Holy Word. You can never know Me outside of My Word because this is where I have hidden the Truth of Who I AM and how I think and feel about you. The more you read My Word, the more I reveal Myself to you. Throughout My Word, I expose My heart, My feelings, and My desires for you. I make it very clear that I long to be your Father and to draw you towards Me as My child. When you make yourself vulnerable to Me, you will never be disappointed! I always answer your cry for more understanding of Me. I will always fill your open heart. True freedom comes from knowing Me. Oh, how I long for you to seek Me with your whole heart. Wisdom says: Only those who seek Me with all their hearts will have true intimacy with Me, not just knowledge. ***For those who desire Me, I will impart the deep and intimate secrets of My heart.***

"Call to me and I will answer you and tell you great and unsearchable things you do not know."
— Jeremiah 33:3

Till heaven and earth pass, one jot or one tittle shall in no wise pass from the law, till all be fulfilled.
— Matthew 5:18 KJV

You are not to circle the mountain. You are to speak to the mountain!

A mountain is any obstacle that keeps you from victory or an answered prayer. Those who are unsure of their authority will keep circling the mountain, tolerating its presence, rather than telling it to be removed. Notice that I do not tell you to get a shovel and physically move the mountain because it cannot be done with manual labor. I said to speak to the mountain and give it instructions. Many of My children have been held back from great destinies because they neglect to speak with authority to what stands in their way. Wisdom says: Trust My Word and trust My instructions. ***Do not maintain the mountain; move it!***

"Truly I tell you, if anyone says to this mountain, 'Go, throw yourself into the sea,' and does not doubt in their heart but believes that what they say will happen, it will be done for them."
— MARK 11:23

"You have circled this mountain long enough. Now turn North."
— DEUTERONOMY 2:3 NASB

SEE ALSO: PSALM 97:5

I AM the Father of Lights; the enemy is the father of lies.

I AM Truth. I AM Life! Every lie is death, darkness, and deception. My Word is pure and total uncontaminated Truth. Agreeing with anything contrary to My Word is the same as giving life or agreement to a lie. Do not let lies twist or pervert My character. If it is contrary to My Word, it is a lie. To agree with poverty, sickness, or any part of the curse, you are enacting the Law of Agreement which gives life to a lie. To agree with something means you have *faith* that it is truth. Wisdom says: When you agree with My Word, you deprive a *lie* of the oxygen it needs to come alive. If you agree with a lie, it is like giving CPR to something that is dead, giving it life to affect and kill you. Know this: The enemy can only defeat you by lying to you! *I AM the Father of Lights and the enemy is the father of lies.* Today, ask for My Light to expose any area that the enemy is trying to pose as truth!

"Again, truly I tell you that if two of you on earth agree about anything they ask for, it will be done for them by my Father in heaven." — MATTHEW 18:19

Sanctify them [purify, consecrate, separate them for Yourself, make them holy] by Truth; Your Word is Truth. — JOHN 17:17 AMP

SEE ALSO: ISAIAH 28:15; 1 JOHN 5:8; REVELATION 21:8

Having an **idol** will make your life **idle**.

My vision and destiny for you are too large for you to achieve without Me! You will never become what I have created you to be if you put other gods — idols — before Me. I refuse to share your heart with anyone or anything else. Idols make your life fruitless and without purpose. A fruitless life is a faithless life. A faithless life speaks idle, inoperative words. You will be held accountable one day soon for every idle word you speak. Wisdom says: If your life seems to be idle, check your heart to see if anything has taken My place as your first love. Today, do not allow anything to take My place in your heart. Because you are My temple, when I dwell solely in your heart, My Holy of Holies is within your heart.

> *But I tell you, on the day of judgment men will have to give account for **every idle (inoperative, non-working) word** they speak.*
> — MATTHEW 12:36 AMP

> *Little children, keep yourselves from idols (false gods) — [from anything and everything that would occupy the place in your heart due to God, from any sort of substitute for Him that would take first place in your life].*
> — 1 JOHN 5:21 AMP

> *They spout empty words and make covenants they don't intend to keep.*
> — HOSEA 10:4

The only thing that can keep you from a **bright future** is living in a **dark past!**

When you embrace the new, you embrace Me. The present is My gift to you. Behold! I AM doing a new thing! *I have planned a bright future for you!* Choose to live a faith-filled life that will catapult you into your promising future. When you cling to the past, you cling to death. *When you live in the past, you live among the tombs. Leave the past in the grave and not in your soul.* The grave is the only place for the past to be rightfully buried. When you dig up your past, it is like digging up a corpse. Every time your past is exhumed, the stench becomes worse and worse. When you live in the past, the dead, dark past lives in you. When you live in the present, My Presence lives in you. Wisdom says: Take the time to make new memories with Me. I want to show you a fresh and new perspective of Me today.

See, I am doing a new thing! Now it springs up; do you not perceive it? — Isaiah 43:19

Morning by morning he dispenses his justice, and every new day he does not fail. — Zephaniah 3:5

See also: 2 Corinthians 4:16

Get My instruction
to avoid destruction.

Seek Me first before anyone else. When you are in a serious battle, get clear instructions from Me about who to tell, who not to tell, and whether or not to stay quiet and keep this battle between you and Me. Even get instructions about who to ask for prayer. Get My battle plan and My way of escape. If you continue to speak about the problem, then the problem continues to speak about you and becomes even larger in your mind. Do not talk carelessly and freely about any trial over which you do not yet have complete victory. This is strategy! Other people's words of fear and unbelief can make your victory harder to attain! I AM certainly not telling you to never tell anyone or not to ask for prayer! I AM saying: Get My instructions first on the specifics of My Way of escape. I always have a good plan and a way out. Wisdom says: To avoid destruction in a trial, seek My instructions first.

Take firm hold of instruction, do not let go; guard her, for she is your life.
— Proverbs 4:13 AMP

God is faithful, who will not suffer you to be tempted above that ye are able; but will with the temptation also make a way to escape, that ye may be able to bear it.
— 1 Corinthians 10:13 KJV

See also: Proverbs 8:33; Proverbs 8:10

Lowliness is as holiness.

Do you have what it takes to be the greatest in My Kingdom? I AM not talking about believing you have enough power and strength to be the greatest. I AM asking if you have the lowliness and meekness to be the greatest. Having a meek and lowly spirit is characterized by a quiet and gentle nature, not provoking fights and arguments, having a servant's heart, and putting the interests of others ahead of your own. Those who do these things are the greatest in My Kingdom, and they will inherit the earth. I AM calling forth a shift in attitudes in My Body that will shift the ranks in My Kingdom. Wisdom says: Look inside your heart this day and ask yourself: "Do I have what it takes to be the greatest?" This is true holiness! In this end-time harvest, like never before, I need servants to surface!

The meek and lowly are fortunate! for the whole wide world belongs to them.

— MATTHEW 5:5 TLB

Do nothing out of selfish ambition or vain conceit. Rather, in humility value others above yourselves, not looking to your own interests but each of you to the interests of the others.

— PHILIPPIANS 2:3-4

In holiness [being set apart] and righteousness [being upright] before Him all our days.

— LUKE 1:75 AMP

SEE ALSO: MATTHEW 18:1-4; PROVERBS 16:19

Sickness and disease
are as terrorist spirits.

Sickness and disease attack like terrorists do. They need fear to survive. Disease and terrorists both want to rule. They never want to just cohabit. There is no way to negotiate with a terrorist. The same is true with disease. Whenever you attempt to negotiate with a terrorist or disease, you have just lost the war. If you do not view disease as a terrorist, you may tolerate it and try to make a peace treaty with it. Both disease and terrorists laugh in the face of peace treaties. Both have an agenda to steal, kill, and destroy everything they touch. Neither are satisfied with the territory they occupy. Just as terrorism wants the entire world, disease wants the entire body. Wisdom says: Disease did not originate from Me! I created Life, not death. I give My Peace and My Rest, not terror! You have the right to live free! Remember that I AM the Lord Who heals you! You were recreated to rule over sickness and fear because of My Son's victory over sin, sickness, fear, and death.

By his wounds we are healed.

—Isaiah 53:5

See also: Psalm 91:5-10; 1 Peter 2:24; Isaiah 53:4-5

Am I in the heart of your Sabbath?

"Come to Me, all who are weary and heavily burdened [by religious rituals that provide no peace], and I will give you rest [refreshing your souls with salvation]."
— Matthew 11:28 AMP

I AM the heart of your **Sabba**th rest! I call all unto Me who are feeling overloaded with the pressures of life. And I promise to give you My rest! My rest does not mean inactivity. My Sabbath rest is that of returning you to a state of peace and tranquility as was in the Garden of Eden. My Sabbath rest is not striving, but resting from all the works of trying to earn a place in The Garden with Me, and just enjoying your rightful place as an heir in My family. Wisdom says: When I AM in the heart of your rest, there is peace, joy, love, and blessing. Bathe today in My Love, in My Sabbath Rest.

*So then there is still awaiting a full and complete **Sabbath-rest** for the [true] people of God. For he who has once entered [God's] rest also has ceased from [the weariness and pain] of human labors, just as God rested from those labors peculiarly His own.*
— Hebrews 4:9-10 AMP

See also: Mark 2:27; Matthew 12:8; Luke 6:2-28

Travel light, so you can be a Light traveler.

Be cautious if you feel the need to accumulate "things." The more things you have, the more things you will have to maintain and repair. This is more clutter on your mind. Do not allow a spirit of discontentment to creep into your life, where you keep needing more and more. There is nothing wrong with being blessed with My blessings; this is part of My Covenant Promise to you. Just remember, when things take over your thinking, that is how you know you have stepped into bondage. You are meant to travel light so that you can go at a moment's notice when I call you to go, then you will not be so heavy with possessions. If you notice you are becoming weary in your journey in life, perhaps you are carrying more than possessions; you are carrying the cares of your possessions. Lighten up! Wisdom says: Today, remember that life is too short to just fill it with things. ***Be sure to fill your life with the treasures of heaven, not just the pleasures of earth. Don't carry things; carry My Light!***

*I have learned the secret of being **content** in any and every situation, whether well fed or hungry, whether living in plenty or in want.* — PHILIPPIANS 4:12

SEE ALSO: ISAIAH 40:31; MARK 10:21; MARK 6:8; JOHN 8:12; EXODUS 13:21; 1 TIMOTHY 6:7

How do I measure success?

I do not measure a successful and productive day as some would. By the world's standards, a mother with small children may not seem to accomplish much in a typical day. But by My standards, I call a day of diaper-changing, feeding, and loving children a very successful and effective day of accomplishments with much fruit. Here's how I measure productivity in My Kingdom: ***Did you take advantage of each opportunity I presented to you today? Did you love and serve those I positioned around you?*** Did you treat your spouse with respect? Did you help those who needed your help when I put them in your path? When you are loving and serving one another, in My Book, that is a very successful day. Wisdom says: Be sure to take the time to notice the people I place in your sphere of influence. Love them as if this were the last day you will ever see them. Since Love never fails, then in My eyes, My children who love never fail!

Love never fails [never fades out or becomes obsolete or comes to an end]. — 1 Corinthians 13:8 AMP

Have sincere love for each other, love one another deeply, from the heart. — 1 Peter 1:22

See also: Romans 12:10

November 26

Every time I correct you, it is because I want to promote you.

Only parents who love their children will discipline them. Discipline is a sign of love. So many jerk back from My correcting guidance, not recognizing this as My loving hand. I AM not trying to expose failures or mistakes; I AM saving you from a wrong path of destruction or pain. Consider this correction My mercy, not anger! I AM your Father, and how I raise you is something I take seriously! My intention is to keep you from all harm. Wisdom says: When correction comes, it is for your growth and promotion! Discipline precedes a higher position in My Kingdom. *So remember, every time I correct you, it is to redirect you for promotion!*

> *My son, do not reject or take lightly the discipline of*
> *the Lord [learn from your mistakes and the testing*
> *that comes from **His correction** through discipline];*
> *Nor despise His rebuke.*
> — PROVERBS 3:11 AMPC

> *Endure hardship as discipline; God is treating you*
> *as sons. For what son is not disciplined by his father?*
> *If you are not disciplined (and everyone undergoes*
> *discipline), then you are illegitimate children and*
> *not true sons.*
> — HEBREWS 12:7

348

SEE ALSO: PROVERBS 10:17

When you **pray** for those who hurt you, hurt cannot **prey** upon you.

Hurt stalks its prey like an animal stalking its victim. To be prey of hurt means you are helpless or unable to resist the attack of hurt. When you pray for those who hurt you, this gives Me supernatural access to heal you. In fact, the only way you can heal from hurt is to forgive and then pray for the one who hurt you. This is a holy act that releases the Law of Love upon both parties involved. To pray for those who hurt you is to praise Me. Wisdom says: Loving your enemies and praying for those who misuse you takes you out of the enemy's clutches and makes you untouchable — and that hurt can no longer *prey* upon you.

They have tracked me down, they now surround me, with eyes alert, to throw me to the ground. They are like a lion hungry for prey, like a fierce lion crouching in cover.

— Psalm 17:11-12

Love your enemies and pray for those who persecute you.

— Matthew 5:44 AMP

Be alert and cautious at all times. That enemy of yours, the devil, prowls around like a roaring lion [fiercely hungry], seeking someone to devour.

— 1 Peter 5:8 AMP

349

Do you want **Me** to have a following, or do **you** want a following?

Are you wanting a movement for Me or a ministry for you? In this holy, end-time hour, motives and agendas will be revealed like never before. I can no longer afford to have those in leadership who have been seduced by crowds, money, and fame. My Kingdom must look on earth like it does in heaven. King Jesus is the One who is the center of all honor and focus! Many good people start out with such sincerity in wanting to serve Me, but then they become drunk with the wine of power! I AM asking you to judge yourself, and not others. Wisdom says: *I AM asking every one of My children to look carefully at their motivations in this hour.* Ask yourself the hard questions. Come before Me with a sincere heart, for My help, grace, and mercy to heal your heart of anything that could cause you to stumble. *When you get people to follow you, they will become disillusioned. When you get people to follow My Son, Jesus, they will become disciples.*

As they were going along the road, someone said to Him, "I will follow You wherever You go." — LUKE 9:57

SEE ALSO: 1 CORINTHIANS 11:1-2

You are created to ride the storm, not just ride out the storm!

When you can find joy, even in the midst of the storm, then you cannot be defeated! When you live and are nourished on the revelation that the sun is always shining, even on a dark and stormy day, then you will survive every storm of life. Have you noticed that the strongest and most violent storms happen when life is bursting forth and is in full display during the months where spring overpowers the months of winter? ***Know this: When Life is springing forth in your life, there will always be dark storms to discourage you and try to stop you!*** Wisdom says: Anchor yourself to Me alone. How can a storm defeat you when your Father is the One Who calms the storms to a whisper? Rise with Me above the storm, where My Son is always shining and My Peace will stabilize your heart. I ride the storm clouds — and, in Me, you will ride them too! When you ride *out* the storm, you are subject to the storm. ***When you ride the storm, the storm is subject to you. The storms in your life are very temporary, but I AM Eternal.*** Can you see Me shining through this storm today? Your survival depends upon your ability to see Me surrounding you. ***I AM your Storm Shelter!***

He stilled the storm to a whisper.

— Psalm 107:29

See also: Psalm 91:1; Isaiah 25:4; Isaiah 32:2; Proverbs 1:33; Proverbs 3:2

Walk over the enemy. Do not allow the enemy to walk over you!

You are crowned with My Glory and honor to rule and have dominion over the earth and everything My hands have created. You are a joint heir with My Son, Jesus, in My Kingdom. You have been given all power and authority over the enemy when you use My Son's name. If you fail to walk over the enemy, he will walk over you! If you are being attacked, get into My Presence and get My battle plan for victory. I will reveal secrets from My war room over the battle that is raging around you. Use My Word and My weapons to walk over the enemy. If you are allowing him to trample you, it is because you do not understand who you are and Whose you are. You have been given power to tread on serpents and scorpions, and over all the power of the enemy, and nothing shall by any means harm you. Wisdom says: Get the enemy off your back and crush him, in Jesus' name! Do not walk around him; walk over him!

Now Jesus called together the twelve [disciples] and gave them [the right to exercise] power and authority over all the demons and to heal diseases. — LUKE 9:1 AMPC

SEE ALSO: LUKE 10:19

How do you know that I will do what I say? You have My Word!

Take comfort in knowing I AM honor-bound to My Word and will not violate My Promises! My Word is My Love letter to you, expressed through Promises that will never fail. You may sometimes fail, but My Word never fails. When I say something will happen, you have My guarantee that it will come to pass, just as I said. Look at how many prophecies have happened just as My Word said they would. They were fulfilled with exact precision and were not a second late! My Word is the Constitution and the Law of My Kingdom. *When I speak, everything on earth must shift to accommodate My Word.* Wisdom says: My Word is My Son, clothed with flesh; your constant Companion leading you to My Peace; your Bread and Water; your Sword. I AM My Word! So you may ask, "But Father, how do I know that you will do as you say you will?" *My response, with great love, is: "You have My Word!"*

As for God, His way is perfect! The word of the Lord is tested and tried; He is a shield to all those who take refuge and put their trust in Him. — Psalm 18:30 AMP

353

See also: Luke 16:17; John 1:1; Isaiah 55:11; Psalm 138:2

December 2

When you are taking Communion, I AM saying, 'Come union!'

Every time you take Comm**union**, I call you to remember the New Covenant sanctified in the Body and Blood of My Son, Jesus. When you are taking Communion with other believers, it is such a holy time! During Communion, I AM reminding you that there are to be no divisions among you, but you are to be perfectly united. Division among members of My Body has so grieved My heart! Division makes My Body weak and ineffective. Where strife and division exist, evil abounds. But where the state of agreement exists, anything is possible! Wisdom says: When there is unity, especially during Communion, My power and miracles can be released. I AM calling My Body into union as One with Me, My Son, and My Spirit. *The next time you take Communion, seek holy union with Me! Remember, the more unification, the more of My manifestation!*

For we [no matter how] numerous we are, are one body because we all partake of the one Bread [the One Whom the communion bread represents].
— 1 Corinthians 10:17 AMP

SEE ALSO: *1 Corinthians 11:17-26; 1 John 4:17; 1 Corinthians 12:12*

The weapon of worry is designed to keep you weak.

Worry and thinking about your weaknesses are not only a waste of time and energy, but they are weapons to keep you from future successes. How can you step out in confidence when you have been meditating on past failure? It is impossible! Worry is a strategic way to keep you stationary and afraid to move forward. It is designed to keep you weak. Worry steals your joy — and joy is your strength! Wisdom says: Meditate on the power of My Word! If you feel deficient today, judge your heart to see if you have been worrying about something that happened in the past, instead of meditating on the excitement of victories that are yours to possess today! Know this: The attack of worry is to make you weary. If you have become weary, it may be that you have become leary of My Love for you. Never doubt that I love you with Love that never ends!

*"Therefore I tell you, do not worry about your life, what you will eat or drink; or about your body, what you will wear. Is not life more than food, and the body more than clothes? Look at the birds of the air; they do not sow or reap or store away in barns, and yet your heavenly Father feeds them. Are you not much more valuable than they? **Can any one of you by worrying add a single hour to your life?**"* —Matthew 6:25-27

See also: Matthew 6:34

355

Unity means that you forfeit the fight.

To unite My Kingdom is to expand My Kingdom! So many in My Body cannot let go of small differences of opinions and insignificant details for the sake of unity! This is so grieving to My heart! The problem is: All believe they are right — which means that most are not! To walk in unity, you must agree on foundational issues, not necessarily on culture and tradition. ***My Kingdom has suffered such violence because of division.*** You will not lose your individuality just because you decide to be in agreement. Why would the world want to be part of an army that wounds its own instead of leaving no man behind. When My Body comes together to ***make*** a difference instead of to ***expose*** its differences, My Body will rapidly change the world! Wisdom says: ***Be part of the solution, not part of the confusion! When you are united in Me, you lay down your differences, not your identity.***

Keep the unity of the Spirit through the bond of peace.
– Ephesians 4:3

Behold, How good and how pleasant it is for brethren to dwell together in unity!

– Psalm 133:1 AMP

See also: Colossians 3:14; Hebrews 6:1-2

I AM as generous on earth as I AM in heaven.

Thy kingdom come, Thy will be done in earth, as it is in heaven.
— MATTHEW 6:10 KJV

I AM your Father. I do not change! In heaven, you are healed, whole, delivered, blessed, and have every need provided. You lack no good thing! Since I *do not change*, these same blessings are available for you on earth. *I desire that My Kingdom be manifest on earth! But My will for My Kingdom does not change just because you are on the earth.* Many have been deceived into thinking they must die before they can be healed or blessed extravagantly! I said in My Word that in heaven there are many mansions so you would understand My nature and will for you. To walk in these blessings *on earth* now, you *must* learn to operate within the Laws of My Kingdom. The Laws are the same for anyone who applies and enforces them. *I love you as much now as I will in heaven!* I AM intimately acquainted with your every need *now*! Wisdom says: Why would I love you and take care of you more in heaven than on earth? I AM just as generous and giving now as I will be in heaven.

In my Father's house are many mansions. — JOHN 14:2

Jesus Christ is the same yesterday and today and forever. — HEBREWS 13:8

SEE ALSO: *MALACHI 3:6; MATTHEW 6:10; TITUS 3:6*

December 6

Do not underestimate the importance of My little ones!

How important are My "Little Ones"! Never underestimate how valuable children are to Me! I have entrusted them to you! I have called My Body to be Guardians of Life and to champion their cause for protection. *Little children are the purest reflection of Me!* They are innocent, trusting, pure, loving, full of wonder. There is no deceit or guile in them. Wisdom says: Little children are a picture of My Kingdom. I give very severe warning to anyone who causes one of *My* Little Ones to stumble! *I also gave a profound blessing to anyone who welcomes one such child in My name; they welcome Me!* Look for ways to love My Little Ones. When you love My children, you love Me. Do not despise their inconvenience. Never forget: Their angels have access to Me face to face! When you take care of the least of these, I will take care of even the least of your needs.

> *"If anyone causes one of these little ones — those who believe in me — to stumble, it would be better for them if a large millstone were hung around their neck and they were thrown into the sea."*
> —MARK 9:42

SEE ALSO: MATTHEW 18:2-10

Love opens the door to access My power.

To love is to have power. Love is the key that releases My power to flow through you. The more you love, the more I can use you in My Kingdom. The enemy shivers at the power of My Love that flows through you to raise the dead, heal the sick, and love the unlovely. If you are not seeing miracles when you pray, check your love level. Not even faith will work without love. Wisdom says: The more revelation you have of My Love for you, the more of My power that will flow through you. Never forget: I AM also bound by My own Law. Since My Mouth speaks from the overflow of My heart, I speak many great loving things about you because I think and store beautiful thoughts of you daily.

We have heard of your faith in Christ Jesus [how you lean on Him with absolute confidence in His power, wisdom, and goodness], and of the [unselfish] love which you have for all the saints (God's people).
— Colossians 1:4 AMPC

*But **love your enemies**, do good to them, and lend to them without expecting to get anything back. Then your reward will be great, and you will be children of the Most High.*
— Luke 6:35

See also: 1 John 4:16; 1 John 4:9

December *8*

Expect and protect
My promise with your faith.

❧

Do not allow pressure to ever catch you off guard again! With every promise, whether it comes through My Word or it is given prophetically, know there will be opposition from the enemy to steal that Word! Pressure and attacks are strategically planned by the enemy, but carried out through people. The purpose of the enemy's attack is to abort My Seed — to get you to quit or stop believing that My promise will come to pass. So many rejoice when the prophetic word is given — and rightfully so! Then many are completely caught off guard when attacks come from every side. This is the Kingdom suffering violence. Wisdom says: The enemy knows that the only way My Word can fail is when you allow it to be stolen with unbelief or offense. My Word produces one hundred percent of the time when you protect My Word with your faith! Be steadfast today in the fight over My promise in you!

The ones along the path that those who have the Word sown [in their hearts], but when they hear, Satan comes at once and [by force] takes away the message which is sown in them.

– Mark 4:15 AMP

See also: 2 Corinthians 12:10; 2 Thessalonians 1:4; Mark 4:4-20; James 1:2-4

Are you minding your business? Or is your business your mind?

There is a war raging in your mind. Be alert! Are you just going about your day, minding your own business? So many in My Body are filling their minds with all the pressures, projects, and plans of work. *With the schedules and appointments you must keep every day, it can be difficult to remember that this day is about My Kingdom and My work.* When your business *is your mind*, then you are listening to, guarding, and are aware of the bombardment of thoughts and spiritual warfare around you! This is where Life and death collide in an epic battle for strongholds and territory — in your mind! Some are too busy to even consider the war that is raging. I AM giving instructions and answers to their problems, and the enemy is trying to deceive and distract to keep them from hearing My still, small voice. Wisdom says: When you keep your mind on Me and open to Me, the rewards are limitless! Know that you are listening to someone today. Be sure it is Me, your Father, and not your enemy!

> But I see another law at work in me, waging war against the law of my mind and making me a prisoner of the law of sin at work within me.
>
> — ROMANS 7:23

SEE ALSO: *2 CORINTHIANS 4:4*

A settler's world encompasses only his own posterity and land. A pilgrim's posterity and land encompasses the **world**.

My Son, Jesus, lived His life on earth as a Pilgrim. Jesus was focused on those who would enjoy the fruits of His sacrifice and labor. I AM calling *you* to live in My Kingdom as a pilgrim, not as a settler! Pilgrims live a life without compromise. They will not be swayed or talked out of their destiny. Their only fear is not fulfilling their destiny from Me. Pilgrims see no limits; the world is theirs for the taking. A pilgrim's life is marked for service to a generation they may never know. They have the heart and tenacity to sow seed for the next generation's harvest! Wisdom says: Pilgrims rarely see the impact of their hard work. They persevere, knowing they may never see the honor due them in their lifetime. Let your reward be to see that the path where you are laboring will make easier the lives of those who dare to follow.

These all died in faith ... confessing that they were strangers and pilgrims on the earth. — HEBREWS 11:13 JUB

SEE ALSO: PSALM 119:19; HEBREWS 2:10; PSALM 84:5

Settlers are content to maintain their territory. Pilgrims are only content when they are expanding My territory.

There is nothing about being in My Army and in My Kingdom that denotes being a settler! I give orders to occupy the territory that I assign to you. When I give the command to advance, I intend for you to expand and occupy. This is a never-ending process. *You are not to quit and settle in an area that I did not assign to you.* This is not just about physical territory, but also spiritual and emotional territory. Settlers put down roots to stay for a long time in an area or in the same place. They sow for themselves, and they labor to maintain themselves. This separates the pilgrims from the settlers. Wisdom says: The settlers want to eat the fruit of their labor *now*. Pilgrims labor for the future. Do not be a settler when you can be a pilgrim like My Son, Jesus. Know that when you settle, My Kingdom suffers.

Blessed is the man whose strength is in You,
Whose heart is set on pilgrimage.
— Psalm 84:5 NKJV

See also: Isaiah 54:2-3; Psalm 94:17

Is your brother a bother?

To serve Me is to serve your brother! How I long to see the brothers and sisters in My Body serving one another in unity! I have asked that you love one another with brotherly love and affection! Consider it an honor, and no less than a privilege, to serve one another as you would My Son, Jesus. *When you serve one another, you get the credit as if you were actually there ministering to My Son! If you could see serving one other as I see it, with brotherly love, you would never again see it as a bother!* Those who serve are the greatest in My Kingdom. Those who serve "the least of these" get compensation from Me! Wisdom says: Today, serve others as if they were Me — because they represent Me. To serve anyone is to serve The King of kings! *When you tend to your brother, you tend to Me — and I will tend to you. Are you tending to your brother, or contending with your brother?* When you tend to your brother and sister, I send to you honor and reward.

There is a friend who sticks closer than a brother.
— Proverbs 18:24

"If you love each other, all men will know you are My followers."
— John 13:35 NLV

See also: 1 John 4:20-21; 2 Peter 1:6-8; Hebrews 13:1; Proverbs 19:17

Every destructive lifestyle started with a destructive thought.

All deception is introduced as a ***thought*** that appears to be truth. Oh, how Eve's decision to act upon a single thought changed the entire world! If only Eve had seen how dangerous it was to entertain the thought that the enemy was planting. She loved Me and wanted to be more like Me! The deception was that she already was like Me! Deceptive and destructive thoughts may seem innocent and harmless, but I tell you: ***There is no such thing as an innocent and harmless thought!*** All thoughts have the power to change and redirect your life! Your mind is the command center of your heart and your entire physical being. ***Thoughts are alive! If thoughts were powerless, why would I tell you to take every thought captive to the obedience of Christ?*** You will never do or say anything that you have not thought first. Wisdom says: My Word is exposing, sifting, analyzing, and judging the very thoughts and purposes of your heart! Guard your thoughts today. This is where every battle is won or lost!

We have the mind of Christ.

— 1 Corinthians 2:16

See also: Hebrews 4:12; Psalm 139:23; Jeremiah 12:3; 1 Corinthians 2:11

The entire world can lie about you and it may hurt. But a lie you believe **about yourself** can be deadly.

All lies are deadly because they open the door to deception, I warn you this day: If you do not believe that you can be deceived, then you already are! You cannot violate the Laws in My Word. What you believe in your heart, so you will be. What you believe about yourself will ***govern*** your entire being throughout your life. If you are having a hard time changing a behavior, consider this: You must first change the thoughts and lies that you believe about yourself, then watch the behavior change. Wisdom says: Today, ask Me to uncover areas in your life where you have been deceived. Change your mind to align with My Word. A renewed mind is a renewed life!

What he thinks is what he really is.

— Proverbs 23:7 GNT

Do not be conformed to this world (this age), [fashioned after and adapted to its external, superficial customs], but be transformed (changed) by the [entire] renewal of your mind [by its new ideals and its new attitude], so that you may prove [for yourselves] what is the good and acceptable and perfect will of God.

— Romans 12:2 AMP

Neither victory nor defeat can happen without your cooperation!

Defeat is someehing very unnatural in My Kingdom. Defeat can come in several ways — if you quit, if you do not know My Word, or if you choose not to apply My Word to situations that exist in your life. ***Regardless of how it presents itself, defeat can only happen with your cooperation.*** The same principle applies to victory. You have the option to choose victory! The enemy does not have the power to defeat you; he is defeated! I AM The Most High God. How can a defeated enemy triumph over you, My child? He cannot — unless you allow it by failing to believe and speak My Word or by lack of knowledge of My Kingdom Laws. Wisdom says: Today, do not accept or participate in defeat! Cooperate with My Word to gain true victory!

> *For Christ will be King until he has defeated all his enemies, including the last enemy — death. This too must be defeated and ended.*
> – 1 CORINTHIANS 15: 25-26 TLB

> *Yet in all these things we are more than conquerors and gain an overwhelming victory through Him who loved us [so much that He died for us].*
> – ROMANS 8:37 AMP

SEE ALSO: 1 PETER 5:4

If you do not forgive, you will have to deal with temptation!

Many of My beloved children wonder how they wind up in a difficult situation, trial, or wilderness season. In some cases, My children have chosen unforgiveness, which has caused them to step into the enemy's dangerous territory. Conduct yourself as I say in My Word: *Forgive us our debts, as we also have forgiven our debtors; and lead us not into temptation, but deliver us from the evil one.* Know this: If you do not forgive, you will open yourself to temptation from the enemy! He then has a legal right to torment you. If you are in a hard season, ask yourself if there is the possibility that you have stepped into unforgivness. Wisdom says: You can run to Me with all of your hurts and pain of rejection. I AM eager to help you. I cannot resist a contrite heart! Borrow My eyes! Ask and I will help you see with My vision regarding the one who hurt you. This person is My child also — so I will give you the grace to see good in them. Do not allow the enemy to drag you into temptation today! When you forgive, you look just like My Son, Jesus. This is where I see The Best in you — My Son, Jesus.

And forgive us our debts, as we also have forgiven our debtors. And lead us not into temptation.

— Matthew 6:12-13

See also: Matthew 6:15

Are you **saying** a prayer, or are you **being** a pray-er?

Are you in My army of prayer warriors, or are you just one who tosses up a prayer every now and then when you are in trouble? I need an army of intercessors who are willing to empower My Kingdom through prayer. Your prayers give Me legal access to change conditions on earth and also in your personal life. I have given you the power of free will and choices, so I cannot intervene in your life without your permission. I gave Adam complete authority over creation and over the earth. Now that you are in Jesus, you have that same restored authority. Prayer is giving Me rights to move on your behalf. If you really understood the power of prayer, you would not want to do anything else! Wisdom says: ***Today, do not just say a prayer, be My prayer warrior! You will succeed when you intercede!***

> *Then God said, "Let Us (Father, Son, Holy Spirit) make man in Our image, according to Our likeness [not physical, but a spiritual personality and moral likeness]; and let them have complete authority over the fish of the sea, the birds of the air, the cattle, and **over the entire earth**, and over everything that creeps and crawls on the earth."*
> — GENESIS 1:26 AMP

SEE ALSO: MATTHEW 28:18-19; MATTHEW 6:5; ACTS 1:14

Am I getting the glory in your story?

When you cry out to Me, I answer you. When you receive miracles and answers to your prayers, I AM asking that you testify of My glorious love and power! For so many in this world, this is the only time that I can confront them with the reality that I exist! The world can debate opinions and theology, but when they witness or hear of unexplained supernatural miracles and encounters, it confronts their ideology. When you testify of My Goodness, this is high praise to Me. ***Do not just be a miracle taker and forget the Miracle Maker!*** Wisdom says: When you are given a gift of a miracle from Me, please child, do not forget the Miracle Maker! Am I getting the glory in your story? When you *take* credit from Me, you *lose* credit with Me! Tell someone of My Goodness towards you today!

He who speaks on his own accord seeks glory and honor for himself. But He who seeks the glory and the honor of the One who sent Him, He is true, and there is no unrighteousness or deception in Him.

— JOHN 7:18 AMPC

SEE ALSO: *PSALM 115:1; ISAIAH 61:3; PSALM 29:2*

You are the most expensive gift that has ever been, or ever will be, purchased!

If you are ever tempted to think that I AM against you, or disappointed in you for any reason, then remember the price I paid to redeem you. *Your price was paid with the Blood of the One I loved the most, My Son, Jesus! The price I paid for you could not be measured; therefore, your value cannot be measured. This makes you the most valuable treasure without measure!* The more you love someone, the easier it is for you to spend a higher price for a gift to them. When you buy gifts for acquaintances, however, notice how you become more reluctant to spend. Know this: I did not haggle over the price for you! My gift for you was extravagant. This shows that you are much more than just an acquaintance to Me; you are priceless! I was more than willing to pay the highest price in heaven and on earth for you! Wisdom says: Know this day that in spite of the extragavant price I paid for you, I still say, *"You are worth it!"*

You were bought for a price.

— 1 Corinthians 6:20 GW

See also: John 3:16; Galatians 3:27

December 20

Malice was birthed in hell.
Mercy was birthed in heaven.

The enemy is full of malice! He curses and harms people, making them suffer with spite and ill will! When someone does something to hurt you, whether knowingly or unknowingly, you will either choose to show My mercy or choose to bear malice. When you sow mercy, you forgive them. This ensures that when you are in need of mercy, you will reap that mercy from Me and from man. *When you show My mercy, you allow the world to see Jesus! Likewise, when you bear malice, the world sees the expression of the enemy and you put yourself into the enemy's territory.* You will not only reap malice, but you are giving the enemy a foothold into your entire being because of the curse and sin of malice. The enemy has no hold on you when you sow mercy. Wisdom says: Today, be the living sacrifice of My mercy to those who have hurt you or have shown you malice.

Turn to me and have mercy on me, as you always do to those who love your name.
— Psalm 119:132

See also: Romans 1:29; Matthew 5:7; Ephesians 2:4; Ephesians 4:31

Only pigs are content in the pigpen!

Seek My face and study My Word. This allows Me to reveal to you who you are and how My heart values you. I long to show you what you are made of — Me! You are made in My image and re-born into royalty. When you lose your perspective of your value to Me, you will find yourself in places you were never meant to dwell. Just as the prodigal son went from living with pigs back to his rightful place as son in his father's palace, so I AM calling all of My children out of the pigpen. Wisdom says: It is time to get up, wash yourself, and return to your rightful place at My table. Stop being content in the pigpen. Disappointment and deception will keep you there, but I have created you to rule and reign with My Son, Jesus. A king rules from his palace, so stop trying to reign from the level of the pigs. ***Just because I sculpted man from mud does not mean you are to wallow in it!*** Leave the company of the pigs and be secure feasting at My table.

> *After he had spent everything, ... he ... hired himself out to a citizen ... who sent him to his fields to feed pigs. He longed to fill his stomach with the pods that the pigs were eating.*
> – LUKE 15:14-16

SEE ALSO: LUKE 15:13-24; PSALM 23:5

This is a test!
Will your integrity carry you
when I bless your enemies?

I have commanded that you love your enemies and pray for those who despitefully use you. When you pray, I answer your prayers! But when your enemies are blessed because of your prayers, how will you act? Know that this is a test! Please, pass this test because I really want to impart blessings to you as rewards for your sacrificial obedience and love. There are times that I will allow an enemy, or someone from your past who has deeply hurt you, to re-enter your life. Why? I AM seeing how you will treat them. Wisdom says: I AM testing your heart and motives because I want to promote those who will not hurt My children, no matter what hurt they have been through themselves. Love always comes with great rewards. ***Will your integrity show when I bless your foe?***

The crucible for silver and the furnace for gold, but the Lord tests the heart.

– Proverbs 17:3

See also: Matthew 5:43-45

If you disqualify others because of their differences, you disqualify yourself because of your uniqueness.

Uniqueness is My plan to keep competition out of My Body. I hate division and the spirit of competition! *I made everyone different, very different, so there would be no comparing to one another. How can one human be compared to another?* This is impossible! To disqualify anyone who is different disqualifies you! This is the evil scheming from the enemy. Wisdom says: Unity is vital in My Kingdom. People are not your competition! You have *no competition* — especially with Me! Insecurity breeds division and disqualifying one another! This is hate. Security breeds unity and accepting one another as gifts and expressions of *Me*! *How can you compete when you are all unique?* Today, in order to unify My Kingdom, cherish one another's differences. Also, cherish what makes you so special to Me!

Just as a body, though one, has many parts, but all its many parts form one body, so it is with Christ.

— 1 Corinthians 12:12

See also: John 17:23; Psalm 133:1

December *24*

If you cannot enjoy the present, then you will never truly enjoy the future.

When you focus on what you *were*, you miss out on all that you *are*. When you focus on all you *could be*, you miss out on all that you *are*. You will never appreciate the treasured gift of life that I have given to you unless you focus on what is happening right now. If you cannot enjoy the present, then you will never truly enjoy the future. If you are living in the past or future, you are not ruling your present; you are *being ruled* by your past and by the what-ifs of the future. Therefore, do not miss the gift of today! If you are not living in the *now*, you are missing Me! *The key to loving your life is loving the moment you are in — for I AM with you there!* I AM in the present. That is why My name is I AM! This is so important that I said it twice: *I AM Who I AM.* Wisdom says: Spend time with Me today and enjoy the gift of now. Be at peace. I AM pleased with you. In My Presence is fullness of joy.

This is the day the Lord has made; We will rejoice and be glad in it.
— Psalm 118:24 nkjv

376

See also: Exodus 3:13-14; Isaiah 43:18

Will you bethroth or betray My Son, Jesus?

My Son, Jesus, kissed the world with His Presence and the world kissed Him back with betrayal. His love was poured out as a deluge on all of mankind. He loves with perfect love as He is hated with perfect hatred. His heart beat with the deepest of love, even as He was beaten with blows of the deepest of hate. His spit opened the eyes of the blind and they could see, yet the world spit on Him in disgust because they were blind and could not see. As He asked Me, your Father, for your hand in marriage, the world nailed His hands to a cross. Can you still see His beauty beyond the marring and scarring inflicted by this angry world? He died so you could live. He wept so you could laugh. He fell so you could stand in My Presence. Wisdom says: Give My precious Son the love, honor, and glory that He most certainly deserves. The sun looks dim next to Him because His love for you outshines the sun! He walked across the water, climbed mountains, and even descended to the bowels of the earth just to find you! I treasure Him and ask you to treasure Him with all your heart! Do not hurt Him with your indifference! Know that He carried all of your shame; are you ashamed of Him? I ask you as His Father, will you betroth or betray My beautiful Son?

> *On his robe and on his thigh he has this written: KING OF KINGS AND LORD OF LORDS.*
> – REVELATION 19:16

377

SEE ALSO: REVELATION 17:14; REVELATION 21:23-24; MATTHEW 26:67; ISAIAH 50:6; JOHN 11:35; JOHN 3:16-17; MATTHEW 20:28; MATTHEW 17:12

To rejoice is always by choice.

To rejoice is a decision to praise Me for My answer and My faithfulness, no matter what your situation looks like. It is not a natural response to rejoice when you are in a crisis. It is a supernatural response that ushers in My help. *This is not about denying there is a problem; it is about confirming that I AM the solution! When you choose to rejoice, even when it is a sacrifice, then I have access to change what you could not!* You are reminding yourself that when I AM *for* you, who or what can be *against* you? So many lose the battle in this crossroad of decision! What you say in the midst of a problem could mean the difference between victory or defeat! Do not complain about the problem. If you do, then you just enlarge it! When you make the choice to rejoice, despite the trouble that you are in, know this: I AM quick to respond to the joyful and faith-filled response of rejoicing! Wisdom says: *When you rejoice, you give faith a voice! Let Me hear your faith today — rejoice!* Know that I rejoice over you without restraint.

Rejoice in the Lord always [delight, gladden yourself in Him]; again I say, Rejoice! — Philippians 4:4 AMP

See also: Psalm 105:3; Psalm 32:11; Psalm 64:10

To quit is to admit that everyone who has said you 'could not' would be right!

You are made in My image, and I AM not a quitter! *Quitting is such an expensive option!* It may seem like a simple decision, but the results are not simple. Quitting can become a lifestyle. Many opt out too quickly without thinking about the consequences to themselves, others, and My Kingdom. If you quit on My destiny for you, then all those who have said you could not do it would be right! Let those words cause the fight to rise up in you to protect what I placed in you before the foundations of the world! When the idea or dream is from Me, then it will seem large and feel impossible. Only *I* make the impossible possible! The enemy will always bring pressure to tempt you to quit on the destiny that I placed in you because he fears the damage you will do to him. He is the only winner when you quit on My destiny! Everyone else loses! Wisdom says: Those who persevere will reap My rewards! Remember, when you are in a difficult time, call on My help. I can even command the ravens to feed you if that were your last option. But know that I AM never out of options or mercy when it comes to taking care of you!

Stand firm in the faith; be courageous; be strong.
– 1 Corinthians 16:13

See also: Revelation 2:2-3; 1 Samuel 7:8

Money is a powerful **servant**, but a vicious **master**.

To love Me is to trust Me! To love money is to trust money. If you love money, then you despise Me. You cannot serve two masters. Choose My insight over income. Wisdom says: If money is your master, then you are *serving* it! Money is designed to serve you in My Kingdom. You are to serve Me alone! If you think of money more than you think of Me, then you are mastered by it. To be *mastered* by money brings torment through thoughts of not having enough or worrying how to keep it. I have promised to meet all of your needs. I do not take being your Father lightly! *My very nature is to provide, not withhold! Provider is Who I AM!* If you really understood My nature as your Father, you would never again waste your time thinking about money! Your thoughts would rest in the fact that when you are Mine, you have access to *all* that is Mine!

Whoever loves money never has enough. Whoever loves wealth is never satisfied with their income.
— Ecclesiastes 5:10

See also: Matthew 6:24

If you are only entertaining a dream, you are remaining asleep.

It pleases Me when you set your sights on a dream of your heart! But, if you are just hoping and dreaming without activating your dream, then you are doing nothing but simply sleeping. Dreams are not accidentally formed. You **create** them by purposely seeing them in your mind. Desiring the fulfillment of a dream is only the first step in the process of aspiring to achieve a dream. It takes My help and hard work to fulfill a dream. You have to actively pursue it until you achieve your dream. Wisdom says: *A hope or dream that is truly from Me will always require My help, along with your obedience, to accomplish. Together we will do more than you can imagine in your wildest dreams!* A dream in your heart is a set destination. With a dream from Me, you can thrive! True dreamers are always active in their pursuit of the dream. So dream with Me today! Allow Me to revive the dreams that you thought had expired.

Faith without works is dead. — JAMES 2:20

When dreams come true at last, there is life and joy. — PROVERBS 13:12 TLB

God can do anything, you know — far more than you could ever imagine or guess or request in your wildest dreams! — EPHESIANS 3:20 MSG

Consider the source — Me!

Even though your blessing comes ***through*** man, look to Me, not man, as the source of all your needs! When you look to a person, you are completely limited to what they can ***spare***! If your eyes are on people, then your harvest becomes limited to ***leftovers*** that people no longer need! From My view, this looks like beggars who beg from other beggars! Even the wealthiest men look like beggars compared to Me! I never give out of what I can spare or out of leftovers! I gave My Only Son, Jesus. I AM Generosity! Be cautious that you do not look to people or to your job to be your source. I AM your Father Who takes care of you. When you sow, I AM honor-bound as your Father to open My windows of heaven and pour out such a large blessing that you will hardly be able to contain it. Wisdom says: I will use people to give to you and to bless you, but I AM always ***your*** source, because I AM ***the*** source! ***When you seek My vision, I will always reward you with My provision.***

*... the Father of sympathy (pity and mercy) and the God [Who is the **Source**] of every comfort (consolation and encouragement).* – 2 Corinthians 1:3

May he be pleased by all these thoughts about him, for he is the source of all my joy. – Psalm 104:34 TLB

See also: Psalm 87:7

It is easy to submit an unknown future to a Father you know.

Humbly submit yourself completely unto Me so that you can actively resist the work of the enemy, knowing that he must flee from you. When you *know* Me and understand how loved you are, it is easy to have peace about an *unknown* future. Just because the future is unknown does not mean it should invoke fear. I have promised to take care of you and never leave you. Wisdom says: I AM your Peace, your Security, your Solid Rock. Submit your future to Me. To know Me is to trust Me. I guarantee your best is yet to come! Today, see your future in Me — in Peace, not pieces. Never forget: The future is My responsibility when you are My child. Your responsibility is to be obedient and to trust Me. When you understand My character and integrity as your Father, you will never again waste time worrying about the future. Because of Me, your future is very secure!

*Because he has set his love upon Me, therefore will I deliver him; I will set him on high, because he **knows and understands** My name [has a personal knowledge of My mercy, love, and kindness — trusts and relies on Me, **knowing** I will never forsake him, no, never].*
— PSALM 91:14 AMP

Submit yourselves, then, to God. Resist the devil, and he will flee from you.
— JAMES 4:7

Contact the author

Maribeth Eickhoff welcomes your comments!
She can be reached via e-mail at
365lifesentences@gmail.com
regarding speaking engagements.

CPSIA
at www.
Printed i
FFOW02
39135FF